THE **TRUE CRIME FILE**

THE TRUE CRIME FILE

Serial Killers • Famous Kidnappings •
Great Cons • Survivors & Their Stories •
Forensics • Oddities & Absurdities •
Quotes & Quizzes

COMPILED BY **KIM DALY**

WORKMAN PUBLISHING | **NEW YORK**

Copyright © 2022 Workman Publishing Co., Inc.

Library of Congress Cataloging-in-Publication Data

Names: Daly, Kimberly E.- editor.
Title: The true crime file : serial killings, famous kidnappings, great cons, survivors & their stories, forensics, and more / compiled by Kim Daly.
Description: New York, NY : Workman Publishing, [2022] | Identifiers: LCCN 2021040980 | ISBN 9781523514113 (paperback)
Subjects: LCSH: Crime—Case studies. | Criminals—Case studies.
Classification: LCC HV6233 .T78 2022 | DDC 364—dc23
LC record available at https://lccn.loc.gov/2021040980

Text by Kim Daly, Sam O'Brien, and Steven Buscok
Design by Galen Smith
Photo research by Sophia Rieth
Cover credit (fingerprints): artemiya/Shutterstock

Workman books are available at special discounts when purchased in bulk for premiums and sales promotions as well as for fundraising or educational use. Special editions or book excerpts can also be created to specification. For details, contact the Special Sales Director at specialmarkets@workman.com.

Workman Publishing Co., Inc.
225 Varick Street
New York, NY 10014-4381

workman.com

WORKMAN is a registered trademark of Workman Publishing Co., Inc.

Printed in the USA on responsibly sourced paper.
First printing March 2022

10 9 8 7 6 5 4 3 2 1

CONTENTS

KILLERS:

SURVIVORS:

BIZARRE BRUTALITY:

CON ARTISTS:

THIEVES:

ANTICS & ACCIDENTS:

CRIME THROUGH TIME:

FORENSIC FACTS:

LEGAL CONCEPTS:

QUICK FACTS:

RECS:

QUIZZES:

INTRODUCTION

True crime stories have probably been around since there were people to tell them. Or at least a press to print them.

Pamphlets exploring domestic/intimate partner violence, psychosexual motives, crimes against—and by—women, as well as remarkable survivor stories date back to the mid-sixteenth century, evidence of mass media's lasting fascination with the darkness that lurks among us.

This early form of true crime narrative was heavy with themes of morality and divine justice. However, there were also glimmers of contemporary themes that would resonate with today's true crime fans, including the systemic oppression of women, marginalized groups, and poor people. These early stories were often presented in "ballads," printed accounts of murder and mayhem written through the lens of a perpetrator that explored the inner motives behind their shocking crimes, including the psychological and social ills at play.

These themes are at the heart of our ongoing obsession with crime—from the most terrifying attacks to the amateur bandit holding up a local bank at cucumberpoint (page 214). They fuel our fascination and set our minds reeling: *Why* do these things happen? *How* could they happen? *What* can we do to prevent them?

With each question, a new avenue of true crime opens up to us, and it's usually a two-way street. While new investigative and forensic techniques develop to advance justice, flaws overlooked in older methods reveal large cracks in a system that must be repaired. DNA analysis via genetic genealogy is solving cold cases at a record rate but also raising questions about genetic discrimination (page 60) and privacy. Advances in basic technology lead to revolutionary tools like the Amber Alert (page 137) but also create new avenues for predators.

Re-explorations of the most highly publicized crimes in recent history—think: the trials of Lorena and John Bobbitt (page 255)—highlight how ignorant the media was about sexual, physical, and psychological abuse, not to mention how cruel and commonplace victim-blaming was just a few decades ago. Exploring the effects of abuse, particularly on children, adds a new dimension to the psychological and social study of crimes old and new. And with the shame of crime increasingly put rightly on perpetrator rather than victim, survivor tales like those of Mary Vincent (page 74) and Erica Pratt (page 44) get the awe and attention they deserve.

The role bias plays in the concepts of law is being explored like never before, leading to much-needed reform. In 1989, Jeffrey Dahmer (page 45) talked himself out of a conviction for molesting a thirteen-year-old Laotian boy. Almost exactly two years later, by coincidence, he raped and murdered that boy's younger brother despite another brush with the law on the night of that crime. And yet, decades earlier, the entirely singular con artist and suspected murderer Linda Taylor (page 291) became an enduring racialized symbol of Black low-income motherhood used by politicians for decades.

And yet there's still so much to explore in true crime. Prolific rapists and serial murderers like the Golden State Killer (page 96) live among unsuspecting neighbors for years while evading justice for their horrific acts, renewing the horror of our own hometown crimes (check out mine—still unsolved—on page 193). On the other end of the spectrum, seemingly average citizens get their 15 minutes of fame with random acts of nonviolent crime committed during nights of drunken revelry (see page 54) or extremely misguided pranks (page 113).

This endless well of crime, modern and historic, earth-shattering and simply foolish, collides with today's media fishbowl to create a rich platform on which true crime fascination is growing. The nonstop news cycle, books, documentaries, podcasts, long-form journalism, social media, Reddit, and even genealogy websites all serve as a vehicle to drive true crime consumption. If you're just beginning to explore the thrilling vagaries of true crime or you've been a deep fan for years, whether your fascinations lie with serial killers, survivors, forensics, con artists, heists, robbery, law, criminal justice, or just the downright strange ways humans skirt legal systems—there's something in here for you. And if you're into all of it, as so many of us are, even better. Turn to any page and tumble down the rabbit hole. Whatever you seek, you'll find it in *The True Crime File*.

Kim Daly

Proceed with caution—much of this content is disturbing and potentially triggering. Every effort has been made to approach these stories with sensitivity and respect, but tales of rape, murder, torture, and violence are not appropriate for everyone. Even the most diehard true crime fans have their limits. If you ever find yourself in need of support as you try to make sense of the dark side of humanity, please don't hesitate to reach out to the resources listed here:

National Organization for Victim Assistance referral information: 800-TRY-NOVA

Rape, Incest & Abuse National Network (RAINN) sexual assault hotline: 800-656-HOPE

National Suicide Prevention Lifeline: 800-273-8255

CHARLES MANSON AND HIS "FAMILY": TO HELTER SKELTER AND BACK

n New Year's Eve 1968, people in the US and around the world reflected on a year of mounting racial tensions. Spring arrived with tragedy: Martin Luther King Jr. had been assassinated in April. Summer brought protest: Tommie Smith and John Carlos raised their fists in a Black Power salute at the Olympics in Mexico City. And then winter came, with a polarizing pop culture breakthrough: *Star Trek* aired the first-ever televised interracial kiss.

New Year's Eve that year was also when Charles Manson huddled with his followers—his "Family"—at their Death Valley ranch, allegedly discussing what he believed was an inevitable and imminent race war. He named the war "Helter Skelter," after the Beatles' song. Manson's plan was to wait out the war in a hidden bunker with his Family, then emerge at the right moment and seize power. But after several months, Manson grew impatient and decided to speed things along.

On July 25, 1969, Manson sparked his summer of Helter Skelter by ordering Family members Bobby Beausoleil, Mary Brunner, and Susan Atkins to kidnap Gary Allen Hinman, a music teacher and PhD student at UCLA. Hinman had befriended Manson Family members and occasionally let them stay at his house. Manson believed that Hinman owned the house, along with significant amounts of stocks and bonds. The plan was to persuade Hinman to turn his assets over to the Family.

But Hinman wouldn't cooperate. Manson joined the three Family members, holding Hinman hostage in his own home for two days, during which time Manson slashed Hinman's ear with a sword, before Beausoleil eventually stabbed Hinman to death. The group then wrote *political piggy* and drew a panther's paw in Hinman's blood on the wall before leaving.

Beausoleil was arrested on August 6, 1969, caught driving Hinman's car, which had the murder weapon stashed in the tire well. Two days later, Manson announced, "Now is the time for

Manson appears at trial in 1971 with a shaved head.

Helter Skelter." Just after midnight on August 9, four Manson Family members—Susan Atkins, Patricia Krenwinkel, Charles "Tex" Watson, and Linda Kasabian—pulled up to the Bel Air, California, home of film director Roman Polanski and his wife, actress Sharon Tate.

While Kasabian stood guard, Watson climbed through a window and let the others inside. They bound Jay Sebring, Wojciech Frykowski, Abigail Folger, Steven Parent, and Tate, who was eight and a half months pregnant. In a flurry of stabbing, shooting, and extreme brutality, they murdered all five victims. The group had ignored Tate's pleas for the life of her unborn child and stabbed her 16 times. Before leaving, they wrote *PIG* on the door in her blood.

Why the message written in blood? Manson allegedly thought the anti-police sentiments would make authorities believe the murders were the work of Black militants, which he hoped would spark a race-fueled Helter Skelter war.

Just to be sure that authorities/police would believe the crimes were the work of Black militants, Manson decided to strike again. The following night, a larger group of Family members descended on a house seemingly at random, breaking in on

"Many people I know in Los Angeles believe that the Sixties ended abruptly on August 9, 1969, ended at the exact moment when word of the murders . . . traveled like brushfire through the community, and in a sense this is true. . . . The paranoia was fulfilled."
—*Joan Didion, writing about the Manson murders in* The White Album

Leno and Rosemary LaBianca. Manson bound the couple, once again delegating the murders. Along with the four Family members from the previous night, Manson brought along Leslie Van Houten and Steve "Clem" Grogan. Together and separately, the group stabbed the couple to death, carved *WAR* into Leno's abdomen, and wrote *DEATH TO PIGS* and *HEALTER SKELTER* [sic] on the walls in the victims' blood.

In addition to writing the messages, Manson instructed Kasabian to leave Rosemary LaBianca's wallet in a neighborhood that had mostly Black residents. Kasabian later testified that Manson "wanted a Black person to pick it up and use the credit cards so that the people, the Establishment, would think it was some sort of an organized group that killed these people."

Manson's plot to frame the Black community for the murders didn't work. A combination of other crimes committed by the Family and Atkins's sharing the story widely meant it wasn't long before the police found and arrested the true murderers.

The trial of Charles Manson took nine and a half months and was a circus from start to finish. On July 24, 1970, the first day of testimony, Manson entered the courtroom with an X

Linda Kasabian, a former Manson Family member, at a press conference in 1970 after being granted immunity in the murder trial of Charles Manson.

carved into his forehead because he had "X'd [him]self from [the Establishment's] world." His fellow female defendants also appeared with the mark.

Manson Family members who weren't on trial continually disrupted the proceedings, held vigils outside the courthouse, and threatened witnesses. On October 5, Manson leapt over the defense table to attack the judge. As bailiffs tackled him, his female codefendants cheered him on.

Most of Manson's followers remained loyal to him for years after the Helter Skelter summer of 1969. But not Linda Kasabian, who turned against him before the murders at the Tate house were even finished. As the only member of the Manson Family with a valid driver's license at the time, Kasabian provided transport and was present at both the Tate and LaBianca houses, but claimed to not participate in any of the killings. She

Before he started planning for Helter Skelter and instructing his followers to go on a brutal murder spree, Charles Manson was an aspiring folk musician. One of his songs, "Cease to Exist," was altered and recorded by the Beach Boys under the new name "Never Learn Not to Love."

also maintained that she tried to thwart the murder of screenwriter Wojciech Frykowski on August 9 by telling Tex Watson, a high-ranking Family member who helped lead the murders that night, that she heard "people coming" up the property. She further claimed that she went along to the LaBianca residence the next night only out of fear. She was not present in the houses during either set of murders.

Kasabian fled to her parents' house in New Hampshire after the killings and turned herself in to authorities after learning of a warrant for her arrest. She testified against Manson and other Family members in exchange for full immunity. "I started to run toward the house, I wanted them to stop," she said during her testimony. "I knew what they had done to that man [Steven Parent], that they were killing these people. I wanted them to stop."

On January 25, 1971, the jury returned guilty verdicts for Manson and his codefendants.

Manson received the death penalty, later commuted to a life sentence when the death penalty was ruled unconstitutional in 1972 by the California Supreme Court. Seemingly unrepentant, Manson continued his sometimes brutal, but more often petty, attention-seeking criminal activities in prison for the next four decades. In one instance, he poured paint thinner over a fellow inmate and set him on fire (supposedly, he didn't like the inmate's Hare Krishna chants), but he also trafficked drugs and modified the X on his forehead into a swastika.

Bobby Beausoleil was also found guilty of first-degree murder for killing Gary Allen Hinman, and got the death penalty but later had his sentence commuted to life in prison. In interviews he gave to Truman Capote and Ann Louise Bardach in 1981, Beausoleil insisted the reason behind the Tate-LaBianca murders was *not* Manson's purported Helter Skelter race wars, but to convince police that the real killer, not Beausoleil, was still at large. No other member of the Manson Family corroborated the story.

Beausoleil began to distance himself from Manson a year or so into his prison term, after he was stabbed by other inmates.

MANSON: RACIST, DEALER, MOLE?

In recent years, Manson's supposed race-war–Helter-Skelter motives have been thoroughly questioned, including by filmmaker Buddy Day, whose documentary *Manson: The Voice of Madness* suggests that copious drugs, a run-in with a dealer, and good old-fashioned paranoia led to the crimes. Journalist Tom O'Neill's book *Chaos: Charles Manson, the CIA, and the Secret History of the Sixties* also rejects the race wars theory as a construction of the prosecution, proposing instead that Manson may have been recruited by the CIA for LSD experiments.

Manson continued to correspond with his many admirers from prison, and even managed to incite further violence from behind bars. On September 5, 1975, in Sacramento, California, a woman in a red robe reached her hand out from the crowd as President Gerald Ford walked to the Capitol building from his hotel. Ford went to shake it, then noticed a gun. Lynette "Squeaky" Fromme, one of Manson's most ardent disciples, attempted to fire her gun two feet away from the president, but she'd failed to chamber a bullet. Secret Service agents quickly subdued her. Fromme, sentenced to life in prison and paroled in 2009, said her assassination attempt was meant to draw attention to Manson's plight.

Manson's ability to control various former female disciples lasted throughout his life behind bars—he even obtained a marriage license to wed 26-year-old Afton Elaine Burton in 2014 (though a ceremony never took place). Manson died of heart and respiratory failure related to colon cancer on November 19, 2017, at age 83.

THE PSYCHOPATH TEST

A quick online search reveals plenty of amateur "psychopath tests" that promise quick (and unscientific) diagnoses. But a better way of identifying psychopaths is by studying brain scans. In 2005, neurologist James Fallon, who was evaluating thousands of brain scans of murderers and schizophrenics, made a startling diagnosis: He himself was a psychopath.

Fallon inadvertently mixed his own brain scan, along with those of his family, within his psychopath studies. Genetic analysis confirmed the scans. In keeping with the idea that psychopaths lack inhibition, rather than hide, Fallon shared his finding with the world. His discovery helped demonstrate that, while psychopaths may be cold and calculating, they're not all murderers—and it might be worth exploring why some become celebrated doctors while others end up as serial killers.

DEE DEE BLANCHARD: MUNCHAUSEN TO MURDER

he words were posted in Dee Dee Blanchard's Facebook account in July 2015: "That bitch is Dead!" The post was unusual for the 48-year-old single mother. Blanchard lived in Springfield, Missouri, with her daughter, Gypsy Rose, who was critically ill, used a wheelchair, and was being fed through a tube and breathing only with the help of an oxygen tank. As friends debated the post, another comment arrived from Blanchard's account. This one implied that she was dead and that Gypsy had been sexually assaulted.

A crowd quickly gathered outside the Blanchards' house. Blanchard's car was in the driveway, but the house was dark and nobody answered the door. Neighbors called the police, but it took until almost 11:00 p.m. for them to get a search warrant. Once inside, they found Blanchard in the bedroom, stabbed to death. Gypsy was nowhere to be found.

As the police began to document the crime scene, they were approached by one of Gypsy's friends, Aleah Woodmansee, who said Gypsy told her that she had a secret online boyfriend. Woodmansee said they had met on a Christian dating site, fell in love, and were planning to get married. But he was six years older than Gypsy and Dee Dee would not have approved, so Gypsy had kept it a secret. His name, Woodmansee told them, was Nicholas Godejohn, and he lived in Big Bend, Wisconsin. Police traced the IP address that posted the messages from Dee Dee's account and confirmed that it belonged to Godejohn.

Officers were dispatched to Godejohn's house, where he was arrested after a short standoff. Gypsy was found unharmed inside. In fact, she was healthier than anyone had previously known her to be. Despite being without her medications and oxygen tank, Gypsy's hair was growing back and she was able to walk. It turned out Gypsy wasn't ill at all.

Since she was three months old, her mom was convinced that Gypsy was sick. She took her to the hospital frequently, though doctors never found anything wrong. But Dee Dee once worked as a nursing aide and knew the right medical lingo, so her act was convincing. Despite tests to the contrary, doctors treated Gypsy for conditions she didn't have. She was given drugs and had surgeries, including the removal of her teeth. When doctors got suspicious, Blanchard would move. When Hurricane Katrina hit their home in Louisiana, they relocated to Missouri, where Blanchard then claimed that Gypsy's medical records were destroyed.

Blanchard likely had a case of Munchausen syndrome by proxy, a psychological disorder in which a person induces symptoms of illness in others for personal gain. Through her daughter, Blanchard got attention, sympathy, and donations for Gypsy's care.

In 2011, while at a science-fiction convention, Gypsy met a 35-year-old man and went to his room with him. Blanchard tracked them down and made Gypsy leave with her. Although Gypsy was 19 at the time, Blanchard told everyone (including Gypsy) that she was 15. It was the first time Gypsy realized something was truly wrong with their relationship—her mother was controlling to the extreme. Gypsy didn't need Blanchard to take care of her. She was sick, she believed, but she could still walk and eat. In fact, Gypsy only went along with the wheelchair and feeding tube charade so she didn't hurt her mother's feelings.

Ultimately, Gypsy turned to the internet for escape, where she met Godejohn. She told him about her mother, and they crafted a fantasy in which he killed her. That fantasy soon became reality.

In 2015, after police located Gypsy at Godejohn's house, the two were arrested and charged with first-degree murder. Police found texts in which Gypsy asked Godejohn to murder her mother and where Godejohn confessed to stabbing Dee Dee to death.

Friends of the Blanchards were hurt and angry. Dee Dee had deceived them all for years. But their feelings toward Gypsy were more complicated. Clearly, she was a victim of her mother's abuse. But did Gypsy ever become complicit in her mother's lies? And why did she resort to murder?

"I think she would have been the perfect mom for someone that actually was sick," said Gypsy of her mother. "But I'm not sick. There's that big, big difference."

After reviewing evidence of decades of abuse, the prosecutor on Gypsy's case offered her a deal: If she pleaded guilty to second-degree murder, she would serve 10 years in jail with the opportunity for parole. Gypsy accepted. In a *20/20* interview that aired in 2018 she said, "I feel like I'm more free in prison, than with living with my mom. Because now, I'm allowed to just live like a normal woman." Godejohn was found guilty of first-degree murder and armed criminal action in November 2018. He was sentenced to life in prison.

JAYCEE LEE DUGARD

C lad in her favorite all-pink outfit, 11-year-old Jaycee Lee Dugard was walking to the bus stop on June 10, 1991, when a car stopped beside her. Expecting the driver to ask for directions, Dugard turned toward the car as the driver rolled down the window. The next thing Dugard recalled was being held down in the back seat by a woman, drifting in and out of consciousness during a three-hour car ride to a residence in Antioch, California. The couple that abducted Dugard knocked her out with a stun gun. Her stepfather, Carl Probyn, witnessed the abduction and gave chase on his bicycle, but he couldn't keep up with the car.

Within days, national press outlets descended on Dugard's hometown of Meyers, California. Dozens of volunteers searched for Dugard daily. Flyers were mailed across the country, and pink ribbons blanketed the town in remembrance and to show support for her family. The case was featured on *America's Most Wanted* within a week. But Dugard didn't turn up, despite the national attention and support. Her mother, Terry Probyn, continued the effort for the next 18 years.

Dugard was kidnapped by Phillip and Nancy Garrido. Phillip had a record that stretched back to 1972, when he was charged with sexually assaulting a 14-year-old girl. (The girl declined to testify, and the case never went to trial.) Garrido married his first wife the following year; she later claimed he was abusive and had kidnapped her when she tried to leave him. In 1976, he kidnapped and raped 25-year-old Katherine Callaway. While in court for that crime, he admitted to masturbating in his car while parked in front of elementary and high schools. A court-ordered psychiatric evaluation labeled him a "sexual deviant and chronic drug abuser." Garrido was sentenced to 50 years and began serving time at Leavenworth Penitentiary in Kansas.

It was at Leavenworth where Garrido met Nancy Bocanegra while she was visiting her uncle. They married at the prison on October 5, 1981. Garrido was released from federal custody into state custody on January 22, 1988, and then released on probation from state prison seven months later. The Garridos moved to Antioch to live with Phillip's mother, who had dementia. It was there that they kept Dugard prisoner.

LEAVENWORTH PENITENTIARY

This prison was completed in the mid-1920s. Its walls are 40 feet high and descend 40 feet below ground, with a total distance of 3,030 feet long, enclosing almost 23 acres. Leavenworth was the largest maximum-security prison in the United States until 2005, when it was downgraded to medium-security, now housing approximately 1,670 inmates. The imposing structure can be viewed and photographed only from a distance (across the street, on the south side of Metropolitan Avenue).

Some of its more famous inmates were "Machine Gun Kelly," Anthony "Tony Ducks" Corallo, Tom Pendergast, Carl Panzram, George Moran, John Franzese, Robert Stroud (the "Bird Man of Alcatraz"), James Earl Ray, James Joseph "Whitey" Bulger Jr., Michael Vick, just to name a few.

By the time the Garridos arrived at their home in Antioch on the day of Dugard's kidnapping, they'd stripped her of her clothes. They put a blanket over her head and ushered her into a tiny soundproof shed in the backyard, where Phillip raped her for the first time. Afterward, he left her naked and handcuffed, locked in the shed, and with a warning that guard dogs would attack if she tried to escape. Phillip visited her in the shed, bringing her food and talking to her—sometimes telling her amusing stories, but other times ranting at her or tearfully apologizing.

Phillip eventually moved Dugard into a larger room in a shed next door. It was in this room that Dugard would give birth to her and Phillip's two daughters, in 1994 and 1997. As the

A family photo of Jaycee Lee Dugard, before she was kidnapped in 1991.

CLOSE CALLS AND MISSED CHANCES

After Dugard was found, authorities were criticized for several missed opportunities to rescue her:

• Police failed to make the connection that Dugard was taken from the same area as Phillip Garrido's previous kidnapping victim, Katherine Callaway.

• In 2002, the fire department responded to an incident involving a minor with a shoulder injury in a swimming pool on the Garridos' property. This information was not relayed to the parole office.

• A neighbor called the police on Phillip in 2006, claiming he was psychotic and had people living in his backyard. Officers spoke with Phillip at the front door for 30 minutes, but did not search the property and let him off with a warning.

daughters grew, Dugard did her best to homeschool them, though she herself had only a fifth-grade education, and to protect them from Phillip's continued rants and lectures.

On August 24, 2009, 18 years after Dugard's kidnapping, Phillip went to a UC Berkeley police station with Dugard's daughters to inquire about a permit for an event. An officer there took note of Phillip's erratic behavior and the girls' sullen demeanor. After a follow-up meeting the next day, officers phoned the parole board; they believed Phillip was in violation of his parole terms. Officers visited his home, finding only Phillip, his elderly mother, and Nancy. Because Phillip had driven more than 25 miles from his home and was alone in the company of minors (Dugard's children)—both violations of his parole—they asked him to visit the parole office the next day.

Phillip arrived at the office on August 26 with Nancy, Dugard (introduced as "Allissa"), and her daughters. After officers separated them, Dugard maintained her false identity until she heard that Phillip admitted he kidnapped and raped her. She then identified herself as Jaycee Dugard.

Dugard said that she wished to see her mother every day of her captivity. After 18 years, she and Terry were reunited. Dugard's stepfather and aunt reported that the reunion went smoothly and that Dugard's daughters seemed well adjusted. Dugard went on to write the memoirs *A Stolen Life* and *Freedom: My Book of Firsts* about her captivity and reintegration into the world. She works with horses as part of her therapy to help her trust people again.

The Garridos initially pleaded not guilty to rape, kidnapping, and false imprisonment. On April 28, 2011, they both changed their pleas to guilty. Phillip received 431 years, and Nancy received 36 years to life.

In July 2010, the State of California issued a $20 million settlement to Dugard to compensate her for the "various lapses by the Corrections Department [that contributed to] Dugard's continued captivity, ongoing sexual assault and mental and/or physical abuse." Dugard also filed a lawsuit against the federal government, but it was dismissed in 2016.

DNA PROFILING

O n September 10, 1984, geneticist Alec Jeffreys was conducting an experiment at the University of Leicester in England on how inherited diseases passed through families. The experiment involved attaching DNA cells extracted from a technician's family to photographic film, and then leaving the film in a developing tank. What emerged was a DNA fingerprint—a sequence of bars attached to the film that could precisely identify an individual and establish kinship between people.

Though it wasn't his intent, Jeffreys invented DNA profiling. He and his team first used the technology to resolve contested paternities for the UK's Home Office. Jeffreys later gave talks on how his discovery could also be useful in solving crimes and apprehending criminals. Ironically, the idea was met with skepticism.

In 1986, the rape and murder of 15-year-old Dawn Ashworth in southwest Leicestershire went unsolved by police. The crime bore undeniable similarities to the 1983 killing of 15-year-old Lynda Mann, but the person who eventually confessed to Ashworth's killing, a local teenager with learning disabilities named Richard Buckland, insisted he hadn't killed Mann. Police decided to contact DNA profiling inventor Alec Jeffreys to see if he could confirm that Buckland was the killer. Jeffreys tested semen found on Ashworth and Mann alongside a blood sample from Buckland and came to two conclusions: Ashworth and

Mann *had* been killed by the same man, but it wasn't Richard Buckland.

A call for DNA samples from men in the Leicestershire community eventually led police to Colin Pitchfork, who had asked a coworker to give a DNA sample under his name. When this information got back to police, they confronted Pitchfork and obtained a genuine sample, which confirmed that he had killed both girls. Pitchfork pleaded guilty to two counts each of murder, rape, and indecent assault and one count of conspiring to pervert the course of justice. He was sentenced to life in prison.

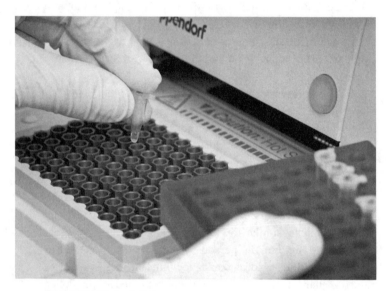

A tube of DNA is loaded into a PCR (polymerase chain reaction) thermocycler for analysis.

FAMOUS REMAINS

Since their discovery, genetic fingerprints have been used to make many historic matches.

- Josef Mengele—The infamous Nazi physician known for his grotesque human experiments was identified in 1990 from remains found in a Brazilian graveyard.

- Tsar Nicholas II—The last Russian tsar, killed during the Bolshevik Revolution in 1918, was identified in 1991 from remains found in a burial pit 850 miles east of Moscow.

- Henry McCollum—After 32 years in prison, McCollum was exonerated of the 1983 rape and murder of a young girl. He is one of at least 17 death row inmates in the United States exonerated by DNA fingerprints.

- Christopher Hampton—In 2016, the 1984 murder of Melanie Road was finally solved after DNA taken from Hampton's daughter, who had been arrested during a domestic dispute, matched samples taken from the crime scene and led police to Christopher Hampton.

In 1994, Jeffreys was knighted for his discovery. When discussing the legacy of DNA fingerprinting, Jeffreys likes to mention that "the first time DNA fingerprinting was used in a criminal case was to exonerate and not establish guilt—that's a really important point."

A BOMBING IN BIRMINGHAM

On September 15, 1963, a bomb detonated during Sunday school at the 16th Street Baptist Church in Birmingham, Alabama, a house of worship with a large Black congregation. The blast killed 14-year-olds Addie Mae Collins, Cynthia Wesley, and Carole Robertson, and 11-year-old Carol Denise McNair. In addition, 20 other people were injured. Two more Black men were later killed during protests, one by police and one by a racist mob.

Ku Klux Klan member Robert Chambliss was charged with the murders of the girls, but received only a six-month sentence. Three other men—Bobby Frank Cherry, Herman Cash, and Thomas E. Blanton Jr.—were involved in the bombing, but FBI director J. Edgar Hoover blocked their prosecution. A battle for justice lasted for decades. Cash died in 1994 without being charged. Chambliss was retried and sentenced to life in prison for murder in 1977, and Cherry and Blanton both received the same sentence after finally being charged in 2000.

The aftermath of the 16th Street Baptist Church bombing in Birmingham, Alabama, 1963.

TED BUNDY: ESCAPEE (AND SERIAL KILLER)

The scene: The Pitkin County Courthouse, Aspen, Colorado, June 7, 1977

The plot: The preliminary hearing for the murder of Caryn Campbell

The villain: Ted Bundy, defendant and—by his own request—his own defense attorney

 undy elected to represent himself, which meant he didn't have to wear the requisite shackles or handcuffs when he appeared in the courtroom. During a recess, he asked that he be allowed to visit the library to do further research for his defense. There, behind the cover of a bookcase, Bundy opened a window and jumped out. Then, with a sprained ankle, he ran.

Bundy wandered the woods for six days, breaking into homes to steal food, clothes, and a rifle. After he stole a car, the escapee's fatigue proved too much for him, and his veering car attracted patrollers' attention. He was apprehended on June 13, 1977, and returned to Garfield County Jail in Glenwood Springs, Colorado. Despite the setback, he hadn't given up planning his escape.

Back in jail, Bundy hatched a new escape plot. Armed with a detailed floor plan of the jail and a hacksaw blade, he gradually chipped away at his ceiling until he could slip through to the crawl space above. (How he acquired the floor plan and hacksaw blade remains unknown.)

On December 30, 1977, the jail was quiet. Most of the staff was still on holiday break. Bundy seized the opportunity, creating a makeshift "body" under his sheets by using books and files. Then he climbed into the crawl space again and broke through the floor above it, which led to the apartment of the chief jailor. From there, he changed his clothes and left the prison.

By the time guards realized he was no longer in his cell, Bundy had already hopped on a plane to Chicago.

After road-tripping through Michigan (where he watched a football game at a local bar), Bundy made his way to Florida. Although he'd intended to lie low and refrain from crime, it wasn't long before he reverted to form. On the morning of January 15, 1978, he broke into the Chi Omega sorority house near the Florida State University campus.

Kathy Kleiner and Karen Chandler were sophomores at FSU living together as roommates in the Chi Omega house— Kleiner's parents thought it would be safer than the dorm she lived in as a freshman. January 14 had been a normal day: Kleiner attended a friend's wedding and then returned to her room in the Chi Omega house after the reception to study. Chandler read in her bed across their room. They turned off the lights around 10:30 p.m. At around 3:00 a.m., Kleiner heard someone trip over the trunk between their beds and awoke with a start. Bundy, only a dark, human-shaped mass to Kleiner's eyes, loomed above her, brandishing a club above his head, and then began beating her and Chandler.

Suddenly light flooded the room, and Bundy fled. Chi Omega sister Nita Neary had returned home from a date just in time to save Chandler's and Kleiner's lives. Neary watched Bundy

Bundy in an Aspen, Colorado, courthouse during his 1977 murder trial.

run from the house, noticing his distinct profile, and called the paramedics as Chandler stumbled into the hallway and Kleiner rocked and moaned in her bed.

By the time he entered Kleiner and Chandler's room, Bundy had already killed two Chi Omega sisters, Margaret Bowman and Lisa Levy. Though Chandler and Kleiner were gravely injured, they were lucky to escape with their lives.

Chandler suffered a concussion, a broken jaw, loss of teeth, and a crushed finger. Kleiner also had a broken jaw, along with a deep cut in her shoulder, and she'd half bitten off her own tongue. She spent a week in the hospital with her jaw wired shut. An oral surgeon would later have to rebreak, realign, and rewire it, and

Kleiner spent more than two months healing at her parents' house in South Miami.

After the attack, Bundy stole a van and drove east. In broad daylight on the morning of February 9, 1978, he abducted 12-year-

old Kimberly Diane Leach from Lake City Junior High School. It wasn't until April 7, after an exhaustive two-month search, that Leach's partially decomposed body was discovered in a state park in Suwannee County.

On February 15, Bundy's auto theft finally caught up with him. A "wants and warrants" check by Pensacola police officer David Lee revealed that the Volkswagen Beetle Bundy was driving had been stolen.

Bundy did not go down without a fight. He kicked Lee and ran. The officer fired a warning shot, chased after Bundy, and tackled him to the ground. After a struggle in which Bundy tried to get Lee's gun, the officer eventually overcame him. Inside the stolen car, Lee found three women's FSU IDs and 21 stolen credit cards. Lee reported that as he drove Bundy to jail, the killer said to him, "I wish you had killed me."

Kleiner became an outspoken force for the prosecution of her attacker. The *Tallahassee Democrat* published a story about the Chi Omega attacks calling Kleiner a "belligerent survivor." At Bundy's trial in the spring of 1979, Kleiner testified against him and didn't wince as Bundy, who again provided his own counsel, stared her down. Though she recalled the frustration she felt when she couldn't identify Bundy as the shadowy figure who had been in the room that night, it didn't matter. Bundy was found guilty on July 24, 1979, and sentenced to death. He wouldn't escape again. He was executed on January 24, 1989.

Kleiner went on to live a full, happy life. She married, had a son, divorced, and remarried. A 2019 article called her and her husband "extraordinarily happy people." Her only remaining complaint: too much focus on Bundy in the media, and not enough on his victims.

Her old roommate Chandler no longer considers herself a victim: "I was a victim until I walked out of that hospital. I was a survivor until he was executed. . . . We gotta come up with something that's after that. It's not part of me anymore."

PRO SE REPRESENTATION

ro se (meaning "for oneself," or "in one's own behalf") refers to the process of acting as your own lawyer at trial. Criminals who have represented themselves include:

• **Lenny Bruce**—The comedian was charged with obscenity multiple times throughout the 1960s. In 1964, he represented himself in one such case and was convicted. He was posthumously pardoned in 2003 on the grounds of the First Amendment.

• **James Traficant**—The politician defended himself against racketeering charges twice, with mixed results: He was acquitted in 1983 and convicted in 2002.

• **Ted Bundy**—Bundy (see page 21) was studying to become a lawyer before he was arrested and tried for the 1978 assault at a sorority house that left two women dead. He grilled some of the survivors on the stand, but was ultimately convicted and sentenced to death.

• **Charles Manson**—During Manson's trial (see page 1) for the first-degree murders of pregnant actress Sharon Tate and six others, he carved an X on his forehead and argued that it removed him from the court's jurisdiction. He was convicted on all seven counts.

• Abraham Lincoln said, "He who represents himself has a fool for a client," but not every person who represents himself is such a fool. In 2011, 58-year-old **Lee Anthony Evans** was tried for the 1978 murder of five teenage boys. Evans was accused by his cousin, Philander Hampton, who received a plea bargain in exchange for his testimony. Hampton claimed that the boys had stolen marijuana from Evans, so Hampton helped him trap them inside a house that Evans then set on fire. However, the bodies were never found, and there was no DNA evidence linking Evans to the crime. With that as a foundation for his case, Evans went on to successfully discredit Hampton, who previously served 10 years in prison for robbery, had a history of heroin addiction, and sold drugs out of the house that was burned down. Hampton was also unable to keep his story consistent. Evans was acquitted of all charges, but the trial left its mark: "It's a situation where I heard them say not guilty, but the way they put a horrible thing on you, you still feel guilty," Evans explained.

Lenny Bruce being arrested in 1961 in San Francisco for using obscene language during his comedy act.

THE GREAT FEATHER HEIST

In the summer of 2009, administrators at the Tring branch of the Natural History Museum, London, discovered that a room containing some of the collection's 750,000 bird specimens had been broken into, and 299 rare tropical bird skins had been stolen. Fifteen months later, 22-year-old Edwin Rist, an American studying the flute at London's Royal Academy of Music, was arrested in his apartment, surrounded by ziplock bags filled with colorful plumes and boxes of what remained of the skins.

Rist was charged with orchestrating the heist. Posing as a photographer, Rist first cased the room. Months later, he returned with a glass cutter, latex gloves, and a large suitcase. Rist began selling the feathers and skins on the black market, known as the "feather underground." Most of the buyers were "fly-tyers," people who were obsessed with re-creating nineteenth-century instructions for fishing lures. Rist used the tens of thousands of dollars he made on the feather underground to buy a new flute. He never served jail time and now lives in Germany, where he makes heavy metal flute videos.

KITTY GENOVESE AND THE BYSTANDER EFFECT

"37 WHO SAW MURDER DIDN'T CALL THE POLICE"
—New York Times, March 27, 1964

So read the 1964 *New York Times* headline reporting the murder of 28-year-old Kitty Genovese in Kew Gardens, Queens, New York. The article claimed that 38 neighbors (one more than the headline stated) watched as a man, later identified as Winston Moseley, returned to attack Genovese three times. This story was the basis of the psychological theory of the "bystander effect"—that people are less likely to intervene in a crime if other people are present.

In the years since, many of the details surrounding the Genovese case have been disproven. Genovese was attacked two times, not three. There were not 38 eyewitnesses to the attacks; in fact, most reported hearing screams but were unsure of the source. Many of the "witnesses" were elderly, and still more heard the 3:15 a.m. attack only through the fog of sleep. Also, after Moseley pierced Genovese's lung, it was unlikely

A mug shot of Kitty Genovese created by the NYPD in Queens, 1961.

that anyone heard her screaming. A neighbor did call the police during the attack, but the call was never logged. Two more neighbors called the police afterward, as Genovese staggered into the building where she lived. One woman ran out of her apartment and cradled her in the hallway as she lay dying. There were several witnesses who did nothing, but not to the extent the media reported at the time. In October 2016, the *New York Times* amended the original article to reexamine the facts of the story.

BEHIND THE HEADLINES

Match the newspaper headline to the accused.

---

1. "Wife does not recall cutting off man's penis"

2. "Body parts litter apartment"

3. "Obsessive Love for His Mother Drove [Redacted] to Slay, Rob Graves"

4. "Double Murder: Wealthy Resident of Fall River and His Wife Killed"

A. Jeffrey Dahmer

B. Lizzie Borden

C. Ed Gein

D. Lorena Bobbitt

Answers: 1D: Bobbitt was accused of cutting off her husband John Wayne's penis in 1993 (see page 255). She was eventually acquitted due to a combination defense of PTSD and temporary insanity from the abuse she suffered at John's hands. **2A:** When Dahmer (see page 45) was caught in 1991, police extracted numerous decomposing body parts from his fly-infested apartment. **3C:** Gein's legendary obsession with his mother (see page 172) was the inspiration for the character of Norman Bates in Psycho. **4B:** Borden was later acquitted of the double murder of her parents.

THE ABDUCTIONS OF SHIN SANG-OK AND CHOI EUN-HEE

n 1967, before Kim Jong-Il was Supreme Leader of North Korea, he was the cultural arts director of the Propaganda and Agitation Department. At the age 25, he oversaw all movies, plays, and books produced in North Korea, ensuring they offered the correct ideological guidance and presented his father, Kim Il-Sung, in a positive light.

The job was a good fit for him. Since he was a child, Kim loved movies. He had an underground network to smuggle banned Western films into North Korea, and would spend hours watching them in the Cultural Film Distribution Center. He burned to make films that were just as good as those. And while the films he produced became known as the Immortal Classics, they were only good by the standards of North Koreans, who (unlike Kim) had nothing against which to compare them. If he wanted to win international awards, Kim would need outside help. So he turned to the south.

Shin Sang-ok was one of the most famous directors in South Korea, and his wife, Choi Eun-hee, was one of its most popular actresses. But their fortunes would turn in the early 1970s, when President Park Chung-hee made himself dictator of South Korea and placed restrictions on the film industry. Shin and Park were friends, so Shin thought he could talk his way out of his movies getting censored. But when news leaked that Shin had a secret child with another woman, Park couldn't ignore his friend's disregard for the law and stripped Shin's studio of its production license.

Choi divorced Shin and focused on raising their two adopted children and running her Academy of Cinematic Arts. When Shin declared bankruptcy, Choi knew she was at risk of losing the school. That's when she got a call inviting her to Hong Kong.

The man on the phone claimed he ran a film studio and wanted Choi to direct a movie for him. She needed the money for her school, so she accepted. In 1977, she flew to Hong Kong to discuss the project. Instead, she was chauffeured around by a woman and her daughter, who took her to an empty stretch of beach called Repulse Bay. There, men forced her onto a boat. When it docked six days later, Kim Jong-Il met her on the pier.

When Shin heard Choi was missing, he flew to Hong Kong but found no trace of her. There were rumors that agents of North Korea were abducting people, but the press and police

South Korean actress Choi Eun-hee with her film director husband Shin Sang-ok in Tokyo in 1989, about three years after they escaped almost a decade of captivity in North Korea.

suspected Shin was responsible for Choi's disappearance. When Choi's trail went cold, Shin tried to find work again, but he didn't have a passport. A friend took him to Repulse Bay to buy one illegally, but their car was stopped by men with knives who put a bag over Shin's head and dragged him onto a boat. Six days later, he too arrived in North Korea.

Despite both being held captive by Kim Jong-Il, Choi and Shin were kept separated for the next five years. Choi, ever the actress, played along with Kim's demands. She watched and discussed his movies with him, sang at his parties, and took his reeducation classes. She was rewarded with a nice villa but was closely watched by her housekeeper and guards. Shin was harder to break. He tried escaping twice and was sent to Prison Number Six, where he sat in a torture position 16 hours a day for two and a half years.

Finally, in 1983, Shin was broken enough for Kim's liking. He was dressed in a suit and taken to his first party with the North Korean dictator. Choi was there. They locked eyes across the room and Kim made them embrace. After a movie screening, Kim then sent them home together. Alone, they told each other everything that had happened and confessed their mutual love. They talked of escape but knew the dangers and decided instead to wait for the perfect moment.

Six months after their reunion, Kim told Shin and Choi that he kidnapped them to help him improve the North Korean film industry. In order for everyone to believe they defected voluntarily, Kim would allow them to travel to Eastern Bloc countries, watched closely by guards, to film and show their movies at festivals.

Over the next three years, Shin and Choi made seven films, winning awards for Best Director and Best Actress. The press questioned their seven-year absence and sudden reappearance, but they stuck with Kim's lie. Their final film, *Pulgasari*, a Communist take on *Godzilla*, was a hit in North Korea. Kim was thrilled with the attention. With every success, restrictions loosened slightly. After *Pulgasari*, Kim permitted them to travel together to Vienna, Austria, a gateway to the West, to find backers for a film about Genghis Khan.

Choi and Shin went to Vienna in March 1986 with three guards. They arranged a lunch meeting with a journalist friend and convinced the guards to follow them in a separate car. But when they left the next morning, Shin told the driver to take them to the US embassy. The guards tried to follow but lost them at an intersection.

Fearing for their safety, Shin and Choi moved to Virginia, where they were reunited with their children; they later moved to California. Eventually, they returned to South Korea, where they retired after a few small jobs. Shin died in 2005 and Choi in 2018.

THE RESURRECTION OF ANNE GREENE

I n 1650, Anne Greene was working as a scullery maid in Duns Tew, Oxfordshire, England, when she was raped by her employer's grandson and became pregnant. The 22-year-old later gave birth to a stillborn boy and attempted to conceal his body. The child was soon discovered, and although medical examiners confirmed that he was born lifeless, Greene was still charged with murdering her baby and sentenced to death. She was hanged on December 14, 1650. At Greene's request, her friends pulled down and struck her hanging body to ensure she was dead. Her body was then given to a medical school for dissection.

The next day, the three physicians due to dissect Greene were shocked to discover she had a slight pulse and was breathing weakly. The doctors set to work reviving her, using "tried-and-true" methods like bloodletting and a tobacco-smoke enema. Greene made a complete recovery over the next two weeks. She was granted a full pardon and went on to marry and have three children before dying in 1665.

TRUE CRIME BY THE BOOK

When it comes to true crime, there are lots of stories published but only a small number of them are told exceptionally well. Here are the enduring classics.

• *In Cold Blood* by Truman Capote. Capote's 1965 nonfiction novel pioneered the genre of true crime writing.

• *The Stranger Beside Me* by Ann Rule. This masterpiece by the queen of true crime writing details her firsthand experience with serial killer Ted Bundy.

• *Helter Skelter* by Vincent Bugliosi. A definitive guide to the 1969 Manson murders.

• *My Dark Places* by James Ellroy. A riveting autobiography that talks about the murder of the author's mother.

• *Midnight in the Garden of Good and Evil* by John Berendt. A young man is shot dead in the mansion of an antiques dealer in Savannah, Georgia, in 1981. Was he murdered, or was he killed in self-defense?

• *Columbine* by Dave Cullen. An examination of the high school shooting that ended in 15 people dead (including the 2 boys who carried it out) and left a nation reeling.

• *Zodiac* by Robert Graysmith. Graysmith, a cartoonist working for the newspaper where the Zodiac Killer sent his taunting letters, unravels his crimes, the evidence, and potential suspects.

• *Under the Banner of Heaven* by Jon Krakauer. Two brothers who are part of a radical religious sect of Mormon fundamentalists kill a woman and her child.

• *The Executioner's Song* by Norman Mailer. Mailer examines Gary Gilmore, who robbed and killed two men in 1976, and his insistence on being executed for the crime.

THE MURDER OF STANFORD WHITE

I n 1906, Harry K. Thaw infamously murdered the prominent New York City architect Stanford White. The trial, which took place a year later, was the first to reach such a sensational media frenzy that it was dubbed the now commonly known "trial of the century." The focus of the trial was neither murderer nor victim, but a young model and chorus girl named Evelyn Nesbit, who was perhaps best remembered in print as one of illustrator Charles Gibson's iconic Gibson Girls, particularly for one of Gibson's most famous works, *Women: The Eternal Question*, which depicts Nesbit in profile.

White and Thaw both had an affinity for young chorus girls like Nesbit. White met and wooed Nesbit first in 1901, when he was 48 and she was just 16. But it was Thaw whom she would go on to marry, when she was 19. Thaw's obsession with Nesbit and White's previous relationship, combined with his tenuous grip on reality, would soon turn deadly.

After seeing Nesbit in a Broadway show, White urged another young chorus girl he knew to invite her to lunch. Nesbit disliked White, but White's infatuation with

Charles Gibson's iconic drawing *Woman: The Eternal Question*, modeled off Evelyn Nesbit.

her was unstoppable. He began buying her lavish gifts and inviting her to parties at his luxurious apartment. One night, after Nesbit's mother had left town, he invited her to one such party. When Nesbit arrived, White was the only person there. He plied her with champagne and then raped her. Afterward, he continued to show her affection for a time, and she believed he would ask her to marry him. But his attention soon began to wander to other young, attractive chorus girls.

Thaw quickly picked up where White left off. Nesbit disliked Thaw as well, but he wooed her in a similar fashion, even taking her and her mother on a trip to Europe. Her mother returned to the US early, and the young girl was again alone with a powerful, wealthy older man. Thaw appeared in her room one night, begging her to tell him what White had done to her. He broke down in tears when she told him the story. Several nights later, he appeared in her room again, this time beating and raping her.

Thaw's obsession with Nesbit and how White defiled her continued. In 1905, Thaw and Nesbit married; the bride wore black. They fell into a predictable domestic existence with Thaw's family in Pittsburgh. In 1906, Thaw told Nesbit he was taking her on another trip to Europe. They stopped in New York to see a musical, *Mam'zelle Champagne*, on June 25, the night before they were to leave. Despite the extremely hot weather, Thaw wore a heavy overcoat all night.

The show was at the rooftop theater at Madison Square Garden, which White, who was present that night, had designed. During the show's final number, "I Could Love a Million Girls," Thaw walked up to White, pulled a gun from his overcoat, and shot him three times, killing him in front of 900 witnesses.

At the first of Thaw's two trials, his mother blocked his lawyers from employing an insanity defense. Instead, the defense argued a type of temporary insanity they called Dementia Americana, which they claimed drove Thaw to kill out of a primal drive to protect his wife's honor. To support the theory, Thaw's mother hired alienists (early psychologists, often relied on in courtrooms) to explain exactly how Thaw was insane only in the moment of the murder, but completely sane before and afterward. Nesbit was also compelled to testify in excruciating detail about what White had done to her, as well as endure accusatory cross-examination that questioned why she accepted gifts from White and attended his parties if he was so brutal to her.

Evelyn Nesbit, 1903, in a studio shot arranged by Stanford White.

American journalist and humorist Irvin S. Cobb commented on the extreme sensationalism of the trial: "You see, it had in it wealth, degeneracy, rich old wasters, delectable young chorus girls and adolescent artists' models; the behind-the-scenes of Theatredom and the Underworld, and the Great White Way . . . the abnormal pastimes and weird orgies of overly aesthetic artists and jaded debauchees. In the cast of the motley show were Bowery toughs, Harlem gangsters, Tenderloin panderers, Broadway leading men, Fifth Avenue clubmen, Wall Street manipulators, uptown voluptuaries and downtown thugs."

The jury in the first trial was deadlocked after nearly two days and led to a mistrial. In the second trial, the defense convinced Thaw's mother that her son would go to the electric chair if they didn't argue insanity. He was found not guilty by reason of insanity and sentenced to life in Matteawan State Hospital for the Criminally Insane.

Thaw used his wealth to live in luxury at Matteawan. He was released on July 16, 1915, after a jury declared him no longer insane. In 1916, he was arrested for beating and raping 19-year-old Frederick Gump. Thaw was again declared insane at trial and sent to Kirkbride Asylum in Philadelphia, where he remained until 1924. He was repeatedly accused of such attacks, usually on chorus girls, until his death in 1947. Monetary settlements were reached with most of his accusers.

Nesbit became pregnant in 1910, while Thaw was still at Matteawan. She claimed the pregnancy was the result of a conjugal visit, but Thaw denied paternity. They divorced in 1915. She struggled to make ends meet for many years before becoming a ceramics and sculpting teacher in California.

ESCAPE FROM ALCATRAZ

From 1934 to 1963, 36 prisoners braved the icy waters of the San Francisco Bay as they attempted to escape from Alcatraz Federal Penitentiary. Prison officials claimed there were no successful escapes, though five prisoners are listed as "missing and presumed dead." Bank robbers Frank Morris and John and Clarence Anglin are perhaps the most well-known of this bunch. In the early hours of June 12, 1962, the three escaped through the air ducts in their cells, which they had been widening for three months with sharpened spoons. The three climbed up 30 feet of plumbing, then escaped across the roof and back down the exterior piping. All that remained was their trip across the bay, with a makeshift raft and life preservers made from 50 raincoats donated by or stolen from fellow inmates.

Guards were alerted when Morris's "head" rolled off the bed the next morning—the escapees had fashioned decoys out of soap, paper, and human hair from the prison barbershop.

The bodies of the escaped prisoners were never recovered. In 2013, San Francisco police received a letter that read, in part:

> *My name is John Anglin. I escape [sic] from Alcatraz in June 1962 with my brother Clarence and Frank Morris. I'm 83 years old and in bad shape. I have cancer. Yes we all made it that night but barely!*

Handwriting analysis of the letter was inconclusive, but it added fuel to the longtime speculation that the escape was successful.

ERICA PRATT:
SUPER SEVEN-YEAR-OLD

Erica Pratt was playing with her sister in front of their Southwest Philadelphia home on a summer evening in 2002 when two men abducted her. They bound the seven-year-old's hands and feet with duct tape and left her in the basement of an empty house. That's where the courageous little girl took matters into her own hands, chewing through the tape for hours until she freed herself, kicking out a panel in the basement door and wriggling through, punching out a window, and then screaming for help until two boys playing nearby led police to her. Less than 24 hours after her kidnappers demanded $150,000 ransom for her return, Erica was back with her family, having sustained only a minor eye injury.

Edward Johnson and James Burns were arrested and convicted of the kidnapping. The supposed motive was a local rumor the two had overheard that Erica's family had received a life insurance payout.

JEFFREY DAHMER: THE MILWAUKEE CANNIBAL

I n 1985, Jeffrey Lionel Dahmer began meeting men for sex at bathhouses in Wisconsin. In his mind, there was only one problem with this: A living body moved a bit too much. He preferred to dehumanize his partners. "I trained myself to view people as objects of pleasure instead of people," he'd say later. His solution? Drugging the men with sedative-laced liquor. This would become Dahmer's chosen method to commit both rape and, eventually, murder. When the staff at the bathhouse discovered what he was doing, they revoked his membership but initiated no legal consequences. So Dahmer simply relocated his predatory act to more private environs.

Between 1987 and 1991, Dahmer lured 15 men to his apartment, usually with an offer of money for sex or posing for nude photographs. Then he drugged and strangled them before having sex with their corpses.

As part of his early murders, Dahmer attempted to retain a piece of each victim's body, though they often decomposed. It wasn't until March 25, 1989, that Dahmer figured out how to permanently retain parts of his victims. Dahmer found 25-year-old victim Anthony Sears exceptionally attractive, so he preserved Sears's head and genitalia in acetone and stored other parts of him in his locker at work.

But Sears was just the beginning of Dahmer's fixation on preserving and keeping pieces of his victims. By 1991, Dahmer's neighbors at the Oxford Apartments in Milwaukee started to complain to management about terrible smells coming from Apartment 213. But Dahmer's landlord accepted his explanation of food spoiling in a broken freezer.

Dahmer experienced several close calls with law enforcement as well—including a 1998 sentence for molesting 13-year-old Keison Sinthasomphone, which he successfully argued down to one-year work release and five years probation—pleading to the judge, in a display of false contrition, that he needed treatment, not punishment. Then in May 1991, by coincidence, Dahmer lured Keison's younger brother, 14-year-old Konerak Sinthasomphone, to his home, offering Sinthasomphone money in exchange for pictures of him. The boy reluctantly agreed, and Dahmer took nude photos of Sinthasomphone before drugging and molesting him. Once the boy was unconscious, Dahmer drilled a hole into his skull, injected hydrochloric acid into his frontal lobe, then led Sinthasomphone into his bedroom, where the body of Tony Hughes, a man Dahmer had killed three days

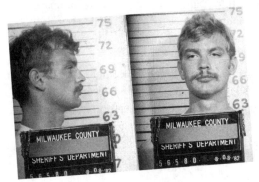

Jeffrey Dahmer's 1982 mug shot.

prior, was rotting on the floor. Dahmer left Sinthasomphone there and went out to drink at a bar.

When Dahmer returned early in the morning, Sinthasomphone was sitting naked outside Dahmer's apartment complex, bleeding and muttering in Lao, surrounded by three women who had called 911. Then the police showed up.

When police officers John Balcerzak and Joseph Gabrish arrived at the scene, Dahmer explained that Sinthasomphone was his 19-year-old lover, and that he typically acted disoriented when he drank too much. When the women protested that Sinthasomphone was clearly in distress and struggling against Dahmer, the officers snapped at them to "butt out" and "shut the hell up." The women grew exasperated as the officers covered Sinthasomphone with a towel and walked him back to Dahmer's apartment.

Once there, the officers noticed the smell of Hughes's decomposing body, but made no attempt to investigate. They did not ask for Sinthasomphone's or Dahmer's identification. They did not run a background check on Dahmer—if they had they would have learned he was a registered sex offender. Instead, the officers left Sinthasomphone with Dahmer, who molested, killed, and dismembered the boy that night.

Balcerzak and Gabrish were later heard on tape making homophobic jokes to dispatch, saying they reunited the "lovers." Both officers were fired but later reinstated.

On July 22, 1991, Dahmer offered Tracy Edwards $100 to pose for nude photographs and keep him company for the evening. Almost immediately upon entering Dahmer's apartment, Edwards knew something was wrong. There were boxes of hydrochloric acid and a foul-smelling 57-gallon drum, in which police would later discover three torsos dissolving in acid. Then Dahmer suddenly snapped handcuffs on Edwards, produced a knife, and casually mentioned that he wanted to eat his heart.

Edwards waited until Dahmer was distracted, then punched him in the face and ran out of the apartment. He was able to flag down two police officers who, though skeptical of Edwards's story, accompanied him back to Dahmer's apartment. Once there, Dahmer tried to convince the police that the whole thing was a misunderstanding. The officers almost believed him—until they spotted Polaroids of dismembered body parts. When Dahmer saw the police had made this discovery, he tried to fight them but he was quickly subdued. Pinned down and defeated, Dahmer said, "For what I did I should be dead."

Eleven victims were found inside Dahmer's apartment, the first of whom disappeared in March 1989, months after Dahmer escaped a sentence for child molestation. There was also evidence that he'd eaten some of his victims. Dahmer eventually confessed to killing 17 men and boys. He was given 15 life sentences.

Dahmer was very unpopular among his fellow inmates because, among other things, he sculpted his prison food into severed limbs and slathered them with ketchup "blood." One prisoner—Christopher Scarver—was particularly disturbed by Dahmer's behavior, as well as his crimes.

On November 28, 1994, Scarver was left unsupervised in the prison showers with Dahmer. Guards soon discovered both Dahmer and another inmate, Jesse Anderson, on the bathroom floor with severe wounds. Scarver had bludgeoned both with a metal bar. Dahmer was rushed to the hospital but pronounced dead one hour later. As guards escorted him back to his cell, Scarver said, "God told me to do it. Jesse Anderson and Jeffrey Dahmer are dead."

MOST CRIMES ARE NOT REPORTED (AND MANY THAT ARE WILL NOT BE SOLVED)

A question on the annual survey from the US Bureau of Justice Statistics asks victims of crime if they reported the crime to the police. Fifty-seven percent of victims of violent crimes, such as rape, robbery, and assault, said they did not. The number of victims who did not report property crime, including burglary, theft, and auto theft, was even higher—66 percent. Among the reasons given for not reporting were feeling that police couldn't or wouldn't do anything to help, believing that the crime was a personal issue, or thinking it was too trivial to report.

A 2018 FBI study of clearance rate, or how many crimes were solved, found that police solved about 46 percent of reported violent crimes and only about 18 percent of property crimes nationwide.

PATTY HEARST AND THE SLA

O n February 4, 1974, a college sophomore at the University of California, Berkeley, was kidnapped from her apartment by a group of domestic terrorists who called themselves the Symbionese Liberation Army, or SLA. But it wasn't just any student they kidnapped: It was Patty Hearst, a scion of the wealthy and powerful Hearst family, abducted from the apartment she shared with her fiancé, Steven Weed. During the abduction she was beaten, warning shots were fired, and Hearst lost consciousness.

The SLA kidnapped Hearst because they wanted access to her family's influence—*and* its money. But their efforts didn't quite pan out—Hearst wasn't enough to leverage for the release of two SLA members from prison. And when Hearst's father donated $2 million in food to the Bay Area poor at the group's behest, the effort turned to chaos.

What exactly was the Symbionese Liberation Army? The small, radical group was founded in 1973 and led by escaped prisoner Donald DeFreeze, aka General Field Marshal Cinque. Its manifesto called for the unity, or *symbiosis*, of all leftist movements. SLA members practiced urban guerrilla warfare, and had already robbed homes in the San Francisco Bay Area and murdered a school superintendent before kidnapping Patty Hearst.

After the Hearst family failed to meet the SLA's difficult demands, the group refused to release Patty. In later testimony,

Hearst said she was kept blindfolded, her hands tied, in a closet for a week. She also said she was threatened with death. Eventually, the SLA started to let her out for meals . . . and political discussions.

According to Hearst, she was given a choice by DeFreeze: Join the SLA or die. "I accommodated my thoughts to coincide with theirs," she explained later. She began to study SLA political writings and participate in weapons drills. She was also raped by DeFreeze and SLA cofounder Willie Wolfe.

On April 3, the SLA released a tape in which Hearst announced that she had joined their cause and taken a new name: Tania, the nom de guerre of Che Guevara's companion. Just 12

Patty Hearst's mug shot after she was arrested for bank robbery in 1975.

days later, surveillance cameras recorded Tania taking part in the robbery of the Hibernia Bank in San Francisco. She held a semi-automatic carbine and yelled commands. Two customers were wounded during the robbery where the SLA stole more than $10,000.

Video evidence showed Hearst seemingly helping the SLA rob the bank. Authorities, including the US attorney general, began to consider her not as a victim but as "a common criminal." Hearst then committed additional crimes with the SLA, including firing shots at a store manager, stealing cars, making home-made explosive devices, and driving a getaway car for another bank robbery.

On an audiotape recording after the robbery of San Francisco's Hibernia Bank in 1974, the heiress and kidnapping victim explained her participation in the crime:

My gun was loaded, and at no time did my comrades intentionally point their guns at me. As for being brainwashed, the idea is ridiculous to the point of being beyond belief. I am a soldier in the People's Army.

Soon, though, the SLA was all but destroyed. On May 17, 1974, police tracked members to a hideout. In a violent shoot-out that involved automatic weapons, tear-gas grenades, and a house fire, six members died, including Wolfe and DeFreeze.

Several months later, on September 18, Hearst was apprehended by police. She listed her occupation as "Urban Guerrilla" when she was booked.

At the time of her arrest, Hearst weighed just 87 pounds and had experienced a dramatic drop in IQ. She had huge memory gaps and experienced frequent nightmares. Experts determined that she had lived with severe trauma and brainwashing during her time with the SLA. She claimed that she had been forced to take LSD and was ordered to participate enthusiastically in the robbery of the Hibernia Bank, a crime for which she was charged.

In 1976, the one-time heiress was convicted and sentenced to up to 35 years. She served only 22 months when President Jimmy Carter commuted her sentence. On his last day in office, President Bill Clinton fully pardoned her. In the years that followed, Hearst married, had two children, and became a fundraiser for charities, an actress, and the owner and handler of prizewinning dogs.

WADDLING OFF WITH DIRK THE PENGUIN

On April 15, 2012, Welshmen Rhys Owen Jones and Keri Mules woke up with a peculiar houseguest in their Queensland, Australia, apartment—a seven-year-old fairy penguin named Dirk who was usually found at nearby Sea World on Queensland's Gold Coast. The two men had drunkenly broken into the Sea World the night before, swam with the dolphins, and set off a fire extinguisher in a shark enclosure before making off with Dirk. They briefly tried to care for Dirk at their home by feeding him and putting him in the shower before releasing him into a canal, where they were spotted by locals who called the police. The men were apprehended, chastised for their drunken hijinks, and fined $1,000 AUD each.

Dirk was rescued and returned safely to Sea World, where he was reunited with his partner, Peaches.

THE LINDBERGH BABY: A QUESTIONABLE KIDNAPPING

 Celebrity aviator Charles Lindbergh was home with his wife, Anne Morrow Lindbergh, and their 20-month-old baby on the evening of March 1, 1932. At 10:00 p.m., the child's nurse, Betty Gow, discovered that Charles Jr. was missing from his crib.

Impressions in the ground and pieces of a wooden ladder were found beneath the baby's nursery window, which was located on the second floor. When word of the kidnapping spread, hundreds of people converged at the Lindbergh home in Highfields, New Jersey, inadvertently destroying any footprint evidence. (Experts would not detect any traces of fingerprints or footprints in the baby's room, either.)

However, Lindbergh did find a ransom note on the windowsill demanding $50,000. The letter concluded with a "signature" of a series of circles and three punched holes. Based on the distinctive spelling mistakes, analysts suspected the writers might be German-speaking:

> *Dear Sir!*
> *Have 50.000$ redy 25 000$ in 20$ bills 15000$ in 10$ bills and 10000$ in 5$ bills After 2–4 days we will inform you were to deliver the mony.*

> *We warn you for making anyding public or for notify the Police*
>
> > *The child is in gut care.*

On March 3, a second letter bearing the same "signature" arrived, explaining that the ransom had been increased to $70,000. A third such letter authorized John Condon, a retired Bronx schoolteacher, to serve as the kidnappers' intermediary with the Lindberghs, who'd grown desperate to rescue their child.

Lindbergh's team of investigators believed mobsters might be behind the kidnapping. They contacted Mickey Rosner, a person with ties to organized crime, to ask around. Several convicted criminals, including Al Capone, offered to help return the baby in exchange for money or release from prison. Lindbergh's team declined.

Together with the police, Lindbergh offered a $75,000

Wanted poster pleading for information on Charles Jr.'s disappearance.

A postcard from the Lindbergh kidnapper, 1932

reward for the baby's return, an astonishing sum during the Great Depression, to no avail. Meanwhile, the schoolteacher Condon met with one of the kidnappers, who sounded "foreign" and hid his face. The kidnapper assured Condon that the baby was still alive, and soon afterward mailed his sleeping suit and another ransom note. Condon then delivered $50,000 in a wooden box... but the baby was not returned.

On May 12, delivery truck driver William Allen pulled over to the side of the road in Hopewell Township, New Jersey, to relieve himself. He discovered the badly decomposed body of a young child whose skull had been fractured. Betty Gow identified the remains as Charles Lindbergh Jr., based on his overlapping toes and a handmade shirt. It appeared the baby had been killed by a blow to the head.

Police pursued hundreds of leads. Suspicion eventually fell on Violet Sharpe, a domestic worker at the Morrow household, and Condon himself. The case didn't progress, though, until police traced $20,000 of marked ransom money to a German immigrant named Bruno Richard Hauptmann. After his arrest, police found additional evidence linking him to the crime at his Bronx home, including Condon's address and telephone number as well as a section of wood believed to match the ladder fragments found outside the Lindbergh home.

Hauptmann was charged with capital murder and tried in Flemington, New Jersey, in 1934. The evidence presented appeared to point to him: the similarity between his handwriting and that of the ransom notes; the marked ransom money found in his garage, which Hauptmann claimed was left to him by a fellow German immigrant; the notebook containing a sketch of a homemade ladder; and Inspector John A. Lyons identifying him as the man who received the ransom payment. Hauptmann maintained his innocence throughout the trial, but was found guilty and given the death penalty.

Alternative theories about the Lindbergh case circulate to this day, questioning everything from the validity of the evidence to how the investigation was handled. Some even suggest that Charles Lindbergh himself might have killed his own baby; he had once hidden the baby in a closet as a joke, so the idea was that the kidnapping might have been a prank gone wrong. Or perhaps "Lucky Lindy" had more sinister intentions.

In 2012, history professor Lloyd C. Gardner proposed a new theory: that Lindbergh himself may have helped in orchestrating the kidnapping. Gardner pointed to Lindbergh's belief in social Darwinism and eugenics, his later Nazi sympathies, and affairs with three German women with whom he fathered a total of seven children as possible motives. Also, Charles Jr. was a sickly child. He had a rickets-like condition, a vitamin D deficiency that required a sunlamp kept cribside; hammertoes; an oversized cranium; and unfused skull bones—conditions that Lindbergh hid after the kidnapping. Lindbergh further took control of many parts of the investigation, and isolated household staff who may have known of the boy's health. Another strange turn involved Charles Jr.'s body, which Lindbergh had cremated before an autopsy could be performed.

Finally, the night of the kidnapping was the only time Lindbergh ever missed a speaking engagement. He claimed he came straight home from work "inadvertently." Was it a coincidence or was he at home to help Hauptmann with the abduction by drawing attention away from Charles Jr.'s room?

"The evidence against Hauptmann is quite compelling," says Professor Gardner, "but the evidence of his being the sole kidnapper is less compelling. Once you conclude it was conducted by a group or more than one person, the question becomes, why?"

GINA AND THE DEVIOUS DEFECATOR

GINA, the Genetic Information Nondiscrimination Act, is a 2008 law barring employers and insurance companies from discriminating against people with gene mutations that cause or increase their risk of an inherited disorder. Fear of discrimination is common among those who consider genetic screening. The law has two parts: Title I, which makes it illegal for insurance companies to use or require a person's genetic information when deciding that person's eligibility for coverage, and Title II, which bars employers from using genetic material when making decisions about hiring, promotion, and other terms of employment.

Since the law went into effect, it has been invoked often in legal matters. In 2010, 201 cases were filed that cited GINA. In 2014, that number jumped to 333. Only one case, however, has made its way to court: the Devious Defecator (a nickname coined by US district court judge Amy Totenberg).

In 2012, the Atlanta, Georgia, grocery distributor Atlas Logistics Group Retail Services obtained the DNA of two employees, Dennis Reynolds and Jack Lowe. The men were suspected of a particularly fetid crime: Someone was depositing human feces all over the warehouse. The men, who were suspected based on their work schedules, agreed to submit to a cheek-swab request from their employers, saying they were afraid they would lose their jobs if they declined. Though both were proved innocent, they soon became the subjects of cruel jokes by their coworkers. In 2013, Reynolds and Lowe filed a lawsuit.

Atlas Logistics argued that GINA did not apply to the case—they were just trying to identify the devious defecator, not acquire either man's genetic profile. But the jury rejected this argument, and in 2015 the men were awarded $2.25 million for emotional suffering. It is unknown if the true pooping perpetrator was ever caught.

TRUE CRIME TERMS: DRUG LINGO

ere's a sampling of the Drug Enforcement Administration's (DEA) lexicon of drug slang:

- **Golden Girl** = heroin
- **French Blues** = amphetamines
- **California Pancakes** = cocaine
- **White Girl** = fentanyl
- **Cat Valium** = ketamine
- **Witches' Teeth** = methamphetamines
- **Burritos Verdes** = marijuana
- **Dancing Shoes** = MDMA (or ecstasy)
- **Crystal Tea** = LSD
- **Smoochy Woochy Poochy** = marijuana
- **Alien Sex Fiend** = PCP mixed with heroin
- **Kibbles and Bits** = Ritalin
- **Aunt Emma** = opium
- **Beans** = oxycodone
- **Beam Me Up** = crack cocaine

THE "MR. BIG" TECHNIQUE

In the early hours of December 28, 2005, the body of 36-year-old Paula Gallant was found in the trunk of her car, beaten and strangled. Despite the notably odd behavior of her husband, Jason McRae, following Gallant's death, it would be more than five years before Royal Canadian Mounted Police obtained a confession from him through a 10-month sting operation using the "Mr. Big" Technique.

Also known as the Canadian Technique, because it was developed by the RCMP in British Columbia in the 1990s, this long-term operation involves a team of undercover operatives posing as a crime boss and his gang. The "crime boss" in particular gradually gains the suspect's trust, drawing him into the "gang" by offering money for participation in (staged) crimes. Eventually, the suspect is asked to prove their loyalty by confessing to their (real) crime.

While some critics claim this technique encourages false confession, McRae went so far as to demonstrate a reenactment of his wife's murder, all secretly recorded by the operatives. He pleaded guilty to second-degree murder in 2011.

THE PILL-TOTING PIGEON

I n May 2017, Kuwaiti customs officials on the border of Iraq detained a homing pigeon that was carrying a blue mini backpack filled with 178 ketamine pills. Though law enforcement knew pigeons were being used to smuggle drugs, this was the first bird they caught in the act.

Pigeons, which can home from more than 1,000 miles away at an average speed of 60 miles per hour, have been used to carry messages since Roman times. But more recently they have been recognized for their ability to carry lightweight, high-value narcotics. In 2011, Colombian police discovered a pigeon struggling to fly over a high prison wall, weighed down with packages of cocaine and marijuana. A pigeon carrying the same goods made its way into a Costa Rican prison in 2015 but was discovered by prison guards.

DEAD MAN WALKING... AND WALKING

 n late 1988, Mark Olmsted's older brother, Luke, visited him in New York City. Luke looked pale and thin when he arrived, and joked that he was on a macrobiotic diet of rice and seaweed—but Mark knew better. Mark was first to disclose it, then Luke—both brothers had tested positive for HIV. In early 1990, Mark joined Luke on the West Coast so the two could take care of each other. It was the early days of the AIDS epidemic. Luke, a medical resident who'd been closely following developments in AIDS research, threw himself into his work. He was confident the virus was a scientific problem he could solve. Mark didn't share his brother's optimism, believing that death was inevitable. He resolved to live the rest of his life to the fullest.

Luke died on February 9, 1991. Mark couldn't afford the rent on the Los Angeles apartment without his brother's help, so he signed rent checks in Luke's name, as he had when Luke was too weak to sign them himself. As the executor of Luke's will, Mark was responsible for mailing his brother's death certificate to creditors and agencies. But he didn't, to stave off premonitions of his own imminent death. Mark's friends were dying, too—he barely had time to grieve one before another was gone. So, when Luke's disability checks kept coming, Mark cashed them.

Managing Luke's bank account was easy. The bank itself was in San Diego, and all transactions were done by mail. When Luke's license came up for renewal, Mark went to the DMV. Several weeks later an ID arrived containing Luke's name and information, with Mark's picture. Mark drained Luke's bank account and racked up debt on Luke's credit card. He drank to numb the fear of HIV and did crystal meth to revive his libido, which was inhibited by the meds he took.

One day, Mark noticed a checkbox at the bottom of Luke's credit card bill: *Mark here to insure the full balance in the event of the cardholder's death.* Mark checked the box, and a scam came into focus: He doctored Luke's death certificate, postdated his brother's death to 1992 with a crude but effective cut-and-paste photocopy method, then sent it to the credit card company. Luke's next statement showed a balance of zero dollars. Mark began to use the rest of Luke's credit cards with total disregard for the balances, not knowing how long he had left and wanting the good life.

Mark ran up $50,000 in credit card debt, including on credit cards in both his own and Luke's names. He sent out five death certificates at a time in both his and his brother's names to clear the balances on as many cards as possible. At one point, someone called from one of the credit card companies about a death certificate for Mark. Apparently, the document was missing a seal. "Luke," slightly annoyed, pointed out there was an embossed color seal that read *CC*, meaning "certified copy," on the back. The credit card rep then confirmed it was fine. She didn't look closely enough to see that it actually read *Corona Cougars*, the name of a little league baseball team. Mark had bought the seal at Office Depot.

Another time, while applying for social security as Luke, a clerk told him Luke Olmsted was dead. Mark began to protest, and the clerk quickly apologized: "These things happen."

To pay off his debt, Mark eventually sold an insurance policy he had taken out on himself through a viatical settlement. After paying off his (and "Luke's") credit cards, it left him with about $10,000. He needed a way to make money, and fast.

When Mark's crystal meth supplier offered to help get him started as a dealer, Mark jumped at the chance. He ran a loose operation, buzzing in anyone who came by his apartment, unconcerned about the foot traffic in and out of his place at all hours. One loyal customer made a point to limit his visits, because he was sure the police would shut Mark down at any minute.

In 2002, Mark became seriously ill. He was convinced it was the end for him, but his doctors tried one more combination of antivirals. It worked: Within a year, HIV was undetectable in Mark's blood—he was going to survive. After years of believing his next moments were his last, Mark's anxiety shifted to his criminal activity. In August 2003, narcotics officers raided his apartment. He was sentenced to 300 hours of community service and fined $2,200. Mark wanted to go straight after the bust, but he couldn't stop selling meth—he was addicted to both the drug and the easy money from selling it.

In October 2003, Mark attempted to declare himself dead one more time (he was doctoring death certificates on his computer by this point) to get out of his community service sentence. In February 2004, Mark's apartment was raided again. Officers found six passports in his safe, in Mark's and Luke's names, all with Mark's picture. Mark insisted to officers that he was Luke and that Mark was dead. But his fingerprints told a different story.

Mark pleaded guilty to possession of a controlled substance for sale and manufacturing false documents and was sentenced to 16 months in prison.

Mark spent his time in prison getting clean, writing letters, and making amends. Proficient in five languages, he began working as a subtitler for films upon his release.

Steven Weisman, an expert on scams and identity theft and a professor at Bentley University, said of Mark Olmsted's long-running scam: "This story reminds me why scam artists are the only criminals we call artists."

KILLER MISTAKES

Match the murderer with the minor crime that got them caught.

1. Timothy McVeigh
2. Ted Bundy
3. Peter Sutcliffe
4. Robert Durst
5. David Berkowitz

a. Stealing a chicken salad sandwich
b. Parking in front of a fire hydrant
c. Driving without a license plate
d. Driving with a stolen license plate
e. Driving a stolen car

Answers: 1C: Police connected McVeigh with the truck that was used as a bomb in the 1995 Oklahoma City bombing after arresting him the same day for driving without a license plate and carrying a concealed weapon. **2E:** Bundy was pulled over a month after committing the Chi Omega murders in 1978. He attempted to flee the scene, but was detained. **3D:** When police brought Sutcliffe in for the stolen plates, they noticed his resemblance to the composite sketch of the Yorkshire Ripper. **4A:** Durst had been a fugitive for two weeks when he was caught shoplifting. Police found $40,000 in his car. **5B:** A witness who saw Berkowitz ripping up a parking ticket the night he murdered Stacy Moskowitz led police to the Son of Sam killer.

THE WOMEN OF JUÁREZ: MISSING AND MURDERED

The official toll of women who have been abducted, raped, murdered, and dumped in the desert in Ciudad Juárez since 1993 is 260. But local women's groups believe the actual number is more than 400. Most of the victims are young, impoverished maquiladora (factory) workers, who typically disappear on their way home from work. Alleged motives vary from gang activity to active serial killers to patriarchal resentment over employment opportunities in the region. Whatever the motives, the rash of homicides has gained international attention and led to much criticism of the Mexican government. In some cases, the criticism was so widespread it is believed that desperate local authorities have forced confessions just to get convictions.

RICHARD RAMIREZ:
THE NIGHT STALKER

rom June 1984 to August 1985, residents of Los Angeles and San Francisco were on high alert. A serial killer, rapist, and burglar was at large. The killer was merciless, preying on the elderly (slashing the throat of 79-year-old Jennie Vincow), the young (stabbing 9-year-old Mei Leung), and those with disabilities (raping Lillian Doi). He often surprised couples by shooting them—or simply the husband—in the face while they slept. But the killer also turned to other weapons to attack his victims, including knives, a tire iron, a machete, and a hammer.

Public fear peaked when the killer struck twice in a single night. On March 17, 1985, he shot Maria Hernandez and her roommate, Dayle Okazaki, in their Rosemead, California, home. Hernandez survived. An hour later, in Monterey Park, he fatally shot Tsai-Lian Yu in her car.

The killer, who was described by surviving witnesses as a curly-haired man with rotting teeth and wide eyes, was called the Walk-in Killer and the Valley Intruder.

On August 24, 1985, the killer drove a stolen Toyota to Mission Viejo, where he attempted to break into a family's home. James Romero Jr., just 13 years old, heard the intruder and ran to wake his parents. As Ramirez fled the scene, the teenager raced after him and took note of the color and make of his car, as well as part of the license plate.

Hours later, the killer broke into the bedroom of Bill Carns and Inez Erickson, shooting Carns and raping Erickson before stealing their cash and jewelry. He identified himself to them as the Night Stalker. Both victims survived.

Thanks to a detailed description that Inez Erickson was able to provide, along with a fingerprint taken from a stolen car the Night Stalker used, the police found their man. His name was Richard Muñoz Ramirez, a 24-year-old Texan with previous arrests for car theft and drug violations. Police released Ramirez's mug shot and announced, "We know who you are now, and soon everyone else will. There will be no place you can hide."

On August 31, 1985, Ramirez was returning to Los Angeles from a quick visit to Arizona. Upon finding officers staking out the bus station and his face plastered across newspapers, the killer ducked into a convenience store. But he was not safe: A group of women recognized the curly-haired killer, declaring him "El Matador." Fleeing the store, Ramirez attempted to steal a car but was thwarted by bystanders.

After a chase, the crowd eventually caught and subdued him. The gruesome murders had a powerful effect on the angry crowd, who viciously attacked Ramirez and beat him (including one person who used a metal bar) until police arrived.

The trial of Ramirez was plagued by drama and violence. Most people raise their right hand and pledge to tell the truth before testifying in court; Ramirez raised a pentagram-covered hand and yelled, "Hail, Satan!" There were also reports from corrections officers that Ramirez had mentioned a plan to shoot the prosecutor (leading to the prompt installation of a metal detector outside of the courtroom). If that weren't enough, one of the jurors, Phyllis Singletary, was found fatally shot in her home. It

Richard Ramirez appears in a Los Angeles courtroom in 1986.

turned out her boyfriend, James Melton, who later killed himself, was the murderer, but the effect on the jury was chilling.

Despite the courtroom chaos, the trial continued and eventually concluded on September 20, 1989, with Ramirez being convicted of 13 counts of murder, 5 counts of attempted murder, 11 sexual assaults, and 14 burglaries. He was sentenced to die in the gas chamber. His response? "Big deal. Death always went with the territory. See you in Disneyland."

Thanks to multiple appeals, Ramirez would stay on death row for 23 years. During this time, he garnered many fans and admirers. One such fan was Doreen Lioy. After a long correspondence, the pair was married on October 3, 1996, in San Quentin State Prison. Although Lioy had promised to die by suicide the day Ramirez's death sentence was carried out, the pair eventually separated. Ramirez died at Marin General Hospital on June 7, 2013, from complications of B-cell lymphoma and a chronic hepatitis C infection.

MARY VINCENT HAS HER DAY IN COURT

O n September 29, 1978, Mary Vincent, 15, was hitchhiking outside of Berkeley, California, when Lawrence Singleton offered her a ride. Things turned nightmarish quickly for Vincent: Singleton raped her, hacked off both her forearms with a hatchet, then rolled her off a 30-foot cliff into a culvert. But Vincent survived. She packed mud on her arms to quell the bleeding, climbed back up to the road, and flagged down a couple, who raced her to the hospital.

Vincent used her newly fitted prosthetics to point out Singleton in court. He was sentenced to 14 years in prison but served only 8. After his release Singleton went on to murder Roxanne Hayes, a 31-year-old mother of three, a crime for which he was sentenced to death in 1997.

Mary Vincent in 1999, 21 years after the attack where she lost both her forearms.

RIPPED FROM THE HEADLINES

These shows take their stories from true crime, either directly or in thinly veiled re-creations:

• *Law & Order: SVU*—The classic ripped-from-the-headline series has covered crimes ranging from Chris Brown's beating of Rihanna to the murder of Trayvon Martin.

• *The Good Wife*—The drama is based loosely on the life of former New York governor Eliot Spitzer, who resigned in 2008 over a scandal involving an elite escort service.

• *Scandal*—The political drama would sometimes draw inspiration from suspicious real-life deaths like those of Cody Johnson and Vince Foster.

• *The Newsroom*—Season three of the series mirrored the case of whistleblower-in-exile Edward Snowden.

THE MURDER OF EMMETT TILL

O n August 24, 1955, 14-year-old Emmett Till, a Black boy from Chicago who was spending the summer with his great-uncle in Money, Mississippi, was accused of flirting with a white woman named Carolyn Bryant. Four days later, on August 28, Carolyn's husband, Roy Bryant, and his half brother, J. M. Milam, abducted Till from his great-uncle's home and beat, tortured, and shot him before tying his body to a cotton-gin fan and tossing him into the Tallahatchie River. When Till's body was found three days later, Till's mother, Mamie Till Mobley, insisted her son be returned to Chicago, where she held an open-casket funeral. Photographers from *Jet* magazine published a photo of Till's body and the story soon gained traction. Till became the devastating face of the lynching epidemic, and the threat of violence that innocent Black Americans—including children—face in the United States.

In September 1955, after a five-day trial and a mere hour of deliberation, an all-white jury found Bryant and Milam innocent of Till's murder. Just months later, in January 1956, Bryant and Milam gave a detailed confession to *Look* magazine, receiving $4,000 for their participation in the article "The Shocking Story of Approved Killing in Mississippi." In 2017, Tim Tyson, author of *The Blood of Emmett Till*, revealed that Carolyn Bryant had admitted that Till never touched, threatened, or harassed her.

BELLE GUNNESS: MISTRESS OF MURDER FARM

I n 1884, three years after immigrating to the United States from Norway, Brynhild Paulsdatter Størseth married Mads Sorenson in Chicago. In the early years of her marriage, Brynhild, who came to be known as Belle, learned of the powers of insurance. When the candy store the couple owned burned down, they used the insurance money to purchase a new home. Six years later, on July 30, 1900, Mads died— from either heart failure or strychnine poisoning. But perhaps more important than the cause of death, July 30 was the only day Mads's two life insurance policies overlapped, resulting in a double payout for Belle, who used the money to buy a farm in La Porte, Indiana. She acquired the last name Gunness—and another impressive life insurance payout—from her next husband, who also died under suspicious circumstances.

Gunness placed this ad in the "matrimonial column" of Midwestern Norwegian-language newspapers.

> *WANTED: A woman who owns a beautifully located and valuable farm in first-class condition, wants a good and reliable man as partner in the same. Some little cash is required for which will be furnished first-class security.*

Belle Gunness, c. 1908.

A wealthy, helpless widow with a farm all by herself? It seemed almost too good to be true—and it was.

What followed was a series of at least 25 suitors (though likely more) who were often last seen withdrawing their savings from La Porte Savings Bank as they prepared to meet the widow with whom they had fallen in love through letters. The men then disappeared, one by one, without a trace.

Andrew Helgelien was one of Gunness's unfortunate suitors. With a check for $2,900, he went to meet Gunness in early 1908. After the check was deposited, he disappeared.

Helgelien's brother, Asle, grew concerned and arrived in La Porte in May 1908 to investigate. Around the same time, Gunness was having a falling-out with her farmhand and alleged accomplice, Ray Lamphere. The widow hatched a plan. Stopping at her lawyer's office to make her will, she just happened to mention that Lamphere had been threatening to burn down her house.

Sure enough, on April 28, 1908, Gunness's farm burned. Four bodies were found inside the house: Gunness's three children and a woman who appeared to be Gunness. The woman's body was missing its head.

Lamphere was the obvious suspect for the arson, but Asle Helgelien pressed authorities to investigate further for his missing brother. When they searched the farm, they made a chilling discovery: at least 11 dismembered bodies buried in sacks near a hog pen.

Lamphere was found guilty of the arson, but not the murders. Almost a year after his conviction, withering away from tuberculosis, Lamphere confessed to a priest his involvement in Gunness's plot. He described the trap: A suitor would answer Gunness's ad and meet her on her farm. Over dinner, she would either drug the bachelor or stab him in the head with a meat cleaver, then butcher and dismember the corpse. She'd throw the remains to her hogs or bury them. Lamphere also found a "body double" for Gunness, whom the Black Widow decapitated and left in the fire.

Was there any truth to Lamphere's story? Was the headless body Gunness, or did she live to kill again? In 1931, Esther Carlson, who bore an uncanny resemblance to Gunness, died while awaiting trial in Los Angeles. Her crime? Poisoning a man for his money.

The mystery continues to perplex, disturb, and fascinate the residents of Indiana, where there's even a beer named in honor of Gunness (an Irish dry stout from Back Road Brewery). On November 5, 2007, forensic anthropologists from the University of Indianapolis exhumed the headless body presumed to be the Mistress of Murder Farm. They'd hoped to compare her DNA with that on an envelope found at her farm, but there was not enough of a sample to make a determination.

"HEADLESS BODY IN TOPLESS BAR"

Called "the most anatomically evocative headline in the history of American journalism" by the *New York Times*, "Headless Body in Topless Bar," written by Vincent Musetto, graced the front page of the *New York Post* on April 15, 1983. The story: After arguing with Herbie's Bar owner Herbert Cummings, patron Charles Dingle shot Cummings on April 13. Dingle then took several women hostage, raped a topless dancer, and forced another woman, a mortician, to decapitate Cummings. Dingle was apprehended the following day and sentenced to 25 years to life. He died in prison in 2012, after being denied parole several times.

Musetto's headline stuck in the cultural consciousness, appearing on T-shirts and used as the title of a 1995 movie loosely based on the crime and a 2007 book about the best *New York Post* headlines ever written. Musetto died in 2015.

The original April 15, 1983, cover of the *New York Post*.

UNBELIEVABLE BUT TRUE CRIME HEADLINES

Man Tries Armed Robbery with Knife in Gun Store

Homicide Victims Rarely Talk to Police

Man Eats Underwear to Beat Breathalyzer

Authorities Pursue Man Running with Scissors

THE BITCH OF BUCHENWALD

E ven among World War II Nazi war criminals, Ilse Koch stood out as particularly heinous. The wife of Karl-Otto Koch, commandant of the Nazi concentration camps Buchenwald and Majdanek, Ilse Koch was known as Die Hexe von Buchenwald, the Witch (commonly translated as Bitch) of Buchenwald, because of her especially cruel treatment of prisoners. She rode around the camp on a horse, sadistically whipping and beating prisoners on a whim. She collected the skins of tattooed Holocaust victims, allegedly to help the camp doctor with his dissertation, though many reports suggest that she had them made into lampshades, book covers, and gloves.

In 1943, Koch and her husband were arrested on charges of embezzlement, private enrichment, and murdering prisoners. Koch was acquitted, but her husband was sentenced to death and executed in 1945. After the war, Koch was tried twice. The first time she was pardoned, but after public outrage, she was tried again and sentenced to life in prison. She died by suicide in 1967 at the age of 60.

CHAPPAQUIDDICK: KENNEDY, KOPECHNE, AND A CAR CRASH

s the nation awaited news of the Apollo 11 manned lunar mission on July 18, 1969, the Boiler Room Girls reunited at a cottage on Chappaquiddick Island in Massachusetts. The six women had been key staffers for Robert Kennedy's presidential bid in 1968, before it was cut short by an assassin's bullets. The women were joined by Bobby's brother Senator Edward "Ted" Kennedy and several of his friends, in town for the annual regatta.

Late that evening, Kennedy left the party with one of the staffers, Mary Jo Kopechne. He claimed he was driving her to catch the last ferry to Edgartown on Martha's Vineyard. But she left her purse and room key behind. When two fishermen found Kennedy's car the next morning, upside down in the water next to a narrow bridge, it was in the direction of the private beach, not the ferry. The police chief found Kopechne's body inside the overturned vehicle.

The car was registered to Ted Kennedy. Edgartown police chief James Arena phoned the station and asked his officers to bring the senator in for questioning, but Kennedy was already there, making private phone calls from the chief's office. Arena met Kennedy there, and told him about the crashed vehicle and dead woman.

The story, as Kennedy told it, was this: He had made a wrong turn and accidentally drove off the bridge. He escaped the sinking car, and, realizing Kopechne was still inside, dove down several times in an attempt to save her. Afterward, he went back to the cottage and recruited two friends to help. They, too, failed in the search. Kennedy then swam the mile to Edgartown, where he returned to his hotel room in a daze and changed, stepping out once at 2:25 a.m. to complain to the innkeeper about noise. The two friends confronted him privately the next morning, at which point they went to the police. By the time Kennedy reported the accident, 10 hours had passed.

After giving his statement, Kennedy refused to cooperate further with police, and flew to the family compound in Hyannis Port to consult with his lawyers. Press coverage, which was at first sympathetic, turned scrutinizing as more details emerged.

Eyewitnesses placed Kennedy driving haphazardly on the road well after midnight. In his statement to police, he did not mention the party, attended only by single women and married men. He claimed everyone was sober, yet Kopechne's blood alcohol level was just below the legal limit. The scuba diver who retrieved her body believed she could have clung to life in an air bubble in the overturned car for up to five hours. If Kennedy had immediately gone to the police, or to one of the three occupied houses between the site of the accident and the cottage, she might have survived.

Kopechne was buried in Pennsylvania after a cursory autopsy, citing drowning as her cause of death. Kennedy attended her ceremony in an unneeded neck brace.

In an attempt to put the incident behind him, Kennedy went to court and pleaded guilty to leaving the scene of an accident. He received a suspended two-month sentence. In a televised speech, he blamed a concussion for his strange behavior but said, "I regard as indefensible the fact that I did not report the accident to the police immediately." Though Kopechne's mother supported Kennedy, the speech was met mostly with skepticism.

Kennedy returned to Washington, DC. In the months that followed, the district attorney of Massachusetts would reopen the case, asking Pennsylvania to exhume Kopechne's body for their investigation. But the state refused to do so without her parents' permission. They denied the request after a visit by two parish priests and a $90,000 check from Kennedy. The inquest ultimately found that Kennedy's negligent actions contributed to Kopechne's death but did not recommend further prosecution.

Ted Kennedy continued to serve as senator from Massachusetts until his death from brain cancer in 2009.

Edward Kennedy's car after it was pulled from the water near Edgartown, Massachusetts, with Mary Jo Kopechne's body inside.

CRIME ON WHEELS

hen Ted Kennedy's car plunged off Dike Bridge, killing Mary Jo Kopechne (see page 83), he was driving an Oldsmobile Delta 88. Here are some other infamous cars:

• Bonnie Parker and Clyde Barrow were killed in a hail of policemen's bullets while driving a stolen 1934 Ford Deluxe.

• The Beltway Snipers, John Muhammad and Lee Malvo, turned the trunk of their 1990 Chevy Caprice into a mobile sniper's nest by cutting a hole just above the license plate, through which they killed 17 people and wounded 10.

• John F. Kennedy was assassinated by Lee Harvey Oswald while waving to a crowd through the open top of a 1961 Lincoln Continental. The car was used by US presidents for 14 more years.

• After the murder of his ex-wife, O. J. Simpson forced his friend Al Cowlings to lead the police in a low-speed chase through Los Angeles in a white Ford Bronco.

BODY FARMS

Behind a razor-wire fence in Knoxville, Tennessee, there are two and a half acres of land littered with decaying human bodies. This is an anthropological research center known as a "body farm." There are five other centers like it in the US, but the University of Tennessee Anthropological Research Facility, conceived by anthropologist William M. Bass in 1971 and opened a decade later, was the first. Its purpose is to determine how human bodies decompose in different environments so forensic anthropologists can better estimate time of death. Scientists place donated bodies at various places around the farm and closely monitor them.

Different types of scenarios, such as a car accident undiscovered for several days or a murder victim buried in a shallow grave, are simulated to allow insight into the process of decomposition. Over time, the work at the Body Farm has grown to include other sciences that aid in forensic anthropology, like entomology, the study of insects. Students are also tapped by law enforcement to lend their expertise in real-world cases.

The Body Farm receives more than 100 body donations per year. Skeletal remains go to the farm's Bass Donated Skeletal Collection, where they are a resource for research in forensic taphonomy, which involves the study of decay and fossilization. The Body Farm's first donation arrived in 1981: a 73-year-old man renamed 1-81, who died of emphysema and heart disease. 1-81 provided Bass and his students with crucial information on the four stages of decomposition:

• The fresh stage: Maggots feed and multiply on the body; the skin on the upper and lower jaw stretches; hair and skin remain attached to the skull.

• The bloat stage: After a couple of days of exposure, the body bloats from gases given off by bacteria feeding on the intestines.

• The decay stage: Microbes and insects consume soft tissue like muscle, ligaments, fat, and so on, causing the body to slowly decompose.

• The dry stage: After about a month (or longer if the body is not exposed to the sun) most of the soft tissue is gone and the bones have dried, leaving a skeleton.

While decomposition is understood generally, temperature, humidity, and method of disposal create variations in the process. More body farms are needed to help study other ecosystems. A proposed body farm in Florida, for instance, will study how bodies decompose in water.

FORCED STERILIZATION

n January 1936, 21-year-old socialite and heiress Ann Cooper Hewitt, daughter of electrical engineer and inventor Peter Cooper Hewitt, sued her mother, Maryon, for $500,000—equivalent to about $9 million today—in a San Francisco court. Ann claimed that shortly before her 21st birthday, Maryon paid two doctors $9,000 each to remove Ann's fallopian tubes during a routine appendectomy. The sneaky surgery was an attempt to disinherit Ann, whose two-thirds share of her wealthy father's estate was contingent on her having children. Maryon countered that she had her daughter sterilized because Ann was "feeble-minded" and promiscuous.

Witnesses testified to Ann's intelligence and Maryon's neglectful parenting style, of which Ann lamented, "I had no dolls when I was little, and I'll have no children when I'm old." Ann eventually settled with her mother out of court for $150,000. Maryon attempted suicide and had a brief illness, and then died shortly after the settlement was made. Ann attended her funeral.

In addition to the Cooper Hewitt suit, the doctors accused of performing the sterilization surgery on Ann were brought up on charges of felony mayhem, the act of disabling or disfiguring an individual, by the San Francisco prosecutor. With Maryon unable to give testimony because of her illness, the defense relied mainly on an argument developed with Paul Popenoe, secretary of the Human Betterment Foundation and founder of the

Southern California branch of the American Eugenics Society, that maintained Ann was unfit to be a mother. As evidence, they cited her promiscuity, undermined the witnesses who testified to her intelligence, and even dizzyingly claimed that because Maryon was found to be an unfit mother, it logically followed that Ann would be unfit as well, thereby justifying the doctors' decision to perform the sterilization.

Convinced of the doctors' authority to determine Ann's incapacity, the judge dismissed all charges against the doctors after six days of testimony.

The Cooper Hewitt case repopularized the idea of eugenics, the practice of controlled selective breeding of human populations in the United States. Eugenics had fallen out of favor during the early 1930s because of shoddy science and associations with the Nazi regime, but it was given a platform again as the nation was gripped by the Cooper Hewitt trials. The pseudoscience had mainly targeted poor populations of color in the United States, as well as people with disorders such as epilepsy, people who were intellectually disabled, and those who were unemployed. But the success of the doctors' argument in the Cooper Hewitt case cast a wider net, leaving even more people vulnerable to involuntary sterilization.

California laws authorizing the practice were repealed in 1979, but involuntary sterilization continues today. Between 2006 and 2010, 144 women in the California prison system underwent the same procedure as Ann without their informed consent. Court-ordered sterilizations occur throughout the country, and certain judges have offered reduced sentences in exchange for hormonal implants and other forms of birth control.

DOES THE SENTENCE MATCH THE CRIME?

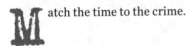

atch the time to the crime.

1. Chamoy Thipyaso, corporate fraud

2. Darron Bennalford Anderson, larceny, robbery, kidnapping, rape

3. Gary Ridgway, murder, tampering with evidence

4. Jamal Zougam, terrorism, mass murder

5. Dudley Wayne Kyzer, triple murder

a. 10,000 years

b. 48 life sentences plus 480 years

c. 12,500 years

d. 141,078 years

e. 42,922 years

Answers: 1D: *The Thai businesswoman served eight years of this massive sentence for defrauding more than 16,000 people.* **2C:** *Initially sentenced to 2,200 years, Anderson fought for a retrial only to have his sentence increase by 10,300 years.* **3B:** *Known as the Green River Killer, Ridgway received a life sentence for each murder conviction, plus 10 years per victim for tampering with evidence.* **4E:** *Convicted for his part in the 2004 Madrid train bombing, Zougam will actually serve only 40 years, according to Spanish law.* **5A:** *Kyzer holds the record for the longest sentence for a single count.*

BAIL

According to the American Bar Association, bail is the amount of money defendants must post to be released from police custody until their trial. The purpose of bail is to ensure that defendants will appear for trial and all pretrial hearings for which they must be present. Bail is returned to defendants when their trial is over, minus a processing fee in some states. Bail is not a fine. It is not supposed to be used as punishment.

However, money bail or cash bail has led to a severe form of wealth-based incarceration in which people who cannot afford to post bail languish in jail while they await trial—sometimes for years. This system disproportionately affects people of color, poor communities, and women. As many as 500,000 people are held across the country in local jails because of their inability to pay bail, mostly for low-level offenses, though many states are beginning to push for and adopt bail reform laws.

THE BANK ROBBER AND THE BAIL LAW

G erod Woodberry was being held in police custody for a string of six bank robberies committed in late 2019. On January 10, 2020, a recently passed New York state law that abolished bail for nonviolent offenses allowed him to walk free pending trial. Less than four hours later, Woodberry passed a note to a teller at a Chase bank in Brooklyn: *THIS IS A ROBBERY BIG BILLS ONLY NO DYE PACKS*. Four days later, he robbed another bank and was rearrested. None of the robberies involved a weapon.

Woodberry's recidivism (or likelihood to reoffend) set off a heated and ongoing debate about the new law. One side argues that abolishing bail for nonviolent offenses could put dangerous criminals back on the street; the other side argues that an interpretation like that is deliberate exaggeration intended to scare the public and prevent the end of mass incarceration. Samuel I. Jacobson, Gerod Woodberry's lawyer from Federal Defenders of New York, noted: "The United States Attorney has said that no sane or rational system would release Mr. Woodberry, but that's not the question. The question is whether a sane or rational system locks people presumed innocent in cages simply because they are too poor to post bail."

The debate continues, encompassing many types of infractions, including nonviolent drug offenses, petty theft, and, apparently, nonviolent bank robberies, as well as more controversial crimes like stalking and assault without grievous injury.

BY THE NUMBERS: INCARCERATION

Roughly 2.2 million Americans are in prison. That's a rate of almost 700 per 100,000 people—the highest of any country in the world. According to the Bureau of Justice Statistics, here's how likely it is that US residents born in 2001 will be imprisoned at some point in their lives, based on binary gender and race.

Men: 1 in 9

White men: 1 in 17

Black men: 1 in 3

Latino men: 1 in 6

Women: 1 in 56

White women: 1 in 111

Black women: 1 in 18

Latina women: 1 in 45

JACKIE NINK PFLUG: SUPER SURVIVOR

On November 23, 1985, three terrorists hijacked EgyptAir Flight 648 just 10 minutes after it took off from Athens, Greece. When the plane stopped to refuel in Malta, an intense standoff took place. The hijackers freed 11 hostages, but then they began shooting others. One of them was Jackie Nink Pflug.

After shooting the special education teacher in the head, the terrorists rolled her down metal stairs from the plane onto the tarmac. Even though the bullet shattered part of her skull and caused it to cave in, she survived. Pflug knew her attackers thought she was dead, so she played dead.

The standoff concluded in a bloody storming of the plane that left both terrorists and passengers killed, after which Pflug was taken to a hospital. Pflug was able to make a near-complete recovery, returning to teaching and even coauthoring a book about her ordeal called *Miles to Go Before I Sleep*.

JOSEPH DEANGELO: THE GOLDEN STATE KILLER

 rom March 1974 until late 1975, the city of Visalia in central California was plagued by a series of bizarre break-ins—120 in total and as many as 12 in one night. The burglar, initially known as the Visalia Ransacker, would, as his nickname suggests, ransack a residence; steal seemingly trivial items such as coins, single earrings, or vacation photos with women in bikinis; and sometimes stay long enough to make himself a snack.

In September 1975, the Ransacker turned deadly when he attempted to kidnap 16-year-old Beth Snelling from her home. Snelling's father, Claude, ran out to confront the Ransacker, who then released Beth and shot Claude twice, killing him. A month later, the Ransacker turned violent again, shooting at Detective William McGowen but only hitting McGowen's flashlight. The Ransacker escaped, and the crimes stopped after the attack.

The East Area Rapist (EAR) terrorized the Sacramento, California, area from mid-1976 to mid-1979. EAR would stalk middle-class neighborhoods, initially in search of women either alone or with their young children. Eventually he escalated to attacking couples, waking them in the middle of the night by shining his flashlight in their faces, separating them, stacking dishes on the man to make sure he wouldn't move, and raping the woman in the next room. He would then linger in the house,

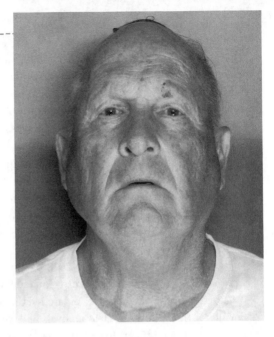

Former police officer and serial killer Joseph DeAngelo was caught in 2018 by way of DNA evidence uploaded to a genealogy website.

sometimes for hours, eating the victims' food, drinking their beer, and rifling through their possessions. If the victims moved, he would pounce and threaten their lives again.

The EAR raped more than 50 women. He was seen a number of times but always fled successfully, one time after shooting and injuring a young man who pursued him on foot. He would also make threatening phone calls to his victims, sometimes years after the attacks.

In October 1979, attacks with MOs similar to the EAR began in Southern California, but with a dark twist—the attacker began killing his victims. Unaware of the crimes in Sacramento, authorities dubbed this prowler the Night Stalker, now known as the Original Night Stalker (ONS), because serial killer Richard Ramirez (see page 71) received the former name.

The ONS first attacked a couple in Santa Barbara but they were able to alert a neighbor, forcing the ONS to flee on a stolen bicycle. After that botched attack, nine people were believed to be murder victims of the ONS between 1979 and 1981. An additional victim, 18-year-old Janelle Cruz, was killed in 1986.

In 2001, DNA evidence definitively linked the East Area Rapist and the Original Night Stalker as the same person. Crime writer Michelle McNamara renamed the attacker the Golden State Killer in a 2013 article in *Los Angeles* magazine, and her in-depth reporting sparked new interest in the case. A renewed effort to catch the Golden State Killer was announced on June 15, 2016.

Then, on April 24, 2018, came an unbelievable announcement—the Sacramento County Sheriff's Department arrested a suspect whose DNA matched that of the Golden State Killer. After months of DNA analysis and weeks of surveillance, former police officer Joseph James DeAngelo was taken into custody.

Michelle McNamara chronicled her consuming hunt for the Golden State Killer in her book *I'll Be Gone in the Dark*. Sadly, McNamara passed away in her sleep at the age of 46 on April 21, 2016, just two years before DeAngelo was caught. The book was published posthumously to great acclaim as a consummate work of investigative crime writing. Especially notable is the eerie accuracy with which McNamara imagines the capture of the Golden State Killer in her epilogue "Letter to an Old Man."

The title of the book is taken from a threat made to an EAR victim during an attack: "You'll be silent forever, and I'll be gone in the dark."

Forensic investigator Paul Holes hunted the Golden State Killer for more than 20 years. Shortly before he retired in April

2018, he uploaded DNA from the crime scenes to genealogy website GEDmatch. With the information he received from the site, he was able to identify a pool of the killer's relatives. This began a months-long process of narrowing down suspects until surveillance of DeAngelo led to a direct DNA match. Holes explained: "This investigation lasted over 40 years, but with this course of DNA testing and matching, it took us only four months to get to the right pool of people." Holes has since garnered much attention for his expertise in solving the Golden State Killer crimes and other cold cases.

DeAngelo was ultimately charged with 13 counts of murder and 13 counts of kidnapping. No charges were brought against him for the 50 rapes, due to the statute of limitations on pre-2017 rape cases in California. However, in July 2020, as part of a plea deal to take the death penalty off the table, DeAngelo confessed to all counts and admitted to the rapes as well. The following month, he was sentenced to multiple life sentences without the possibility of parole.

GENDER REVEAL GONE WRONG: THE SAWMILL FIRE

On April 23, 2017, Border Patrol Agent Dennis Dickey aimed his gun at a target filled with the explosive Tannerite, a legal substance that has become increasingly popular at so-called gender-reveal parties, which are thrown to announce the biological sex of a baby. Dickey's party was being held on state-owned land near Tucson, Arizona. The wind was gusting at 40 miles per hour, and the National Weather Service had issued a fire watch, warning that "conditions are ideal for wildland fire combustion and . . . rapid spread." When Dickey pulled the trigger, the target ignited and so did the Sawmill Fire, a weeklong blaze that destroyed 45,000 acres of land, took 800 firefighters to subdue, and caused $8 million in damages.

Dickey pleaded guilty to a misdemeanor violation of US Forest Service regulations and was sentenced to five years' probation and ordered to pay $220,000 in restitution, $100,000 up front, and $500 monthly for 20 years. This wasn't the last gender reveal that ended in criminal charges—in April 2018, a man in Queensland, Australia, was charged with dangerous operation of a car after his vehicle caught fire as his tires billowed colored smoke. Both babies were assigned male at their birth.

JOLLY JANE AND
THE DEATH RATTLE

S erial killer Jane Toppan was born Honora Kelley in Boston on August 17, 1854, to Irish immigrants Bridget and Peter Kelley (the latter was nicknamed "Kelley the Crack"). Bridget died when Toppan was very young, and soon afterward, Peter surrendered Toppan and her older sister to an orphanage, where documents noted that they'd been "rescued from a very miserable home." Two years later, eight-year-old Toppan was placed as an indentured servant in the home of Mrs. Ann C. Toppan, whose name she eventually adopted.

She was given the name Jolly Jane while studying nursing at Cambridge Hospital in Massachusetts, where she was popular and well liked for her cheerful attitude. It was there, during her residency, that Toppan began experimenting on patients with morphine and atropine, altering their doses and falsifying their charts. She would climb into bed with them as they drifted in and out of consciousness, a habit she continued throughout her prolific career as a serial killer.

Toppan eventually confessed to killing 31 people throughout her 10-year nursing career, including an entire family, Mr. and Mrs. Alden P. Davis and their two adult daughters, with whom she was close friends. She continued to poison her victims with morphine and atropine, either dissolved in water or diluted whiskey or injected. Her confession was especially disturbing because of the gleeful way she described how much she enjoyed the death rattle and the passion she felt for watching the life drain from her victims' eyes and faces. She willingly admitted, "That is my ambition, to have killed more people—more helpless people—than any man or woman who has ever lived."

Although she was found not guilty by reason of insanity, Toppan maintained that she was sane and that during the murders she was fully aware that what she was doing was wrong. Toppan was committed to the State Lunatic Hospital at Taunton in Massachusetts (now Taunton State Hospital), where she died in 1938 at age 84.

SURVIVORS ON SCREEN

- *I Am Elizabeth Smart* (2017)—A Lifetime Original reenactment produced and narrated onscreen by Smart (see page 355).

- *Crazy Love* (2007)—Linda Riss survives a chemical attack by her boyfriend; a survivor story with an unbelievable twist (see page 248).

- *Alison* (2017)—The incredible story of Alison Botha, who was abducted and left for dead in a South African nature reserve.

- *Kidnapped: Natascha Kampusch* (2017)—Kampusch retells the harrowing story of her eight-year captivity, with footage from the house and basement where she was held (see page 334).

- *I Survived . . .* (2008 to present)—It's all in the title. . . . The classic series features several first-person survivor stories per episode.

EL FUSILADO AND THE FIRING SQUAD

Wenseslao Moguel was fighting on the side of legendary Mexican revolutionary general Pancho Villa when he was captured by the Federales on March 18, 1915, and sentenced, without a trial, to execution by firing squad. He was shot nine times, once by each member of the firing squad, and received a 10th coup de grâce shot to the head. Though he suffered major injuries and had facial disfigurement, Moguel managed to survive and crawl to safety.

His story was picked up more than two decades later by the *Evening Independent* in St. Petersburg, Florida. On July 16, 1937, he was a guest on *Ripley's Believe It or Not* radio show, where he was given the nickname El Fusilado, the executed one.

ED KEMPER: MATRICIDAL MONSTER

larnell Kemper had been abusive toward her son since he was a child. She locked Edmund in the basement, mocked his imposing size (he'd grow to six feet four as a teenager), and told him no one would ever love him. The young Kemper eventually ran away to his estranged father, who sent him to live with his maternal grandparents, a decision that would prove deadly.

By the time he was 15, Kemper was projecting his anger toward his mother onto his grandmother Maude. On August 27, 1964, he grabbed a hunting rifle and shot her in the kitchen. Afterward, he shot his grandfather in the driveway.

Kemper subsequently received a diagnosis of paranoid schizophrenia and was sentenced to the Atascadero State Hospital. He was released six years later—into his mother's care.

After being released, Kemper lived with his mother and worked odd jobs. The two fought constantly during this time. Even after moving out of his mother's home, Kemper found himself with mounting anger and increasingly difficult-to-control murderous urges, which he called "little zapples." On May 7, 1972, Kemper succumbed to his urges. After picking up hitchhikers Mary Ann Pesce and Anita Mary Luchessa, Kemper drove them to a secluded area and stabbed them to death. He then brought the bodies to his apartment, where he had sex with the corpses. After dismembering the bodies, he left them in the forest.

By January 1973, Kemper was back in his mother's Santa Cruz home, the toxicity of their relationship intensifying alongside Kemper's murder spree. He continued to kill women by shooting them, followed by necrophilic acts and dismemberment of their bodies. He kept one, the body of hitchhiker Cindy Schall, in his bedroom closet. Later, Kemper buried her head in his mother's garden. He made sure the head was facing up in the direction of his mother's bedroom, because his mother "always wanted people to look up to her."

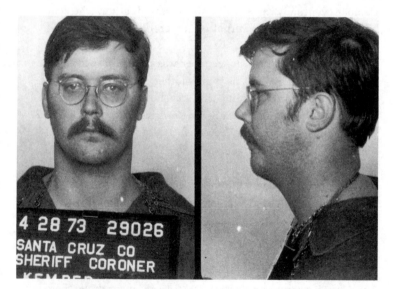

Ed Kemper's mug shot after he turned himself in for killing his mother in 1973.

It was only so long before Kemper stopped murdering his mother's "proxies" and turned on the true object of his hatred. On April 20, 1973, Clarnell Kemper returned home from a party, got into her bed, and started reading a book. When she spotted Kemper in her doorway, she said, "I suppose you're going to want to sit up all night and talk now." Those would be her last words. Kemper waited for her to fall asleep then gruesomely murdered her. His decapitation of his mother was especially grotesque and depraved. Later that same day, he also murdered his mother's friend Sally Hallett.

Kemper fled the scene, leaving a note for the police that read, *Appx. 5:15 a.m. Saturday. No need for her to suffer any more at the hands of this horrible "murderous Butcher." It was quick—asleep—the way I wanted it. Not sloppy and incomplete, gents. Just a "lack of time." I got things to do!!!*

After no reports of his mother's murder made the news, Kemper turned himself in and confessed to everything, including the strangulation of his mother's friend. In a prison interview conducted at a later date, Kemper reflected on the murder of his mother and why he had turned himself in after the deed was done: "Once my mother was dead, it was almost a cathartic process."

He is serving a life sentence at California Medical Facility in Vacaville.

A PURR-FECT MATCH

When Shirley Duguay's body was found in 1977 on Prince Edward Island, Canada, the only clue was a man's leather jacket with her blood and eight white cat hairs on it. Investigator Roger Savoie decided to order a forensic analysis of the cat hair in an attempt to incriminate Duguay's estranged boyfriend, Douglas Beamish, who owned a white cat named Snowball. But when Savoie began calling DNA testing labs, he learned that DNA evidence had never been extracted from a domestic animal before. He persisted, enlisting the aid of Dr. Stephen J. O'Brien, an expert on cats and their genes. The DNA extracted from the hair was a match to Snowball's blood. To prove this wasn't a result of inbreeding among cats on the small island, Savoie tested the blood of 20 neighborhood cats as well.

Beamish's defense attorney, John L. MacDougall, tried to discredit the prosecution's case, saying, "Without the cat, the case falls flat." Nevertheless, Beamish was found guilty of second-degree murder and received a sentence of a minimum of 18 years. Snowball went to live with Beamish's parents. Since its first use in this case, DNA analysis of cat and dog hairs has become a well-established practice.

FORENSIC DATABASES

When forensic scientists find a piece of evidence at a crime scene—a fingerprint, a ransom note, a fleck of paint—they can use various forensic databases to find a match to their sample. Can you match the following forensic databases with the evidence they catalog?

1. IAFIS
2. CODIS
3. IBIS
4. SICAR
5. FISH

a. Handwriting
b. Fingerprints
c. Shoe prints
d. DNA
e. Ballistics

Answers: 1B: Fingerprints (Integrated Automated Fingerprint Identification System). **2D:** DNA (Combined DNA Index System). **3E:** Ballistics (Integrated Ballistic Identification System). **4C:** Shoe prints (Shoeprint Image Capture and Retrieval Database). **5A:** Handwriting (Forensic Information System for Handwriting).

JOHN LIST AND THE ANNIHILATION OF THE LIST FAMILY

 the late 1960s, John Emil List lost his job as an accountant and started having money troubles. By 1971, he was $11,000 behind in mortgage payments on Breeze Knoll, a drafty 19-room Victorian mansion in Westfield, New Jersey, where he lived with his mother, Alma; his wife, Helen; and their three teenage children, John Jr., Patricia, and Frederick. Every morning, List got dressed and pretended to leave for work, then spent the day reading newspapers at the train station before returning home in the evening. Unable to keep another job, List skimmed money from his mother's bank accounts. His family was completely unaware.

As his financial pressures grew, List looked for a way out. On November 9, 1971, he took action. While his children were at school, List shot his wife, Helen, in the back of the head, then his mother, Alma, above her left eye. When Patricia and Frederick returned from school, he shot each of them in the back of the head as well.

List then made lunch, drove to the bank to close his and his mother's accounts, and made his way to Westfield High School, where John Jr. was playing in a soccer game. When they got home, List shot his son more than 10 times, as John Jr. struggled to fight off the attack.

After the murders, List moved the bodies of his wife and children to the mansion's ballroom and wrapped them in sleeping bags. He left Alma in the attic, explaining in a five-page letter to his pastor, "Mother is in the hallway in the attic. She was too heavy to move." In the letter List also insisted that he killed his family to save their souls, and claimed he was sure they were all in heaven. "If things had gone on, who knows if that would be the case," he wrote.

List proceeded to cut his face out of all the family photos in the house. He turned on all the lights in the mansion, set the radio over the intercom system to a religious station, and left. List would not be seen again for more than 17 years.

List was known for being reclusive and antisocial. This, coupled with notes he sent to the children's schools saying that the family was going on vacation, ensured that the bodies in the ballroom were not discovered for nearly a month. A neighbor eventually noticed that all the lights in the house were on day and night, with no activity. When the lights began burning out one by one, the neighbor called the police.

Soon after the bodies were discovered, List's car was found at John F. Kennedy International Airport in New York City. There was no evidence List had boarded a flight—there was no trace of him at all.

Breeze Knoll burned down in 1972. Among the items destroyed: the ballroom's stained-glass window, an original Tiffany that would have been worth $500,000 today. The very window that hovered over the family's bodies was worth more than enough to solve their financial troubles.

In May 1989, List's crimes were profiled on *America's Most Wanted*. The episode featured an age-progressed clay bust by forensic artist Frank Bender that turned out to closely resemble

List. He was apprehended in Virginia less than two weeks after the episode aired.

Where had List been living for the previous 17 years? By 1972, a year after the Breeze Knoll murders, he settled outside Denver, Colorado, living under the name of Bob Clark. He found work as a controller at a box-making company. List remarried in 1985, and he and his wife relocated to Virginia three years later, where he resumed work as an accountant.

List was convicted on five counts of first-degree murder and received five consecutive life sentences. At his sentencing, Superior Court Judge William Wertheimer said, "John Emil List is without remorse and without honor. After 18 years, 5 months, and 22 days, it is now time for the voices of Helen, Alma, Patricia, Frederick, and John F. List to rise from the grave."

ASSAULT WITH A DEADLY GATOR

J oshua James liked a good prank. But on October 11, 2016, he crossed the line when he threw a three-and-a-half-foot American alligator through the drive-thru window at a Wendy's in Florida. The 24-year-old was soon arrested and charged with aggravated assault with a deadly weapon, unlawful sale, possession, or transporting of an alligator, and petty theft. At his arraignment, a judge ordered James to stay away from all Wendy's restaurants, avoid possessing any weapons, and get a mental health evaluation. The judge also asked that he limit his interaction with animals to his mother's dog.

The alligator was captured by responding officers, who temporarily taped the animal's mouth shut for safety before releasing it into a nearby canal.

TERRI HOFFMAN: CONSCIOUS DEVELOPMENT'S TRAIL OF DEATH

erri Hoffman was fascinated by metaphysics, hypnotism, mind control, and clairvoyancy. By the late 1960s she had parlayed these interests into her own movement and begun amassing followers. In 1974, she formed the Conscious Development of Body, Mind and Soul through which she sold lessons and private consultations. Before her hundreds of followers, Hoffman declared herself the reincarnation of St. Teresa of Ávila and claimed that she and her inner circle waged war against the "black lords" on behalf of humanity. The black lords existed on the astral and mental planes, and Hoffman led the effort against them with the help of God and the "twelve masters," including Jesus, who were visible only to Hoffman. She warned her followers against negative energies, which could be fatal. But she also preached that death was not to be feared, as the ultimate goal of Conscious Development was rebirth in the spiritual realm.

By late 1976, Hoffman's second husband, Glenn Cooley, wanted out of their marriage and Conscious Development. He died of a drug overdose in February 1977, five days after their divorce was final. Hoffman produced Cooley's will, naming her as sole beneficiary. She cited Cooley's death as proof that the black lords were poisoning the blood of the group. The only cure for this was bloodletting—a suggestion that caused many members to leave the movement. Still, by the mid-1980s her meditation classes were drawing hundreds.

After a brief third marriage, Hoffman married husband number four, Don Hoffman, in 1980. In 1988, Don was found dead from a drug overdose. A suicide note mentioned inoperable cancer, but an autopsy revealed no such illness. Hoffman said that the black lords had hidden the cancer behind an illusion. She was sole beneficiary of the deceased's estate.

Many of Terri Hoffman's inner circle suffered strange fates, like Conscious Development secretary-treasurer Sandy Cleaver. Cleaver, the beneficiary of an ample trust fund, transferred the title to her house to Hoffman and paid rent to live in her own home. Hoffman convinced Cleaver to distance herself from her family, including her 14-year-old daughter, Susan Devereaux, whose "evil spirits" were infecting Cleaver's energies, according to Hoffman. In February 1979, Cleaver took Devereaux on a vacation to Hawaii, where Devereaux mysteriously drowned while the two were rafting. The girl inexplicably bequeathed her $125,000 trust fund to the cult, but Hoffman didn't receive a penny because wills written by minors were invalid in Texas.

In September 1981, Cleaver drove a Jeep with her housekeeper Louise Watson off a cliff. Both women had updated their wills to name Hoffman as the sole beneficiary. Hoffman was also the sole beneficiary of a $300,000 life insurance policy Cleaver took out.

Hoffman was connected to at least five other stranger-than-fiction deaths, including Robin Otstott. Hoffman had matched both Otstott and Otstott's best friend, Tamara Taylor, with "invisible CIA lovers," but Hoffman warned Otstott that

Taylor's invisible lover was threatening her. Otstott told her ex-husband that she was diagnosed with viral hepatitis and shot herself two days after a meeting with Hoffman. An autopsy found no evidence of the disease. Follower Mary Levinson was found dead of a drug overdose. Her estate was missing $125,000 in cash, and she had recently made her boyfriend—whom she met through Hoffman—the beneficiary of her life insurance policy. Former devotee Jill Bounds was found beaten to death in her home months after she left the movement. Pages had been ripped from her diary. David and Glenda Goodman were found in November 1989, weeks after dying in a ritualistic double suicide. They had allegedly received instructions from God months earlier.

The pattern of deaths that followed Hoffman became apparent to Dallas police after the Goodman case. Hoffman and Conscious Development denied any wrongdoing, and the Dallas district attorney's office stated that it would be difficult to argue that mind control could have been a contributing factor in the deaths.

In 1991, Hoffman declared bankruptcy, and in 1994 she was convicted of bankruptcy fraud and served one year in prison. She died in Dallas on Halloween 2015 at the age of 77.

THE STONEWALL UPRISING

I n the 1960s, New York City's LGBTQIA+ community thrived behind closed doors. It was illegal to dance or hold hands with someone of the same sex in public, so the so-called outcasts and runaways found refuge in unlicensed Mafia-owned bars like the Greenwich Village's Stonewall Inn. These establishments were allowed to exist, with the occasional tipped-off raid, as long as cops were appropriately compensated. But an increase in unexpected raids in 1969, which shuttered several gay bars, was seen as an attempt to snuff out these safe havens for good.

In the early morning hours of June 28, police raided the Stonewall Inn for the second time in a week and arrested 13 people. As they tried loading the patrons into paddy wagons, a protest broke out. Angered over the constant harassment, hundreds of protestors fought with police. Over the next few nights, the number of protesters swelled to the thousands, helping spark the gay rights movement.

Participant Michael Fader described the uprising: "We had a collective feeling like we'd had enough of this kind of shit. It wasn't anything tangible anybody said to anyone else, it was just kind of like everything over the years had come to a head on that one particular night in the one particular place, and it was not an organized demonstration. It was spontaneous. That was the part that was wonderful." Every June, those historic nights are honored with a Pride March that goes past the Stonewall Inn.

THRILLING READS

• *Five Days at Memorial* by Sheri Fink. A chronicle about what happened at New Orleans Memorial Medical Center after Hurricane Katrina hit in 2005.

• *A Kim Jong-Il Production* by Paul Fischer. The story of actress Choi Eun-hee and director Shin Sang-ok, and how they were abducted by future North Korean dictator Kim Jong-Il (see page 32).

• *I'll Be Gone in the Dark* by Michelle McNamara. Published two months before the Golden State Killer was identified through DNA (see page 96), McNamara's book (completed by colleagues after her death) presents a gripping look at the then-unknown serial killer's crimes.

• *Mrs. Sherlock Holmes: The True Story of New York City's Greatest Female Detective and the 1917 Missing Girl Case That Captivated a Nation* by Brad Ricca. An absorbing account of NYPD investigator Grace Humiston and the murder of Ruth Cruger.

SPUMONI GARDENS
AND THE SECRET SAUCE

On June 30, 2016, around 6:30 p.m., Louis Barbati left his popular Brooklyn pizzeria, L&B Spumoni Gardens. Less than a half hour later, his wife found him dead outside their nearby home. He was shot five times.

The crime sent shock waves through the quiet Italian American neighborhood of Dyker Heights. It was the first homicide of the year in the local police precinct, and there was no clear motive. Barbati was wearing flashy jewelry and carrying $15,000 cash—both were left at the scene of the crime. Then there was the matter of the sauce . . .

In 2009, Eugene Lombardo, a former employee who had reportedly stolen Barbati's secret recipe for L&B's famous pizza sauce, opened a pizza place on Staten Island with a sign advertising "Best Pizza: Just like L&B Spumoni Gardens." The feud that ensued was reminiscent of Brooklyn's bygone Mafia days. According to Colombo crime family captain Anthony Russo, he and associate Francis Guerra threatened Lombardo and warned him to stop using the recipe.

A man named Andres Fernandez was eventually charged with Barbati's murder. Federal agents claimed the motive was robbery, though Fernandez didn't take anything from Barbati. No connection to the Mafia was mentioned in Fernandez's indictment, but the lead agent came from the FBI squad that investigates organized crime. The reason the case passed from the NYPD to the FBI was unclear.

JOHN WAYNE GACY:
THE KILLER CLOWN

n the town of Norwood Park, Illinois, John Wayne Gacy was a model citizen. He ran a successful construction company, supported local politicians, and participated in the Jolly Joker Club, whose members dressed up as clowns to entertain sick children in hospitals. For the Jolly Jokers, Gacy appeared as two clown characters, Pogo and Patches. Some of his fellow clowns criticized the way he applied his makeup (Gacy used sharp, pointed edges for the curves of his smile). "That scares the kids," they told him. "The mouth should have rounded edges." Gacy continued painting the same grimace.

Gacy ran his hometown's Polish Constitution Day Parade for three years. For his efforts, he got to meet First Lady Rosalynn Carter on May 6, 1978. A photograph shows Gacy beside a beaming Carter. By that time, the man standing next to the First Lady had murdered 23 young men.

Many of Gacy's victims worked for his construction company and entered his home voluntarily. Others he'd follow in his black Oldsmobile, flashing a spotlight and donning a badge, pretending to be law enforcement. Later, when he confessed, Gacy would describe "the handcuff trick" and "the rope trick" he used to bind and strangle or suffocate his victims.

Nearly all the bodies were then transferred to a crawl space in Gacy's home, where he'd bury them and speed up decomposition with quicklime.

Gacy's mug shot following his arrest on murder charges, 1978.

POLICE DEPT.
DES PLAINES, ILL.
78 - 467 · 12-22-78

On December 11, 1978, 15-year-old Robert Piest left a pharmacy with Gacy to discuss working at his construction company. Piest was never seen again.

The pharmacy's owner, however, knew that Gacy and Piest had left together. During police questioning, Gacy behaved erratically and made false statements. Detectives were confident he was their man—a hunch that grew more certain when they learned of the criminal's earlier conviction for sexual assault.

While searching Gacy's home, detectives found a class ring with the initials J.A.S., male clothing far too small for Gacy, and handcuffs.

As the police investigation continued, a disturbing pattern emerged: Gacy seemed connected to the disappearances of more boys. From Gacy's ex-wife, they learned about a former construction employee who had vanished. Later that same day, they learned that the class ring belonged to John A. Szyc, who disappeared in 1977 shortly after selling his car to Gacy. Police then began surveillance on Gacy.

On December 18, 1978, two young men who'd worked for and temporarily lived with Gacy told police that they'd helped their boss spread quicklime and dig trenches in the crawl space in his home—for "plumbing" purposes. One man mentioned that the trenches were roughly the size of graves.

On December 21, with a new search warrant in hand, detectives arrived at Gacy's home. The killer had flooded the crawl space to thwart investigators. Once it was drained, an evidence technician crawled inside, started digging, and found decaying

GACY'S FINAL VICTIM

Before Gacy's death, he met with one last young man who could be added to his victim count. Like so many of us, Jason Moss was fascinated with crime. For his honors thesis at University of Nevada, Las Vegas, he corresponded with several incarcerated serial killers, including Richard Ramirez, Henry Lee Lucas, Jeffrey Dahmer, and Charles Manson. But it was his relationship with John Wayne Gacy that would prove the most fruitful—and terrifying. Moss met with Gacy twice and was disturbed by the killer's sexual fantasies and attempts to manipulate him. He wrote a book about his experience, titled *The Last Victim*, because he felt like Gacy had victimized him, too. His interactions with Gacy would haunt him for the rest of his life, which sadly wasn't very long. Struggling with depression, Moss took his own life in 2006, at the age of 31.

human flesh and bone. He offered this chilling assessment: "I think this place is full of kids."

On December 22, John Wayne Gacy confessed to committing between 25 and 30 murders. His subsequent trial would be at turns dramatic, infuriating, and tragic. In his closing argument, prosecutor Bill Kunkle held up photos of the 22 identified victims and implored the jury to "show the same sympathy and pity this man showed when he took these lives and put them there."

After less than two hours' deliberation, the jury returned with a guilty verdict—and the death penalty. Gacy was executed on May 10, 1994. "Kiss my ass" were his last words.

THE REAL AMITYVILLE HORROR MURDERS

 onald DeFeo Jr. was frantic when he ran into Henry's Bar in Amityville, New York, on the evening of November 13, 1974, shouting, "You got to help me! I think my mother and father are shot!" The 23-year-old DeFeo pleaded for help and a small group followed him to the home he shared with his family just down the road at 112 Ocean Avenue. There they found a gruesome scene: The entire family was dead. Ronald DeFeo Sr. and his wife, Louise DeFeo, had both been shot twice; their four children—Dawn, Allison, Marc, and John Matthew— had all been shot once. They were all found lying face down in their beds and had been dead since the early hours that morning. Evidence suggested that only Louise and Allison had been awake when they were shot.

DeFeo was taken into protective custody by police after suggesting the murders may have been carried out by a mob hit man—the family had ties to the mob through Ronald Sr.'s uncle Pete, a capo in the Genovese crime family. However, by the next day DeFeo had confessed.

He told police he had bathed and got dressed in clean clothes after killing his entire family, then discarded his blood-stained clothes and the Marlin rifle and cartridges used in the murders before going to work as usual that day. He also disclosed the location of the bloody clothes and weapon, which were cru-cial pieces of evidence.

The DeFeo house in 1978, four years after Ronald DeFeo killed six members of his family there in 1974. The house became the inspirational setting for the book and movie of *The Amityville Horror*.

With a signed confession and the evidence stacked against his client, DeFeo's lawyer, William Weber, decided to mount an insanity defense, claiming that DeFeo killed his family in self-defense after hearing their voices plotting against him. A psychiatrist for the defense gave testimony affirming this. The psychiatrist for the prosecution countered, saying DeFeo abused LSD and heroin and had antisocial personality disorder, but insisted that he was aware of his actions at the time of the murders. The prosecution also pointed out that DeFeo had asked about his father's life insurance policy when he was taken into protective custody. DeFeo was found guilty of six counts of second-degree murder and sentenced to six concurrent sentences of 25 years to life.

Since his conviction, DeFeo has given several variations of what happened the night of the killings:

• Dawn killed their father; their mother, distraught, then killed all the children before DeFeo killed her.

• Dawn and an unknown assailant who fled the house killed the family, and then Dawn was killed accidentally when the gun went off as she and DeFeo wrestled for it.

• After a fight with Ronald Sr., DeFeo and Dawn planned to kill their parents—who DeFeo believed were plotting to kill him—with the help of two friends. Dawn then killed all the children to eliminate them as witnesses. Enraged by what she had done, DeFeo knocked Dawn onto her bed and shot her.

The house on 112 Ocean Avenue is best known as the setting for *The Amityville Horror*, the 1977 book by Jay Anson that was based on claims of paranormal torment made by the Lutz family, who moved into the house just over a year after the murders. The Lutzes—George, Kathy, and Kathy's three young children—moved out just 28 days later. George and Kathy said they were plagued by paranormal activity, including doors slamming, George waking up every night around the time of the murders, Kathy levitating in bed, swarms of flies infesting the house in winter, and cloven hoofprints in the snow, among many other happenings.

DeFeo after his arrest for murdering his parents and four siblings in 1974.

William Weber admitted that he helped George Lutz fabricate the haunting story to garner a book deal and potentially a new trial for his client. In a series of lawsuits brought against the Lutzes by Weber, the publisher of the book, and the Cromartys, who moved into the house after the Lutzes, George admitted that the events were entirely fabricated. But the story was unstoppable—it grew into a franchise of books and movies.

MUMMY ISSUES: THE CASE OF THE PERSIAN PRINCESS

Was the mummified corpse the 2,600-year-old daughter of Xerxes? Or an Egyptian princess married to a Persian prince during the rule of Cyrus I? These were questions archaeologists asked in October 2000 when a mummy was found during a murder investigation in Pakistan. Oddly, the mummy displayed an amalgam of Egyptian and Persian mummification and burial elements, which led to the archaeological debate. A dispute broke out between Pakistan, Iran, and the Taliban regime in Afghanistan over ownership of the mummy.

By January 2001, the mummy's story had unraveled. Petrochemicals and detergents in her body, pencil marks on her coffin, and an inscription on her breastplate in broken ancient Iranian proved she was no mummy at all. A CT scan confirmed that the body was that of a 21- to 25-year-old woman who had been mummified within two years of the discovery. Her organs had been removed and her cavities filled with powder. A report issued in April 2001 by the curator of Pakistan's National Museum officially declared the mummy a fake—and possibly a murder victim.

WHERE DID THEY HIDE?

Some criminals hide in plain sight. Match the criminal to the place where they were found.

1. John List

2. Whitey Bulger

3. Marie Dean Arrington

4. Frank Freshwaters

5. Susan Edith Saxe

a. New Orleans, Louisiana

b. Halifax, Virginia

c. Philadelphia, Pennsylvania

d. Santa Monica, California

e. Melbourne, Florida

Answers: 1B: *List (see page 110) killed his whole family in New Jersey in 1971 and was apprehended more than 17 years later in Virginia.* **2D:** *The mobster went on the lam from Boston in 1994 and was caught, along with his girlfriend, in 2011.* **3A:** *Arrington was in a Florida prison for murder when she cut through a window screen and fled in her pajamas in 1969. She was apprehended three years later, working as a waitress.* **4E:** *Freshwaters, serving time for voluntary manslaughter, escaped prison in Ohio in 1959 and spent a whopping 56 years on the lam until he was recaptured in 2015.* **5C:** *Saxe was wanted for a 1970 bank robbery—she was caught in 1975.*

DAVID BERKOWITZ:
SON OF SAM

 t all began in Pelham Bay in the Bronx, New York. Just after 1:00 a.m. on July 29, 1976, Donna Lauria and Jody Valenti were in their car, ready to head home after a night at a disco. A man approached the car, pulled out a pistol, and fired. Lauria died instantly; Valenti survived but failed to identify the shooter. A similar scene would play out several times over the next few months, as young men and women were similarly shot in the dead of night in their New York neighborhoods.

Forest Hills Gardens, Queens: On March 8, 1977, Columbia University student Virginia Voskerichian was returning from classes when a man shot her in the head, killing her instantly. Immediately afterward, a neighbor turning onto the street almost collided with a person he later described as looking like a husky teenage boy.

After the Voskerichian shooting, New York City mayor Abraham Beame held a press conference, revealing that the same gun had been used to kill Lauria and Voskerichian: a .44 Bulldog revolver.

When two more teenagers—Alexander Esau and Valentina Suriani—were shot dead in the Bronx on April 17, police determined it was the same .44-caliber weapon. This wasn't a string of unrelated incidents. This was a serial killer.

After the murders of Esau and Suriani, the killer left police a handwritten letter—and a name:

I am deeply hurt by your calling me a wemon hater. I am not. But I am a monster. I am the "Son of Sam." . . . [T]o stop me you must kill me. Attention all police: Shoot me first— shoot to kill or else. . . . I love to hunt. Prowling the streets looking for fair game—tasty meat. The wemon of Queens are z prettyist of all. . . . Police—Let me haunt you with these words; I'll be back! I'll be back! To be interrpreted as—bang, bang, bang, bank, bang—ugh!! Yours in murder Mr. Monster

Bath Beach, Brooklyn: The anniversary of the first killings came and went without a suspect. On July 31, 1977, the killer struck again. Stacy Moskowitz and Robert Violante were

David Berkowitz, known as "Son of Sam," in 1977.

kissing in Violante's car when a shooter approached and fired four rounds. Moskowitz later died in the hospital. Violante survived, but with permanent blindness in one eye and limited vision in the other.

But one development that came out of the shooting: several eyewitnesses. A teenager in a nearby car got a full glimpse of the killer, illuminated by a full moon. Later, another woman spotted a similar-looking man sprinting to a car. Thinking he looked "like he just robbed a bank," she recorded the visible part of his license plate.

A neighbor of Violante's saw the same man, holding a "dark object," approach a car that had been ticketed. Police began looking into all cars ticketed in the area that night. One of those cars? A yellow 1970 Ford Galaxie owned by Yonkers resident David Berkowitz, a suspect in other crimes.

On August 10, 1977, police searched Berkowitz's parked car and found a rifle, ammunition, maps of crime scenes, and a threatening letter to a police inspector. At 10:00 p.m., Berkowitz got into his car. Detectives approached with guns drawn.

"Now that I've got you," the lead detective said, "who have I got?"

"You know," Berkowitz answered.

"No, I don't. You tell me."

The man replied, "I'm Sam."

David Berkowitz is serving six consecutive life sentences.

THE BLACK DAHLIA MURDER

One woman. Several scattered body parts. One hundred and fifty suspects. No arrests. The murder of 22-year-old Elizabeth Short, an aspiring actress whose dreams of stardom were ended in January 1947, is one of the greatest unsolved criminal mysteries. Short's murder was notorious for the gruesome mutilation the killer inflicted on her. Her body was severed at the waist, with her lower half nearly a foot away from her top half, completely drained of blood, and her face had been slashed ear to ear.

Newspapers dubbed Short the Black Dahlia, a possible reference to a film noir known as *The Blue Dahlia*. The case gained

a level of media attention so feverish, it may have compromised the investigation. Despite hundreds of confessions by those claiming to be the killer, the case remains unsolved.

Elizabeth Short, who was nicknamed "The Black Dahlia," in 1947. Her gruesome murder was never solved.

TILLIE KLIMEK:
THE PSYCHIC
SERIAL KILLER

 fter 30 years of marriage, Ottilie "Tillie" Mitkiewicz started having nightmares. She told her neighbors in the Little Poland area of Chicago that every night, she dreamed her husband had dropped dead. Sure enough, John died of heart failure in 1919, and Tillie collected a hefty life insurance payment.

Tillie continued to foresee her husbands' deaths. First there was Joe Ruskowski, whom Tillie married two months after Mitkiewicz's death. Husband number three, Frank Kupezyk, died six months after saying "I do." In both instances, Tillie again collected payments.

After she predicted the deaths of three husbands, Tillie's neighbors started to believe she was psychic. So confident was she in her abilities that Tillie even asked her landlady before Kupezyk's death if she could store a casket in the basement.

Frank Kupezyk died on April 25, 1921. At the funeral, Tillie met Joseph Klimek. It didn't take a psychic to predict what happened next. The pair married shortly afterward, and Klimek fell ill in 1922. But there was something Tillie didn't foresee: Klimek's brother stepped in and took him to the hospital. The doctor noted stiffness and "garlic breath," both telltale signs of arsenic poisoning.

Police exhumed the bodies of Tillie's former husbands. All contained significant levels of arsenic. When police came to arrest her, she didn't even try to play innocent. She made threats, hinting at how she'd poisoned her husbands with food. "The next one I want to cook dinner for is you," she told one officer.

Tillie's cousin Nellie Koulik also had a husband who died under mysterious circumstances. By some accounts, it was Nellie who introduced her kin to the Rough on Rats poison that she'd later employ.

After Tillie was arrested, it wasn't long before friends and neighbors started to notice a pattern: Those who had crossed or simply irritated either Tillie or Nellie often disappeared. Children, grandchildren, husbands. The coroner exhumed the body of Nellie's husband. Again, the corpse contained frightening levels of arsenic.

Both cousins were charged with the murder of one husband each, though some accounts estimate that they had poisoned as many as 20 victims.

Tillie was charged with the murder of Frank Kupezyk. She proclaimed her innocence, blaming bad moonshine for his death. But her behavior was damning:

• One nurse testified that when Klimek was in the hospital, Tillie told her, "If he makes any trouble for you, take a two-by-four board and hit him over the head with it."

• Another witness, a neighbor, noted how the widow merrily blasted jazz music on her Victrola the day Kupezyk died.

• At Kupezyk's funeral, Tillie reportedly reached into the casket, tugged on her dead husband's ear, and yelled, "You devil, you won't get up anymore!"

Tillie Klimek before she was arrested for murder in 1921.

After 80 minutes of deliberation, the jury returned a guilty verdict and the judge handed Tillie a life sentence.

Tillie's case shares many similarities with those of Belva Gaertner and Beulah Annan, two other early-twentieth-century Chicago women accused of murdering their husbands. If the women's names sound familiar, it's because a fictionalized account of their trials became the hit musical *Chicago*. One crucial difference between Tillie and these women? They were acquitted. Another difference? They were beautiful.

Of course, the evidence was incriminating, but many believe that Tillie's looks and lower-class nature influenced the jury. Journalists were merciless in describing her. Reporter Genevieve Forbes would write that Tillie was "a fat, squat, Polish peasant woman, 45 years old but looking 55, with a lumpy figure, capacious hands and feet, and dull brown hair skinned back into a knot at the back of her head."

DANGER DAD: THE ISRAELI MOTORCYCLE BANDIT

O ver 18 months in the late 1980s, the Motorcycle Bandit robbed 21 banks in Tel Aviv, Israel, stealing more than $400,000 along with the hearts and minds of the city. He was characterized in the press as a young, attractive Robin Hood figure: Bank tellers slipped him their phone numbers when they handed over the cash and children wore motorcycle helmets for Halloween.

But when he was arrested in October 1990, Ronnie Leibowitz defied these public perceptions. He was 37 and married with two kids. The motorcycle wasn't even his getaway vehicle. He'd ditch it, along with the helmet, in the back of a nearby truck and return to the bank, posing as a curious onlooker until the police shooed him away. He had a few debts, but, because he was from a wealthy family, he didn't need to steal in order to pay them. According to Leibowitz, the robberies were the actions of someone in crisis: "I didn't do it for the money. I was in distress. Some people do drugs, others jump off a roof. This was my way of screaming out, of shocking the world, if you know what I mean."

Leibowitz was sentenced to 20 years but only served 8 after receiving a presidential pardon.

JOHNNY GOSCH, MILK CARTONS, AND THE AMBER ALERT

 welve-year-old Johnny Gosch left home with his dog before dawn on September 5, 1982, for his regular Sunday-morning paper route. By 6:00 a.m., Johnny's parents began receiving calls from neighbors who had not received their deliveries of the *Des Moines Register*. Johnny had vanished, leaving behind his dog and a wagon full of undelivered papers. Witnesses reported seeing a blue car speeding through the neighborhood around the time of Johnny's disappearance, and one neighbor witnessed Johnny speaking to the driver.

Johnny's mother, Noreen Gosch, worked tirelessly to keep Johnny's case in the media, despite and perhaps because of the Des Moines police department's mishandling of the case. Noreen says a 27-year-old Johnny visited her in March 1997, but the case has never officially been solved.

At the time of Johnny's abduction, parents had to wait 72 hours before filing a report that their child was missing—the same procedure followed for missing adults. Police treated most missing-child cases as runaways, even when there was overwhelming evidence of abduction, as in Johnny's case. Though police eventually declared Johnny's case a kidnapping, they were unable to establish a motive, and the delayed reaction only contributed to the trail going cold.

Frustrated with the way her son's abduction was handled, Noreen Gosch lobbied for the Johnny Gosch Bill, which required law enforcement to act immediately when a child goes missing. On July 1, 1984, the bill passed into law in Iowa. Within a year, eight other states had adopted identical or similar laws.

On August 12, 1984, almost two years after the disappearance of Johnny Gosch, another Des Moines–area paperboy, 13-year-old Eugene Martin, also went missing. Inspired by full-page ads of the missing boys run in the *Des Moines Register* and poster-size ads on local trucks, Anderson Erickson Dairy decided to place the faces of Johnny and Eugene on the sides of half-gallon milk cartons. Another Iowa dairy followed suit a week later, and a movement was born.

By 1985, 700 dairies across the nation were participating in the Missing Children Milk Carton Program. Etan Patz, a six-year-old abducted in New York City in 1979, was the first missing child to appear on milk cartons nationally; Johnny Gosch was the second.

Johnny, Eugene, and Etan were never found, though Etan's killer confessed in 2012. There wasn't any data kept on the efficacy of the milk carton program, but the National Child Safety Council reported that sightings of children increased by more than 30 percent. "What it did was raise the level of awareness," said Noreen Gosch. "It didn't necessarily bring us tips or leads we could actually use." It was also a low-tech precursor to the more effective Amber Alert.

The Amber Alert is an international child abduction alert system that originated in the United States in 1996. Though it is a contrived acronym (America's Missing: Broadcast Emergency Response), it was named after nine-year-old kidnapping and murder victim Amber Hagerman. After Hagerman's death in January

1996, her mother, Donna Whitson, began calling for stronger laws protecting children from kidnappers and sex offenders. The alerts were soon adopted by participating radio stations and became mandated nationwide in 2003. In January 2013, Amber Alerts began to be sent through the Wireless Emergency Alerts program.

As of May 2020, 988 children in the United States had been safely recovered as a result of the Amber Alert system.

According to the National Center for Missing & Exploited Children, there are five categories of missing children: 91 percent endangered runaways; 5 percent family abductions; 3 percent critically missing young adults ages 18 to 20; 1 percent nonfamily abductions; and less than 1 percent lost, injured, or otherwise missing children.

Tips about missing or exploited children can be directed to 1-800-THE-LOST (1-800-843-5678), or the NCMEC CyberTipline at missingkids.com/gethelpnow/cybertipline.

GLADYS RICART AND THE BRIDES' MARCH

Gladys Ricart and her family were posing for photos at her Ridgefield, New Jersey, home just hours before Ricart's wedding on September 26, 1999. Moments after Ricart handed out bouquets to her bridesmaids, her abusive ex-boyfriend, Agustin Garcia, charged into the house, shooting and killing Ricart and sending her family running for cover. Garcia was sentenced to life in prison on February 2, 2002, despite his defense team's argument that the murder was a "five-minute lapse" in the life of an otherwise upstanding citizen.

In honor of Ricart and in protest of the legal and media defense of Garcia, the first annual Gladys Ricart and Victims of Domestic Violence Memorial Walk/Brides' March took place in New York City on the second anniversary of Ricart's death. Each year on September 26, participants are encouraged to wear wedding dresses or all white and march to raise awareness for those affected by domestic violence, particularly in the Latinx community. For more information, check out bridesmarch.com.

H. H. HOLMES AND THE MURDER CASTLE

erman Webster Mudgett was born in Gilmanton, New Hampshire, on May 16, 1861. With a growing interest in anatomy and dissection, Mudgett would later enroll in medical school at the University of Michigan. His knowledge and familiarity with cadavers would serve him well in both faking deaths for insurance fraud and disposing of corpses.

After graduating, Mudgett moved around the country, including to Mooers Forks, New York, and Philadelphia. In both places, boys who were seen with Mudgett later went missing. He never stayed long, leaving each area to avoid investigation. Before moving to Chicago, Mudgett made one more change that ensured he would be even more difficult to track. He was no longer Mudgett: He became Dr. Henry Howard Holmes.

In 1887, Holmes began construction on a three-floor building that was going to house a drugstore, apartments, and a hotel. It was perfect timing: Visitors would soon be flooding to Chicago for the 1893 World's Fair, and they would need places to stay.

Unfortunately, many of the visitors who came to Holmes's hotel never left. Holmes would confess to murdering 27 people, but some estimates place the number in the hundreds. Later dubbed the Murder Castle, the building was a literal house of horrors, featuring a gas chamber, dissection table, hidden passages,

Herman Webster Mudgett, aka Dr. H. H. Holmes, a serial killer who was hanged for his crimes in 1896.

and chutes leading to an incinerator that Holmes used to dispose of his victims' corpses.

On August 13, 1893, a fire burned through the third floor of the hotel. Conveniently, Holmes had taken out insurance policies with at least four companies. After the companies refused to pay the claims pending an investigation, he fled to Fort Worth, Texas.

Short on cash, he devised a new scheme with his partner, Benjamin Pitezel: Fake Pitezel's death and split the $10,000 life insurance policy. However, instead of finding a stand-in cadaver for Pitezel, Holmes just killed his partner and collected the insurance policy himself.

Why didn't Pitezel's wife collect the money? Because Holmes didn't tell her he was dead. Instead, he lied to Mrs. Pitezel and persuaded her to give him custody of three of her children, all of whom he would subsequently kill.

By 1894, multiple authorities were searching for Holmes related to theft and missing persons. On November 17, 1894, he was arrested in Boston on an outstanding warrant for a horse theft. By October 1895, Holmes had been tried for the murder of Pitezel, found guilty, and sentenced to death.

While in prison, Holmes confessed to 27 murders and 6 attempted murders. The true total is unknown, however, because some of Holmes's claims later proved false. (In fact, some of his "victims" were alive.) A con man to the end, Holmes continued to indulge in fiction, saying he'd been possessed by Satan throughout his murder spree.

It didn't help his case. Holmes was hanged in Moyamensing Prison in Philadelphia on May 7, 1896.

The Murder Castle hotel burned again in August 1895, when two men broke in and set off several explosions. It was clear the hotel was no more, but could the same be said of Holmes? Stories circulated that Holmes escaped and lived to scheme and kill again. To put these rumors to rest, forensic scientists exhumed the corpse alleged to be Holmes in 2017 and conducted tests. The teeth confirmed it was indeed Holmes.

Even after Holmes's execution, the Murder Castle would claim one more life. The hotel's caretaker, Patrick Quinlan, died by suicide by ingesting strychnine on March 7, 1914, leaving a note that said, "I couldn't sleep."

LOOK BUT DON'T TOUCH: MURDER MUSEUMS

F our must-see museums for dedicated true crime fans.

- **The Museum of Death**—With locations in Los Angeles and New Orleans, this museum houses true crime wonders like a collection of serial killers' artwork, as well as educational material about death in general.

- **Alcatraz Island**—The former federal prison in San Francisco Bay held some of the most notorious criminals of the mid-twentieth century, including mobsters Al Capone and Machine Gun Kelly.

- **The Alcatraz East Crime Museum**—Located in Pigeon Forge, Tennessee, it is home to such true crime artifacts as Ted Bundy's Volkswagen Beetle and O. J. Simpson's Ford Bronco.

- **The Mob Museum**—If it's mob education you're after, this museum in Las Vegas, Nevada, is the place to go. You can even get married there.

- **South Florida Crime Museum**—Maintained by a local attorney, this Lauderdale-by-the-Sea museum in Florida explores state and national crimes, criminals, and law enforcement.

BABY BUMP-OFF: AN ATTEMPTED WOMB SNATCHING

I n 2005, Kentuckian Sarah Brady thought it was a simple mix-up when she received a call from Sarah *Brody* about a package she received that was actually meant for Brady. Brady was nine months pregnant at the time. Brody told her that she was too and assumed their gift registries were confused. The item was indeed something on Brady's registry, though there was no information about who sent it. When Brody called Brady the next day about another package mix-up, they ended up talking for an hour. Brady thought she made a new friend.

But Brady was disabused of that impression quickly when she went to pick up the packages. As she moved in for a goodbye hug, Brody pulled out a knife and attempted to stab her. A struggle ensued, but Brady managed to hit Brody over the head and stabbed her instead. Brody cried, "You stabbed me, you stupid b***h," as Brady fled, uninjured. Brody called 911, but bled to death while waiting for help. When police arrived, they found that Brody, whose real name was Katie Smith, had removed her maternity underwear. Attached to it was a large amount of padding made to look like a pregnant belly. Police believe she had plotted to steal Brady's baby, sending the packages to herself as a ruse. Brady gave birth to a healthy baby girl six days after the attack.

DEAN CORLL:
THE HOUSTON CANDY MAN

 fter being honorably discharged from the army in 1965, Dean Corll returned to his home in Houston, Texas, to work for his family business. The Corll Candy Company happened to be across from an elementary school, which delighted Corll, who loved befriending the students, particularly the boys.

The factory became a popular after-school hangout for boys, because Corll would give out free candy and even installed a pool table for the kids. One frequent visitor was David Brooks, who became a close friend of Corll's. By the time Brooks was 15, Corll was sexually abusing him.

Between 1970 and 1973, at least 28 boys went missing from the Houston area. Corll was a master manipulator who had several ways of luring in his victims:

• Through Brooks: Corll offered the teenager $200 for every boy he could lure into his home. Brooks often brought his own friends.

• Through alcohol and drugs.

• Through a free ride anywhere of their choosing.

No matter how they got there, these boys all ended up bound victims of Corll's sexual and physical assaults and were eventually killed by strangulation or gunshot.

Elmer Wayne Henley knew one of the boys who went missing in May 1971. The 15-year-old even helped hang posters in the area to find him. It was only several months later that Henley found himself in Corll's apartment, having been lured there by Brooks.

Although Henley was likely brought in as a victim, he did not become one. Instead, Corll seemed to see potential in the young man. He made Henley the same offer as Brooks: $200 for every victim. Though he didn't immediately accept, Henley claims financial troubles led him to start bringing boys over in 1972.

On August 7, 1973, Henley brought Timothy Kerley to Corll's home. After first getting drunk, Henley and Kerley picked up Henley's friend Rhonda Williams. When Henley and Kerley arrived with Williams, Corll was furious over the girl's presence, but eventually acquiesced and offered the teens alcohol and marijuana. Later, they appeared to lose consciousness.

When Henley woke up, he, Kerley, and Williams were bound and gagged. Corll admitted he was still upset about Williams and said that he was going to murder all three teenagers as punishment. After some pleading from Henley, Corll agreed that he would let him live if Henley would torture and murder Williams while Corll did the same to

One of the few images of Dean Corll, a serial killer known as the "Candy Man."

Kerley. As Williams woke up, her gag slipped off. She asked her friend, "Is this for real?" When he said it was, she replied, "Are you going to do anything about it?"

Henley took Corll's gun, shouting, "I can't have you kill all my friends!" He fired, striking Corll several times, killing the Candy Man.

After the police arrived, Henley made a full confession, including a description of the first victim he helped ensnare: "I talked him into going to Dean's apartment to smoke some marijuana. . . . Dean then took the boy down and tied his feet and put tape over his mouth. . . . Then the next day, Dean paid me $200. A day or so later, I found out that Dean had killed the boy. . . . [S]ince then, I have helped Dean get eight or ten other boys, I don't remember exactly how many."

He and Brooks cooperated in helping authorities locate the boys' bodies. They are both serving life sentences.

DON'T FOLLOW THE (CULT) LEADER

Match the cult leader to the cult.

1. Vernon Wayne Howell
2. Marshall Applewhite
3. Anne Hamilton-Byrne
4. Keith Raniere
5. Terri Hoffman

a. Conscious Development of Body, Mind and Soul
b. The Family (Australia)
c. The Branch Davidians
d. Heaven's Gate
e. NXIVM

Answers: 1C: *Howell, aka David Koresh, led the Branch Davidians until the tragic Waco siege in 1993.* **2D:** *Applewhite is infamous for leading the Heaven's Gate followers in a mass suicide in the wake of the Comet Hale-Bopp in 1997.* **3B:** *Hamilton-Byrne was a yoga instructor known for adopting children, dressing them uniformly, and, eerily, dyeing their hair blond.* **4E:** *Leader of the pyramid scheme formerly known for its "Executive Success Programs," Raniere was arrested in 2018 for sex trafficking.* **5A:** *Known for selling expensive jewelry to ward off "black lords," Hoffman also left a legacy of dead husbands and wealthy followers who bequeathed her all their money and possessions (see page 114).*

THE MURDER OF DOMINIQUE DUNNE

ominique Dunne was a rising star in the early 1980s. Best known for her role in the film *Poltergeist*, Dunne also appeared in TV shows like *Fame* and *Hill Street Blues*. But her ascent was cut short on November 4, 1982, when she was strangled to death by her former boyfriend John Thomas Sweeney. When police arrived, Sweeney approached them with his hands up, telling them he had just killed his girlfriend and tried to kill himself.

Dunne had ended her relationship with Sweeney because he was repeatedly physically abusive toward her. Sweeney claimed that he and Dunne were planning to reconcile, and he had flown into a rage after she changed her mind. The judge dismissed testimony from Dominque's friends and Sweeney's former girlfriend, all of whom reported that he had a history of violence and abuse. The initial charge of first-degree murder was whittled down to voluntary manslaughter and assault. Sweeney was sentenced to six and a half years in prison but was released after serving just over half that time.

Dominique's father, the writer and producer Dominick Dunne, was encouraged by author Tina Brown to keep a journal during Sweeney's trial. This journal eventually became "Justice: A Father's Account of the Trial of His Daughter's Killer," published in *Vanity Fair* in 1984. This launched a prolific career in investigative journalism for Dunne. He is known for covering such high-profile cases as the O. J. Simpson trials (1994 and 2008), the Menendez brothers murders, and the rape trial of William Kennedy Smith. His daughter's tragic death inspired his career as one of the most well-known crime journalists of the twentieth century, as well as a pioneer in victim-focused crime reporting: "I had never attended a trial until the trial of the man who strangled my daughter. What I witnessed in that courtroom enraged and redirected me . . . I could write about it. I could become an advocate for victims," Dunne noted.

Ellen Griffin Dunne, Dominique's mother, created the victim rights organization Justice for Homicide Victims in 1984 in honor of Dominique and other homicide victims and their families.

THE *POLTERGEIST* CURSE

Dominique Dunne's murder is often cited as the first death in the so-called *Poltergeist* curse—violent or mysterious deaths associated with the film series. Dunne portrayed Dana Freeling in the first film. Six years after her murder, on February 1, 1988, Heather O'Rourke, who played Carol Anne Freeling in all three films, died of a misdiagnosed acute bowel obstruction at age 12. On top of these tragic, unexpected deaths are two not-so-mysterious deaths. Sixty-year-old Julian Beck, who played evil spirit Kane in *Poltergeist II*, died of stomach cancer seven months before the film's release. Will Sampson, who played good spirit Taylor in the same film, died after a heart-lung transplant about a year after the film was released. More coincidence than curse, but eerie nonetheless.

THE ASTRONAUT LOVE TRIANGLE

On February 5, 2007, Colleen Shipman arrived at Orlando International Airport from Houston, Texas. Sensing that she was being followed, she hurried to her car and shut the door when a woman in a black wig began banging on the window. As Shipman rolled down the window, the woman pepper-sprayed her and attempted to get into her car. Shipman was able to escape unharmed.

The woman in the black wig was Lisa Nowak, a US astronaut. Nowak had just spent 14 hours driving the 900 miles from Houston to Orlando to confront Shipman, who had recently started dating Nowak's former love interest, astronaut William Oefelein. Among the items in Nowak's car were latex gloves, a BB gun, a drilling hammer, an eight-inch folding knife, and plastic garbage bags. Police reports said Nowak was wearing space diapers so she wouldn't have to take restroom breaks, but she later denied it. She was arrested for attempted murder and kidnapping but pleaded guilty to reduced charges of burglary and misdemeanor battery. Because of the incident, Nowak and Oefelein became the first astronauts to be dismissed from NASA. Shipman and Oefelein were married in 2010.

MICHAEL AND SUZAN BEAR CARSON: THE SAN FRANCISCO WITCH KILLERS

n 1977, James Clifford Carson began to behave so errati-cally that his wife fled with their daughter, eventually breaking off all contact with both Carson and their mutual acquaintances. Carson soon became involved with divorcée Susan Barnes, and the two changed their names to Michael Bear Carson and Suzan Bear Carson, claiming that the names were given to them by God. Together they moved to the Haight-Ashbury neighborhood in San Francisco and got involved with drugs and mysticism. Then their behavior turned deadly.

The Carsons' killing spree began in March 1981, when they said their roommate, Keryn Barnes (no relation to Suzan), falsely converted to their religion and drained Suzan of her health and yogic powers. In response, they stabbed Barnes 13 times, blud-geoned her, wrapped her in a blanket, and hid her body in the basement of the house they shared in San Francisco.

After they murdered Keryn Barnes, the Carsons fled to the mountains near Grants Pass, Oregon, before returning to California in the spring of 1982 to work on a marijuana farm in Alderpoint. In May, Michael shot and killed Clark Stephens, who also worked on the farm. The two had argued after the

Michael and Suzan Bear Carson in custody, 1983.

Carsons accused Stephens of sexually assaulting Suzan. Michael attempted to burn Stephens's body and then buried him in the woods under chicken fertilizer. The body was found two weeks later.

The Carsons were suspected of the murder, but they'd already fled and police were unable to track them down. They left behind a manifesto calling for the assassination of then-president Ronald Reagan. In November 1982, Michael was picked up by police in Los Angeles but was quickly released because of police error—and the pair vanished again.

In January 1983, the Carsons were picked up by a man named Jon Charles Hellyar while hitchhiking near Bakersfield, California. Suzan quickly decided that Hellyar was a witch, and a fight broke out as Hellyar was driving. He pulled over and the fight continued outside the vehicle. Suzan then stabbed Hellyar as he and Michael wrestled for a gun. Once Michael had the gun, he shot Hellyar in plain view of passing motorists, one of whom alerted the police.

The Carsons attempted to flee in Hellyar's car but were apprehended by police after a brief high-speed chase.

The Carsons held a five-hour press conference and smiled for the cameras as they confessed to the brutal slayings of Keryn Barnes, Clark Stephens, and Jon Charles Hellyar. They claimed to be pacifists despite the murders, vegetarian yoga "Muslim warriors" who were on a crusade to exterminate witches. They said they were disgusted with the American way of life and proclaimed that "witchcraft, homosexuality, and abortion are causes for death," adding that they had no choice but to kill. They kept a hit list of political figures and celebrities and remain suspects in a dozen other murders that occurred during their almost two-year murder spree.

The couple was each sentenced to 25 years, 50 years to life, and 75 years to life for the murders of Barnes, Stephens, and Hellyar, respectively. In 2015, Michael Bear Carson cancelled his parole hearing, stating, "I know this is absurd. No one is going to parole me because I will not and have not renounced my beliefs." As of 2017, neither of the Carsons have expressed a shred of remorse for their crimes.

KILLER'S KIN

Michael Bear Carson's daughter, Jenn, was just eight years old when she was told that her father and his girlfriend were the San Francisco Witch Killers. After a long journey coming to terms with her father's crimes, she eventually became an advocate for children of prisoners, families of violent offenders, and victims of violent crime. She has shared her story far and wide, including on the television show *Snapped: Killer Couples* and the podcast *Criminology*, reminding others that "a serial killer is smart. And much of the energy he puts into deception goes toward the people who are closest to him. Children of such people struggle with that. They struggle with a lot of things. . . . Having such a person in your family isn't easy. It never goes away. It's like a booby trap that keeps going off in your life."

FAMILIAL DNA AND GENETIC GENEALOGY

When genetic material is collected at a crime scene, forensic scientists create a unique DNA profile and try to match it to one of the profiles in CODIS (see page 109), the federal DNA database. But not every search leads to a match. CODIS accounts for only 5 percent of the US population, so an unidentified sample could belong to one of the more than 300 million people *not* in the system.

In recent years, genealogy websites like 23andMe and Ancestry have been building their own DNA databases for users to find distant relatives. If law enforcement submitted a sample to these sites, they could do a familial DNA search, find a close relative, and trace that person's lineage to a suspect. In April 2018, two high-profile cold cases were solved this way, using the genealogy site GEDmatch. The unidentified murder victim known as Buckskin Girl was identified as Marcia L. King through a match to her first cousin once removed, and the Golden State Killer (see page 96) was identified through a match to his third cousin.

CLARK COUNTY JOHN DOE

Bootlegger Joseph Henry Loveless escaped from an Idaho prison in 1916 using a saw he'd hid in his shoe. Loveless was back in prison a few months later for beating his wife to death with an ax, but soon escaped again using his old saw-in-the-shoe trick. He was never seen again.

In 1979, a torso was found in an Idaho cave; a hand, arm, and two legs were discovered in the same cave in 1991. In 2019, Idaho State University began working with the DNA Doe Project, an organization that uses genetic genealogy to identify John and Jane Does, to examine the remains. Due to the cool temperature of the cave, the DNA samples were of high quality—unusual for samples that old.

After a few months of genetic genealogical research, investigators traced the remains to Loveless's 87-year-old grandson. The DNA sample he provided matched the DNA of the remains found in the cave—Joseph Henry Loveless had been found.

Once the remains were identified, the Clark County Sheriff's Department began investigations into Loveless's murder, under the suspicion that he was killed by his slain wife's family as revenge for her brutal murder.

THE DNA DOE PROJECT

The DNA Doe Project (DDP) is a nonprofit volunteer organization that uses forensic genealogy to identify victims of homicide, car accidents, those who died by suicide under an alias, and others who have perished under unusual circumstances. DDP was cofounded in 2017 by Dr. Colleen Fitzpatrick, a nuclear physicist and the founder of forensic genealogy, and Dr. Margaret Press, a novelist, computer programmer, and linguistics specialist. Fitzpatrick previously founded IdentiFinders, an organization that identifies male killers of unsolved homicides through Y-chromosomal testing.

Fitzpatrick and Press work with a group of volunteers and law enforcement agencies and use genetic genealogy and traditional records, along with DNA from unidentified victims, to build family trees through the free DNA database GEDmatch. DDP has solved a growing number of Jane and John Doe cases.

Some well-known cold cases solved by the DNA Doe Project include:

• **Marcia Lenore Sossoman King,** aka "Buckskin Girl"— The murder of the woman named for the deerskin jacket she was found wearing went unsolved for 37 years until DDP matched her DNA to a first cousin.

• **Dana Lynn Dodd,** aka "Lavender Doe"—Joseph Wayne Burnette confessed to killing Dodd in August 2018, but she remained unidentified until January 2019. Her identity was released on February 11, 2019, after Burnette's trial concluded.

• **Mary Edith Silvani,** aka "Washoe County Doe"—Silvani, who had been shot in the head in 1982, remained unidentified for 36 years. By 2019, DDP was able to identify both Silvani and her killer, James Richard Curry, through genetic genealogy techniques. Curry had already died by suicide in prison in 1983.

In 2018, The Trans Doe Task Force (TDTF) was created by Lee and Anthony Redgrave, who were previously volunteers for the DNA Doe Project. The TDTF aims to bridge the gap between lived identity and genetics. Lee and Redgrave discover Doe cases with possible trans or gender-expansive victims, refer them to the DNA Doe Project for genetic identification, and then work from that genetic identity to piece together the Doe's lived name and identity.

The TDTF also works to educate media, law enforcement, and forensic investigators on how to sensitively handle Trans Doe cases, the differences between sex and gender, and the limitations of forensic identification based on sex.

PORTRAYING DARKNESS: SERIAL KILLER MOVIES

These Hollywood stars channeled evil to play real-life serial killers.

• *Extremely Wicked, Shockingly Evil and Vile* (2019)—Zac Efron masters serial killer Ted Bundy's disturbing but undeniable charm.

• *Monster* (2003)—Charlize Theron won an Academy Award for her nuanced portrayal of Aileen Wuornos.

• *My Friend Dahmer* (2017)—Ross Lynch portrays a young Dahmer in this movie based on the 2012 graphic novel by the serial killer's high school friend.

• *10 Rillington Place* (1971)—Richard Attenborough stars as British serial killer John Christie, with John Hurt as Timothy Evans, the neighbor who was hanged for two of Christie's murders.

Charlize Theron won the Academy Award for Best Actress for her portrayal of Aileen Wuornos in *Monster*.

GARY RIDGWAY: THE GREEN RIVER KILLER

 ashington State, 1982: Young runaways and sex workers are disappearing along Pacific Highway South. The bodies, or those that turn up, are found in the forest along the Green River.

The killer—named the Green River Killer for his favorite dumping grounds—had a system. He would show the women photos of his son to earn their trust; then, once they were in his truck, he would rape and strangle them.

As more women disappeared, police grew desperate. They turned to an unlikely source for help: Ted Bundy. Incarcerated

Gary Ridgway in 2011, where he pleaded guilty to the murder of Rebecca Marrero, his 49th confirmed victim.

for his own string of grisly murders, Bundy offered a helpful piece of advice. He thought the killer would likely return to the Green River area to have sex with the corpses. This would prove to be true.

On May 11, 1982, police arrested Gary Ridgway for solicitation of a sex worker. They closely studied the truck painter, giving him a polygraph in 1983 (he passed) and taking DNA samples in 1984. By 1987, Ridgway had wed for the third time, and the number of killings decreased.

In 2001, advances in DNA analysis allowed investigators to revisit Ridgway's samples. His saliva DNA conclusively matched the DNA from semen left on four victims: Marcia Chapman, Opal Mills, Cynthia Hinds, and Carol Ann Christensen. Modern

RIDGWAY'S JANE DOES

Although the victims' families all had to cope with the tragedy of losing their mothers, daughters, sisters, and friends, there are three even more tragic stories: those of the victims who were never identified. Ridgway confessed to killing three young women whose lives, and identities, were erased along the Green River.

Jane Doe B-10, discovered on March 21, 1984, was likely a white female between 12 and 18 years old.

Jane Doe B-17 was a white female between the ages of 14 and 18 years old. Part of her body was found on February 18, 1984, and the rest was found on January 2, 1986.

Jane Doe B-20 was a female between 13 and 24 years old. She was discovered in August 2003.

forensics had yet more to offer: Scientists were also able to match microscopic spray paint aerosol particles on three more victims with a brand used at Ridgway's company.

After eluding police for nearly 20 years, the Green River Killer was finally arrested.

To avoid the death penalty, Ridgway struck a plea bargain in 2003. As part of the deal, he confessed and helped authorities locate the remains of any missing victims. In total, he admitted to 48 murders, though some estimate he may have killed as many as 71 women. Ridgway claimed that he targeted sex workers because they were "easy to pick up" and he "hated most of them." He also described how he lured victims into trusting him: "I would talk to her . . . and get her mind off of the, sex, anything she was nervous about. And think, you know, she thinks, 'Oh, this guy cares' . . . which I didn't."

He was sentenced to 48 consecutive life sentences, plus 10 years per murder for tampering with evidence.

Ridgway was originally set to serve his life sentences at Washington State Penitentiary in Walla Walla but was transferred to a high-security prison in Colorado in 2015. The move prompted a backlash among investigators and the victims' families, who believed keeping Ridgway in Washington could lead to more assistance in both finding additional victims and helping other investigations. The Green River Killer was transferred back to Washington in a matter of months.

Ridgway claimed he didn't hate all women, and that he truly loved his wife, Judith—and his murderous ways largely stopped after their marriage. Now remarried, Judith never suspected her husband of being a murderer. Afterward she said, "I feel I have saved lives . . . by being his wife and making him happy."

WHAT BODY PART HELPS IDENTIFY MORE THAN 93 PERCENT OF REMAINS?

Teeth. Because teeth are among the sturdiest parts of the body, they are often the best-preserved in human remains. Because every individual has a unique dental imprint, teeth come with an extremely reliable form of identification: dental records.

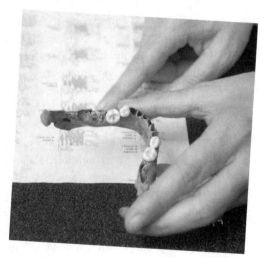

Dental records have helped solve countless crimes.

THE CORPSEWOOD MANOR MURDERS

r. Charles L. Scudder and his partner, Joey Odom, left their run-down mansion in Chicago for a simpler life in 1976. They purchased a plot of land in the Chattahoochee National Forest in Chattooga County, Georgia, where they built a home without amenities—no electricity, no phone, and no television. They laid the bricks themselves, for both their home and a three-story outbuilding, the chicken coop.

Odom cooked gourmet meals in a woodstove using vegetables from their garden; Scudder made wine using grapes from their vineyard. They allowed locals to hunt on their land, hosted guests in the chicken coop, and held a wedding in their rose garden. They named their home Corpsewood Manor after the trees surrounding their property. In the March/April 1981 edition of *Mother Earth News*, Scudder wrote of their idyllic lifestyle: "It's not necessary, you see, to keep piling up the bucks and plodding away at the treadmill until the last crippling coronary takes away your freedom of choice. . . . If we want a different, fuller, more exciting life than we're leading—one closer to this beautiful earth—we can have it. Our only chains are those in our minds! Just promise me that you'll think about it seriously for a while . . . after all, wouldn't *you* like to live in your own kind of 'castle in the country?'"

But there were challenges to being a gay couple in rural Georgia in the '70s and '80s. Scudder had particularly eccentric interests and was a member of the Church of Satan to boot. The sheriff tried to bring charges against both men for their "odd behavior," but Scudder's position as a Satanist protected him because of freedom of religion. Unfortunately, that protection would only go so far.

Odom became famous in the area for his cooking. Locals would often stop by to marvel at the progress of the castlelike structure and indulge in Scudder's homemade wine. Despite these positive relationships, and Odom's Catholic faith, the two became known in the area as "the homosexual devil-worshippers."

On December 12, 1982, Tony West and his nephew, Avery Brock, made their way to Corpsewood Manor with Joey Wells and Teresa Hudgins, two teenagers on a date. Brock had visited the manor before and was under the impression that Scudder and Odom were wealthy. In reality Scudder spent most of his life's earnings on the property and the two lived off just over $200 a month, mostly from a small inheritance of Scudder's. But Brock and West believed they would find a fortune.

When they arrived unannounced, Scudder welcomed them and escorted all four visitors to the "pink room" on the third floor of the chicken coop. Scudder offered them some of his wine, but he didn't partake in any of the "toot-a-lu" (paint thinner and glue) the four were huffing. Only West was in on what was about to happen when Brock excused himself to retrieve more toot-a-lu from the car.

Brock returned to the pink room with a shotgun and pointed it at Scudder, who said "bang bang" in an attempt to diffuse the situation. Wells and Hudgins tried to flee the scene in West's car, but it wouldn't start. West called them back into the pink room, where they found Brock holding a knife to Scudder's neck, demanding that Scudder tell him where the money was. Brock then bound Scudder with a bedsheet and went to the

What's left of the Corpsewood Manor where Scudder and Odom were killed, 2017.

main house, where he shot and killed Odom and the couple's two beloved bullmastiffs. He returned to the pink room one last time to lead the whole group into the house. When Scudder saw Odom's body, he was overcome with grief. His last words before he was shot repeatedly were "I asked for this."

Brock and West ransacked the house. They tried to steal Scudder's harp, but it wouldn't fit in the car. Then they stole the couple's Jeep and fled westward. On December 15, they stopped at a rest stop in Mississippi and stole a car from a navy lieutenant, Kirby Key Phelps, murdering him in the process.

On December 16, a neighbor, Raymond Williams, stopped by Corpsewood Manor to inform Scudder and Odom that a friend of theirs in Rome, Georgia, had passed away. Williams noticed bullet holes in the door, went back down the mountain, and phoned the sheriff's office. The same day, Teresa Hudgins came forward to police, claiming she hadn't come to them earlier because Joey Wells had been holding her hostage. Hudgins and Wells cooperated fully with the investigation and were never charged with a crime.

A nationwide hunt for Brock and West ensued. The two split up in Austin, Texas, after an argument about their plans. Brock turned himself in on December 20 in Marietta, Georgia. West was captured in Chattanooga, Tennessee, four days later, on Christmas Eve. Brock pleaded guilty to the murders and received three consecutive life sentences. West pleaded not guilty and went to trial.

The trial was sensational, in part because of what investigators found in Corpsewood Manor. Though none of it had to do with the actual crimes, the two human skulls, vials of old laboratory LSD, occult tools, gay porn, and library of occult books mixed in with mostly academic and literary titles drew lots of attention, as did a self-portrait of Scudder painted months earlier, depicting himself gagged with blood dripping from five bullet wounds in his head. The couple had broad and eclectic interests and were living their best lives in their dream home.

West's defense used the LSD to try to argue involuntary intoxication—that Scudder had drugged his wine and that "He had a motive because he was a homosexual." But West had already confessed that he and Brock planned the murders and robbery a few days before they committed them. He also claimed that Brock wanted to kill Scudder because he said the two had had a sexual encounter. West was found guilty and sentenced to death. He was retried due to a jury technicality and received three consecutive life sentences.

RUSIK, THE CAVIAR-SNIFFING CAT

The small city of Stavropol near the Caspian Sea in Southern Russia is a hotbed of caviar smuggling—a $1.3 billion industry controlled by local criminal groups. But in 2002, the police found their ultimate caviar-crime-fighting agent after a hungry kitten wandered into a customs checkpoint. His talent was discovered soon after he arrived, when he leapt into the trunk of a car and sniffed out a load of illicit sturgeon. Dubbed Rusik, the Siamese spent the next year on the job. But tragedy struck a few days after a police spokesperson boasted of the feline officer's skill, claiming, "The cat finds the caviar in any hiding place." Rusik was hit by a car on July 12, 2003, dying in the line of duty. Previously, an illegal shipment was found in the car that hit him—which was known to be Mafia-owned.

The police suspected a contract killing.

SERIAL KILLER TROPHIES

Match the serial killer to the trophies they kept from their victims.

1. Ed Gein (page 172)
2. Jerry Brudos
3. Dennis Rader ("BTK")
4. Edmund Kemper (page 105)
5. Jeffrey Dahmer (page 45)

a. Polaroids
b. Driver's licenses
c. Severed heads
d. Gloves made out of human hands
e. A paperweight made from the mold of a severed breast

Answers: 1D: Along with the gloves, several other accessories made of body parts were found in Gein's home, including a belt made of nipples and bowls fashioned from human skulls. **2E:** Brudos brutally murdered and mutilated four women. **3B:** BTK kept the licenses of at least 2 of his 10 victims. **4C:** Kemper's penchant for severed heads started early with pets and his sister's dolls. **5A:** Police found dressers overflowing with Polaroids in his home; Dahmer often lured his victims to his apartment by offering to pay them to take nude photos.

ED GEIN:
THE BUTCHER OF
PLAINFIELD

ugusta Gein was a controlling, God-fearing woman who had a powerful hold over her youngest son, Edward. Though she was stern and sometimes abusive toward Ed, he was driven to please her. After the deaths of her husband and eldest son, Henry, Augusta had a stroke and Ed devoted himself to providing round-the-clock care for her. When she died on December 29, 1945, her son was devastated. He boarded up all the rooms she frequented on their isolated farm in Plainfield, Wisconsin, entombing them just as they were when she was alive.

Ed distracted himself with work and reading horror magazines, but to no avail. He missed Augusta too much. In what he later described as a "daze-like" state, he visited the cemetery. He was looking for corpses who looked like Augusta.

Between 1947 and 1952, Gein visited graveyards at least 40 times, looking for middle-aged women. He would dig, break open the caskets, and bring the corpses back to his farm. There, he would dismember the bodies, tan their skins, and repurpose them for clothing and decorations, including a corset, masks, and a chair covering.

On its own, Gein's grave robbing makes for a horrific story. Unfortunately, corpses weren't enough for Gein. In 1954, tavern owner Mary Hogan went missing. Police wouldn't find her body until three years later while searching for another missing woman.

At 5:00 p.m. on November 16, 1957, the Worden Hardware store mysteriously closed early—its owner, Bernice Worden, was nowhere to be found. Worden's son, Frank, knew that Ed Gein had been in the store the previous evening and mentioned he'd return to buy antifreeze the next day. A check of the store's records revealed that the last receipt Worden wrote that evening was for antifreeze.

Police arrested Gein at a nearby grocery store and prepared to search his farm. What they found there would haunt officers for the rest of their lives. Worden's body had been decapitated, strung up, and sliced open like a butchered animal. It was a small comfort that she'd been fatally shot before being mutilated. Police then found pieces of Mary Hogan, along with a horrific collection of other body parts.

Originally given a diagnosis of schizophrenia, Gein was determined mentally fit to stand trial in 1968. He claimed to not remember much from the morning of Worden's death, but he did recall that his gun discharged accidentally in the hardware store and that he hadn't meant to kill Worden.

In 1968, a judge found Gein not guilty by reason of insanity (the defense had requested no jury) and sent him to the Central State Hospital for the Criminally Insane, where Gein would spend the rest of his life. Three days before his house was set to be auctioned off, it mysteriously burned. A carnival operator bought the car Gein used for grave robbing and charged people a quarter to see it.

After battling lung cancer, Gein died of respiratory failure on July 26, 1984. In an ironic twist, his own gravesite was robbed repeatedly over the years as visitors chipped away pieces of his headstone for a keepsake of the Butcher of Plainfield until the entire headstone was stolen in 2000. The headstone was later recovered and the site is now unmarked.

Gein's legacy includes a large mark on popular culture: His worship of his mother and the gruesome scene at his farm influenced many of the twentieth century's most memorable stories and characters, including *The Silence of the Lambs*, *The Texas Chainsaw Massacre*, and *Psycho*.

Gein's gravestone was vandalized before it was stolen in 2000 from Plainfield Cemetery in Wisconsin.

KELLY HERRON: "NOT TODAY, MOTHERFUCKER!"

On March 5, 2017, Kelly Herron was 4 miles into a 10-mile run through Golden Gardens Park in Seattle, Washington, when she stopped to use a public restroom. As she was drying her hands, a man attacked her, going first for her knees to bring her to the ground. But Herron wasn't going down without a fight. She began yelling, "Not today, motherfucker!" and used every tip she could remember from a self-defense class she took just three weeks earlier: Trust your intuition, respond immediately, be loud and fight hard, and connect hard bones to soft spots. When she found herself cornered in a stall with her attacker hitting her in the head, she scratched his face and was able to escape. She barricaded her attacker in the bathroom with a carabiner borrowed from a passerby and asked another to call 911.

Sex offender Gary Steiner waited in the stall until the police arrived. He pleaded guilty to second-degree assault with sexual motivation and received the maximum sentence of three years to life. Herron continues to run and partnered with Fighting Chance Seattle to offer classes on self-defense geared toward runners.

NANNIE DOSS: THE GIGGLING GRANNY

 annie Doss, born Nancy Hazel in 1905, was always a romantic with a penchant for reading the lonely hearts columns in her mother's magazines. The picture-perfect romance would elude her for decades—but it didn't stop her from serial marriages.

Doss first met Charles Braggs when they both worked at a thread factory. After mere months of dating, the pair wed in 1921. Doss, only 16 years old at the time, moved into Braggs's home. It was far from an ideal situation: Braggs's unmarried mother still lived there, and the marriage was plagued by infidelity.

On a happy note, the couple had four children. Unhappily, two of them died from mysterious cases of food poisoning. Braggs was terrified that his wife had killed their children and he fled with their oldest daughter, leaving their newborn baby with Doss. They divorced several years later, and their oldest daughter returned to Doss in 1928.

Single again, Doss returned to reading the lonely hearts column. An ad from Robert "Frank" Harrelson caught her eye. The pair exchanged letters, including poetry. They married in 1929 and lived together in Jacksonville, Florida. The marriage lasted for 16 years, but Harrelson's alcoholism pushed his wife to the breaking point.

Nannie Doss, who admitted to poisoning four of her five husbands, often laughed and joked in court while detailing her murders.

After a night out celebrating the end of World War II in 1945, Harrelson was deeply intoxicated. He returned home and, by some accounts, raped his wife. The next day, Doss took his whiskey and dosed it with rat poison. Harrelson's life, and Doss's second marriage, ended later that evening.

Once again, Doss used the lonely hearts column to find her next husband. She married Arlie Lanning just days after meeting him in North Carolina. In 1950, Lanning, too, would fall victim to rat poison, though the official cause of death was heart failure.

Doss's next marriage, to Richard L. Morton of Emporia, Kansas, came through the singles club known as the Diamond Circle. Not long after marrying Morton in 1952, Doss became frustrated with his womanizing ways. She also had her hands full with her mother, Lou, who had been living with the couple since the death of Doss's father. It wasn't long before Lou started complaining of severe stomach pains. She died in 1953, with Morton following suit three months later.

Doss's fifth and final marriage was to Samuel Doss, of Tulsa, Oklahoma, in June 1953. Samuel was a devout man who disapproved of Doss's love for romance stories. He forbade her to continue reading them. It didn't take long for Samuel to end up in the hospital with severe digestive problems. After being released on October 5, 1953, he died the same night. An autopsy revealed fatal levels of arsenic in his body. In her confession, Doss would later say she killed Samuel "because he got on my nerves."

Doss confessed to killing four of her husbands, along with various family members. Throughout her trial, she smiled and cracked jokes. The media loved her, giving her nicknames such as the Giggling Granny and the Merry Widow (and also, by some, Lady Blue Beard).

After she was found guilty of murder, Doss faced the death penalty. However, the judge noted that executing a woman would set a "poor precedent" and sentenced Doss to life in prison.

Doss maintained her morbid sense of humor while serving out her prison sentence. Referring to her poisonous ways, she once told a reporter, "When they get shorthanded in the kitchen here, I always offer to help out, but they never let me." She died of leukemia in 1965.

MR. ROGERS'S CAR

"Children aren't the only ones with a soft spot for Mr. Rogers. Two weeks ago, his Oldsmobile sedan was stolen while he was babysitting for his grandson. After looking over papers and props he had left in the car, the thieves apparently realized who the owner was. Mr. Rogers found the car parked in front of his house a day or two later. All that was missing was a director's chair with his name on it."

—*"This Neighborhood Hasn't Changed a Bit Over the Decades" by Peter Pae,* Wall Street Journal, *March 2, 1990*

Fred Rogers on the set of his show *Mister Rogers' Neighborhood*.

THE MURDER OF MARVIN GAYE

 arvin Gaye is known for a successful music career that spanned decades and genres, from Motown to '70s protest music to R & B, earning him the title "Prince of Motown" and "Prince of Soul." But his life was also marred by abuse and tragedy, culminating in his murder.

Gaye's singing success started early. By age 11, he was being encouraged by his mother and others around him to pursue a singing career. Despite his mother's love and support, Gaye's home life was a source of immense suffering. He and his three siblings were subjected to the violent whims of their volatile, alcoholic father. Gaye's family recognized that he bore the brunt of their father's abuse, later detailing the brutal whippings and psychological terror he experienced from age seven well into his teen years. At 17, Gaye dropped out of school and, to escape his father's abuse, enlisted in the United States Air Force.

The air force was Gaye's ticket out of his childhood home, but he wasn't suited to taking orders or performing menial tasks and received a general discharge soon after joining. In 1957, he began climbing the ranks as a singer, achieving steadily increasing success through the '60s. In early 1967, Gaye was paired with Tammi Terrell to record a series of duets, and the duo excelled— Terrell's vivacious stage presence inspired Gaye, who was shy and disliked performing live, to come out of his shell. In October 1967, Terrell collapsed into Gaye's arms onstage. She was diagnosed with a brain tumor and died on March 16, 1970, at the age of 24. Gaye performed her eulogy while their hit duet "You're All I Need to Get By" played.

Compounded with the trauma Gaye experienced as a child, Terrell's death was a turning point in his life. He sunk into a deep depression and began self-medicating with drugs, primarily cocaine and PCP. Though he continued to release critical and commercial hits through the '70s and into the '80s, by 1983 he had reached a low point in his struggle with depression, drug abuse, and debt and moved back into his parents' house. Within a year, he would be dead.

On April 1, 1984, an argument between Gaye's father and him became physical, with Gaye kicking and punching his father. Gaye's mother, Alberta, defused the fight. As Alberta was attempting to calm Gaye in his room, Gaye's father charged in and shot Gaye once, fatally puncturing his heart, lung, and liver. He then shot Gaye again at point-blank range. Fearing for her own life, Alberta fled the house, running to the home of her son Frankie, who lived next door. Frankie rushed to Gaye's side and held him

Marvin Gaye in a studio, circa 1974.

held him until police arrived. Gaye's last words to Frankie were "I got what I wanted . . . I couldn't do it myself, so I had him do it . . . it's good, I ran my race, there's no more left in me." Gaye was taken to the hospital and pronounced dead on arrival. It was the day before his 45th birthday.

Gaye's father, Marvin Gay Sr., was sitting calmly on the porch when police arrested him. During his initial police interview, when Marvin Sr. was asked if he loved his son, he replied, "I didn't dislike him." He was charged with first-degree murder.

Alberta filed for divorce from Marvin Sr. but posted his $30,000 reduced bail. Based on the traces of PCP (later disproven) and cocaine in Gaye's system and pictures of Marvin Sr.'s injuries following the fight he had with his son, Judge Ronald George allowed Marvin Sr. to take a plea bargain. Marvin Sr. pleaded no contest to voluntary manslaughter and received a six-year suspended sentence and five years of probation.

The Gaye siblings believe Gaye's actions were calculated—

Marvin Gay, Sr., the day he was arrested for shooting and killing his son, singer Marvin Gaye.

they knew if they ever attacked Marvin Sr. he would kill them. At the time of Gaye's death, he talked of little but suicide and had actually bought his father the Smith & Wesson .38 pistol used in his murder.

Gaye's sister Jeanne said Gaye "accomplished three things. He put himself out of his misery. He brought relief to Mother by finally getting her husband out of her life. And he punished Father, by making certain that the rest of his life would be miserable. . . . My brother knew just what he was doing."

THE LOST CARNEGIE

Elizabeth "Betty" Bigley committed her first con when she was 13. By forging a letter stating her uncle had died, she received an advance from a bank in Ontario on a small inheritance. When she was caught, Bigley was set free with a warning. In her twenties she posed as an heiress, the sickly niece of a Civil War hero, and a clairvoyant. She conned money out of everyone she met, including her own sister, and left several ex-husbands in her wake.

In 1897, Bigley finally settled in Cleveland, Ohio, where she married a doctor and changed her name to Cassie Chadwick. She told her husband she was the illegitimate daughter of steel magnate Andrew Carnegie, who paid her to stay quiet. With forged promissory notes, Bigley obtained loans from various banks, living in luxury until 1904, when a Boston banker discovered her fraud. Bigley was convicted and sentenced to 14 years in prison but died two years into her sentence. In all, her crimes netted her $16.5 million, adjusted for inflation.

PEDRO ALONSO LÓPEZ:
THE MONSTER
OF THE ANDES

edro Alonso López, who would later go on to rape and murder at least 100 but perhaps more than 300 women, started his life of crime in his own home. At the age of eight, his family kicked him out for molesting his sister. He later explained that the prostitution he witnessed as a child had disturbing effects on him.

Unfortunately, life on the streets likely exacerbated López's violent tendencies. Cycling through foster homes and jail, he was repeatedly assaulted and also raped. Eventually, López fought back. After being gang-raped in prison at age 18, he made a shiv and killed all four of his rapists. His sentence, originally for car theft, was extended by two years.

In 1971, López, 23, was a free man and hungry for new victims. During the height of his spree, López murdered two or three girls every week. He would stalk marketplaces throughout Peru, Ecuador, and Colombia, looking for young, trusting children (typically between ages 7 and 12), approach them, and offer gifts. He'd then lead them to a nearby hideout, where he would imprison them. If it was nighttime, he'd wait—he preferred to rape and kill his victims in the light of day. "When the sun rose I would strangle her," he later told a journalist. "It was only good if I could see her eyes. I never killed anyone at night. It would have been wasted in the dark."

López, who may have killed more than 300 women and girls, was released from a Colombian psychiatric facility in 1998 and was never seen again.

With little police assistance, people in the countries where López killed took matters into their own hands. In 1978, Peruvian village chiefs caught López after he'd murdered two local girls. According to lore, they were just about to kill him when an American missionary intervened and offered to take him to the police. Instead, she released him at the Colombian border.

In 1979, the killer who'd come to be known as the Monster of the Andes was caught trying to kidnap a 10-year-old girl in an Ecuadorian market. The crowd, already outraged by the recent brutal strangling of four young girls (likely López's doing), savagely beat and held him until authorities arrived.

In addition to the 110 girls López was convicted of killing in Ecuador, he confessed to killing 240 more children in Peru and Colombia. Since Ecuador does not permit death sentences and imposes a maximum sentence of 16 years for murder (regardless of body count), López was released 15 years later. Why not 16? Good behavior.

When López walked out of prison a free man on August 31, 1994, he was immediately apprehended by the Colombian police, who'd been waiting to charge him with a separate murder. However, López sidestepped punishment once again, when he was found not guilty by reason of insanity. After being held in a Bogotá psychiatric facility for just four years, he was declared rehabilitated and released. As part of his probation, he needed to report to court every month. But he never showed up.

López slipped into obscurity and had nearly drifted off police radar entirely when he appeared to strike again. In 2002, Colombian authorities and Interpol announced that two fresh murders matched his style. They planned to arrest him, but he was never found.

What happened to Pedro Alonso López? Some believe he may have learned to control his urges and now lives peacefully in a small South American town. Others believe that those who lived in the countries where he operated, twice denied their opportunity to exact vigilante justice, finally caught up with López and killed him. Or, perhaps, the Monster of the Andes is simply biding his time, waiting to kill again.

KNIT, PURL, SPY

Knitting and war have a long history—throughout World War II, women were encouraged to knit socks for soldiers. But pervasive knitting became a great cover for another common wartime activity: espionage. During the Revolutionary War, Patriot spy Molly Rinker sat knitting on a hill, so she could secretly deliver British secrets to American soldiers. She tucked messages into balls of yarn and tossed them to American soldiers who sat below. Frenchwoman Madame Levengle sat knitting in front of her window during World War I, observing the movement of troops while tapping codes with her heel to her children on the floor below, who transposed them. Belgian women observed train patterns and used a knit-purl pattern based on Morse code to pass information to the resistance during the first and second World Wars. Soviet-spy-turned-US-informant Elizabeth Bentley smuggled documents and pictures with information about B-29 bombers and other enemy aircraft in her knitting bag.

This use of knitting to pass codes led the Office of Censorship (an emergency US agency established during World War II) to ban mailing knitting patterns abroad for the duration of the war.

JOHN HINCKLEY JR.: GUNNING FOR THE GIPPER

 ohn Hinckley Jr. is known for attempting to assassinate President Ronald Reagan on March 30, 1981, in a twisted attempt to gain the attention of his celebrity obsession, Jodie Foster. In a letter sent to Foster, he explained:

I will admit to you that the reason I'm going ahead with this attempt now is because I just cannot wait any longer to impress you. I've got to do something now to make you understand, in no uncertain terms, that I am doing all of this for your sake! By sacrificing my freedom and possibly my life, I hope to change your mind about me. This letter is being written only an hour before I leave for the Hilton Hotel. Jodie, I'm asking you to please look into your heart and at least give me the chance, with this historical deed, to gain your respect and love.

Hinckley shot and wounded four people that day: Reagan (hit by a ricochet bullet), police officer Thomas Delahanty, Secret Service agent Timothy McCarthy, and press secretary James Brady, whose death from the injuries he sustained that day was ruled a homicide 33 years later, on August 4, 2014. Hinckley was controversially found not guilty by reason of insanity and

The iconic self-portrait of Hinckley with a gun to his head released by the FBI and used as evidence in his trial.

sentenced to an indefinite term at St. Elizabeths Hospital in Washington, DC, where he was treated for narcissistic and schizotypal personality disorder and major depressive disorder.

On September 10, 2016, Hinckley became the first man to attempt a presidential assassination and walk away a free man. He was ordered to live with his mother in Williamsburg, Virginia, for one year and to continue outpatient treatment.

CRIMES AROUND THE WORLD

Match the crime with the country in which it occurred.

1. B1 Butcher
2. Beer Man
3. Paraquat Murders
4. Paturis Park Murders
5. Sewer Murders

a. Brazil
b. Germany
c. India
d. Japan
e. Namibia

Answers: 1E: *The B1 Butcher killed and dismembered at least three women in Namibia between 2005 and 2007, leaving their body parts alongside the B1 road.* **2C:** *The Beer Man killed at least six homeless men in India in 2006 and 2007, leaving behind an empty can of beer at each scene.* **3D:** *Drinks laced with the herbicide paraquat were found inside vending machines in Japan, killing 10 people and sickening 35 others in 1985.* **4A:** *The bodies of 13 gay men were found shot and dumped in Brazil's Paturis Park in 2007 and 2008.* **5B:** *Between 1976 and 1983, a killer disposed of the bodies of seven adolescent boys in the Frankfurt, Germany, sewage system.*

THE BEAR BROOK MURDERS

I n November 1985, hunters discovered a 55-gallon drum containing the skeletons of an adult woman and a young girl in Bear Brook State Park near Allenstown, New Hampshire. Fifteen years later, another drum containing two more girls was found 100 yards away. The dead woman was related to the oldest and youngest girls but was unrelated to the middle child. They had been beaten to death and put there between 1980 and 1984.

The case of the Allenstown Four went cold until 1986, when Lisa Jensen, then five years old, was abandoned at a California RV park by a drifter named Gordon Curtis Jensen. He had kidnapped and abused her. As an adult, a genetic test showed that Lisa was actually Dawn Beaudin, who went missing along with her mother, Denise, from Manchester, New Hampshire, just 15 miles from Allenstown, in 1981.

When Denise Beaudin and her infant daughter disappeared after Thanksgiving in 1981, her boyfriend, Robert Evans, assured her family that it was by choice. They were not reported missing, and Denise was never seen again. Evans moved to California in 1984 and used the alias Curtis Kimball. In 1986, when he abandoned Dawn, he was calling himself Gordon. Later still, he had run-ins with police as Gerry Mockerman and Lawrence William Vanner. Evans's real name was Terry Peder Rasmussen. By connecting his various aliases and crimes, police determined that he was responsible for at least six murders.

Rasmussen was finally arrested and sentenced in 2003 for killing his girlfriend, Eunsoon Jun. He died of natural causes in prison in 2010. In 2017, DNA obtained from one of Rasmussen's sons identified Rasmussen as the father of the unrelated middle girl in the Bear Brook murders.

In 2019, the Bear Brook woman was identified as Marlyse Honeychurch. The oldest and youngest girls were identified as her daughters, Marie Vaughn and Sarah McWaters. This was made possible through genealogy and genetic DNA, when Rebekah Heath, a librarian in Connecticut with an interest in the case, found a post on Ancestry.com by a man looking for his older half sister—Sarah McWaters. He didn't know what happened to her, but he knew that her mother, Honeychurch, had an older daughter named Marie and had married a man named Rasmussen after divorcing McWaters's father. The three identities were then confirmed with DNA given by Honeychurch's relatives.

Police still don't know the location of Denise Beaudin's body or the identity of the middle Bear Brook child, though it is known that Rasmussen was her father.

SENIOR CENTER: THE NOTE BEFORE THE BLAZE

At 6:00 p.m. on August 22, 2007, firefighters responded to the scene of a fire at a senior citizen apartment complex in Yonkers, New York. By 6:15, the fire was under control, but all that was left of 78-year-old Louise Paciarello's apartment was a black, burned-out hole. Authorities initially believed that Paciarello died in the fire, but in the following days a more sinister narrative unfolded. An autopsy revealed that Paciarello had been strangled, and police suspected the fire was set to cover up the murder. Neighbors revealed Paciarello was worried about an intruder in recent weeks. She changed her locks after reporting that someone had been trying to get into her apartment and expressed anxiety that someone knew she kept money in her freezer. She had even found a note on her kitchen table a month before the fire. It read:

I am here at 4 a.m. You were sleeping. I'll be back.

Paciarello's purse was not found in her apartment and no money was found in the freezer. Her killer remains at large.

BETTY BRODERICK:
LOVE TRIANGLE
TURNED DEADLY

Betty Broderick supported her husband, Dan, and their four children as he made his way through MD and JD degrees. Dan eventually became a successful malpractice lawyer in La Jolla, California, and Broderick continued to work part-time and raise their children. It was not an ideal marriage—Broderick complained that she felt like a single parent while Dan worked long hours.

Not long after Dan hired 21-year-old Linda Kolkena as his legal assistant in 1982, Broderick began accusing Dan of having an affair with her. Dan denied it and told Broderick she was "crazy." Arguments between the two escalated, and Broderick remained suspicious of the relationship between Dan and Linda. She even burned some of Dan's suits when she learned he spent his 38th birthday with Linda.

In 1985, Dan moved out and filed a restraining order against Broderick. Broderick dumped their children on Dan's doorstep one at a time and to her surprise, Dan took full custody of them. Their divorce, *Broderick v. Broderick*, was legendary in its complexity, and its viciousness.

Broderick's response to the divorce was violent and disturbing. She left hundreds of profane messages on Dan's answering machine and showed up to his house—which he shared

Broderick testifying in court in 1990.

with Linda—on numerous occasions despite restraining orders against her. She smeared a Boston cream pie on Dan's suits, spray-painted his walls, and broke his windows. She made demands to her children regarding how they were to treat Dan and Linda. She even drove her car through the front door of Dan's house. After one hearing for violating a restraining order, Broderick spent three days in jail.

By many accounts, Dan egged on Broderick's behavior instead of showing sympathy and encouraging her to get help. He was president of the local bar association, and Broderick struggled to find a lawyer who would work with her. He exploited legal loopholes to drag out the proceedings for five years, and Broderick's behavior became increasingly dangerous.

Their divorce was finalized on January 30, 1989, with Dan, a multimillionaire, paying Broderick $30,000 plus alimony. A few months later, and just 10 days after what would have been the Brodericks' 20-year anniversary, Dan married Linda. Linda was so concerned about Dan's safety, she asked him to wear a bullet-proof vest to their wedding.

A month before Dan and Linda married, Broderick bought a gun, claiming she needed protection now that she was living as a single woman. She took shooting lessons and began regularly threatening to gun down Dan.

On November 5, 1989, Broderick made good on her threats. She drove to Dan and Linda's house in the middle of the night, letting herself in with a key she stole from their daughter. Broderick shot both Dan and Linda as they slept. Linda was killed instantly, but Broderick reported Dan saying "OK, you shot me. I'm dead!" before he died. He was reaching for the phone, but evidence at the trial stated that Broderick had previously removed both the phone and the answering machine from the room.

Broderick immediately turned herself in to the police. She never denied shooting Dan and Linda, but insisted that it was not premeditated. She claimed she was startled because Linda began screaming when Broderick entered their bedroom, despite evidence that suggested Linda was shot in the head and chest and killed without ever waking up.

At Broderick's first trial, her attorney, Jack Earley, depicted his client as a battered woman, driven over the edge after years of psychological, emotional, and mental abuse at the hands of Dan. Earley emphasized how Broderick worked five jobs while Dan

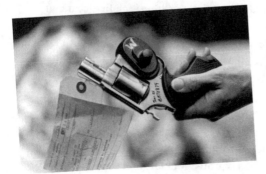

The gun Broderick used to shoot her ex-husband, Dan Broderick, and his new wife, Linda Kolkena.

was in law school and said she was repaid with lies, infidelity, and legal bullying. The prosecution, led by Kerry Wells, insisted that Broderick was a narcissist who had been planning the murders of Dan and Linda for months. Wells called Broderick's older daughter as a witness to testify how angry and unrepentant her mother was.

The case ended in a mistrial after two jurors held out for a manslaughter conviction, one of whom was quoted as saying "I only wonder what took her so long." The second trial was mostly a replay—though Earley insists the judge restricted the defense. The jury found Broderick guilty on two counts of second-degree murder. She was sentenced to 15 years to life. In 2010, two of Broderick's children testified to the parole board, imploring them to release her; the other two asked them to keep her incarcerated. Her parole was turned down because she showed no remorse and refused to admit any responsibility. Broderick said of Dan: "I realize now that he was right when he said our battles would continue until one of us was dead." She has been denied parole two more times since and is eligible again in 2032.

WHISKEY AND CANNIBALISM

I n 1886, James Sligo Jameson, grandson of John Jameson of whiskey fame, set off as the only Irish officer on Henry Morton Stanley's Emin Pasha Relief Expedition—a British exploration up the Congo River. The expedition was ostensibly meant to provide relief to a South Sudanese governor, with the implicit understanding that land would be annexed for British colonization along the way. Jameson is remembered for one horrific incident at the town of Ribakiba (now Lokandu), when he, in conversation with a local chief about the practice of cannibalism, purchased a young girl for six handkerchiefs and made sketches of the scene as locals stabbed, dismembered, and ate her.

Jameson wrote to his wife that it was a misunderstanding, that he handed over the six handkerchiefs as "a joke" and was horrified when the men brought out the young girl. In a letter to the *New York Times* sent by Mrs. Jameson (as she is known to history) in defense of her by-then-deceased husband, Jameson claimed he didn't even have anything to sketch with at the time of the cannibalistic murder he facilitated, and that all the sketches he made of it were done later when he had returned to the safety of his tent.

THE COOPER DO-NUTS UPRISING

The May 1959 uprising at Cooper Do-nuts in Los Angeles is believed to be the first LGBTQIA+ uprising in the United States—a precursor to the Stonewall uprising (see page 117) a decade later in June 1969. The 24-hour Cooper Do-nuts in downtown LA, nestled between two gay bars, was a popular late-night hangout for transgender people. The shop was frequently raided by police, who arrested anyone whose gender presentation didn't match the sex on their ID. On the night of the uprising, officers tried to arrest two drag queens, two sex workers, and a gay man. When those arrested complained about cramped conditions in the police car, onlookers began pelting the car with doughnuts, coffee cups, and trash. The police fled without the detainees, and the uprising continued throughout the night. More police responded, the street was blocked off, and several people were arrested during this early show of resistance from the LGBTQIA+ community.

THE ZODIAC KILLER

he Zodiac Killer, active in the San Francisco Bay area in the 1960s and '70s, was known for his attention-seeking behavior, which included calling police to report his own crimes and sending letters to newspapers. Among the latter were four ciphers, or encrypted messages.

The first cipher was sent in three pieces to two different San Francisco newspapers on July 31, 1969. It was cracked within 24 hours by Bettye Harden and her husband, Donald. Bettye discovered several cribs—words or phrases suspected to appear in the messages—that helped quickly unravel the rest of the code. Bettye believed that the letter began with "I" and likely contained the words "kill" or "killing" or the phrase "I like killing." She was correct on all counts. Police speculate that the killer wasn't very happy that his code was so quickly cracked; subsequent ciphers were less sensical and more difficult to decode.

Unfortunately, the cipher contained little more than the typo-filled ramblings of the killer, and it offered few clues to police.

> *I LIKE KILLING PEOPLE BECAUSE IT IS SO MUCH*
> *FUN IT IS MORE FUN THAN KILLING WILD GAME*
> *IN THE FORREST BECAUSE MAN IS THE MOST*
> *DANGEROUE ANAMAL OF ALL TO KILL SOMETHING*
> *GIVES ME THE MOST THRILLING EXPERENCE IT IS*

*EVEN BETTER THAN GETTING YOUR ROCKS OFF
WITH A GIRL THE BEST PART OF IT IS THAE WHEN I
DIE I WILL BE REBORN IN PARADICE AND ALL THEI
HAVE KILLED WILL BECOME MY SLAVES I WILL NOT
GIVE YOU MY NAME BECAUSE YOU WILL TRY TO
SLOI DOWN OR ATOP MY COLLECTIOG OF SLAVES
FOR MY AFTERLIFE. EBEORIETEMETHHPITI*

The *San Francisco Chronicle* received a subsequent letter from the Zodiac Killer on October 13, 1969, after the murder of cabdriver Paul Stine. Another of his taunting, error-laden missives, it opens as follows:

This is the Zodiac speaking.
I am the murderer of the taxi driver over by
Washington St + Maple St last night, to prove this here is
a blood stained piece of his shirt. I am the same man who
did in the people in the north bay
area.

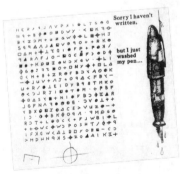

The S.F. Police could have
caught me last night if they
had searched the park properly
instead of holding road races
with their motorcicles seeing
who could make the most noise.
The car drivers should have just
parked their cars and sat there
quietly waiting for me to come
out of cover.

The Z340 cipher from the Zodiac killer was finally decoded in 2020, but the killer's identity still remains a mystery.

In his 2014 book, *The Most Dangerous Animal of All,* Gary Stewart makes the argument that his deceased biological father, Earl Van Best Jr., was the infamous Zodiac Killer. He cites similar handwriting and fingerprints, as well as an uncanny resemblance between his father's mug shot and the police sketch of the killer.

Earl Van Best Jr. was a rare books dealer who tried to elope with Stewart's 14-year-old mother.

Despite much speculation, the case has never been solved.

A 1969 sketch of the Zodiac Killer, who was never caught or definitively identified.

FORENSIC FINGERPRINTING

British missionary doctor Henry Faulds was accompanying his friend on an archaeological dig in Japan in the late 1870s when he noticed something on the pottery fragments being excavated. Delicate impressions of the ancient craftsmen's fingerprints were visible on the clay. After examining his own fingerprints and those of a friend, he was convinced that each individual had unique markers. Faulds proved his theory by exonerating a man arrested for breaking into his hospital by showing police that the man's fingerprints did not match those left at the scene.

By 1880, Faulds published a paper on fingerprinting in *Nature* magazine and forwarded his findings to naturalist Charles Darwin, who passed them along to his cousin Francis Galton.

Shortly after Faulds's paper was published, Sir William Herschel, a British civil servant based in India, wrote a letter to *Nature* claiming that he had been using fingerprints to identify criminals since 1860, though he failed to mention the potential use in conviction.

In 1886, Faulds approached Scotland Yard, London's police headquarters, with his fingerprinting system, but they declined to adopt it. Interest in the idea caught on only when Galton, Darwin's cousin, published a paper in 1888 claiming credit for the invention of forensic fingerprinting, without acknowledging Faulds's work. A bitter battle between Faulds, Herschel, and

Galton ensued until 1917, when it was determined that Faulds had been responsible for the initial research in the field.

On June 19, 1892, Francesca Rojas's children, six-year-old Ponciano and four-year-old Teresa, were brutally murdered in the family's apartment near Buenos Aires, Argentina. Rojas was found with superficial wounds to her neck. She blamed the crime on a neighbor, who allegedly turned violent after she rebuffed his sexual advances. The neighbor insisted he was innocent— local police tortured him for days anyway, including chaining him to the young victims' bodies overnight in an attempt to get a confession.

Word of the murder didn't reach Buenos Aires proper until July 8, at which time Central Police Inspector Alvarez—who had been trained by another fingerprinting pioneer, the Croatian-born Argentinian anthropologist and police official Juan Vucetich—was dispatched to investigate the crime scene. He found a bloody fingerprint on the door to the bedroom and, after calling Rojas in to fingerprint her, determined that the fingerprint matched hers. When confronted with the evidence, Rojas immediately confessed. The reported motive was that her boyfriend, whom she wished to marry, didn't like children, though other reports claim she believed her children were better off dead than with their biological father. Rojas was sentenced to life in prison. The case was the first known instance of fingerprint evidence being used to solve a criminal case.

The case renewed Vucetich's faith in fingerprinting and he continued to research the subject, developing the Juan Vucetich system of fingerprint classification. It was one of the three systems of classifications employed before computers took over, and it was primarily used in Argentina and throughout South America. The other two systems were the Roscher system

THE HENRY CLASSIFICATION SYSTEM

The Henry system divides fingerprints into three basic patterns:

• Loops—This category makes up 60 percent of all fingerprints. Subgroups are radial loops, which point toward the thumb, and ulnar loops, which point toward the pinky.

• Whorls—35 percent of fingerprints. There are four subgroups: plain whorl (concentric circles), central pocket loop (a loop with a whorl at the end), double loop (two loops that create an S-like pattern), and accidental loop (irregularly shaped).

• Arches—5 percent of fingerprints. Subgroups are plain arches and tented arches.

(developed in Germany and used in Germany and Japan) and the Henry Classification System (developed in India and used in most English-speaking countries).

But as forensic science advances, criminals tend to find ways to stay ahead of it. The FBI's answer to this has been Next Generation Identification (NGI). NGI was implemented by the bureau's Criminal Justice Information Services in 2014 to replace the Integrated Automated Fingerprint Identification System started in 1999.

The new methods of fingerprint classification include Advanced Fingerprint Identification Technology, which increased the accuracy of fingerprint retrieval from 92 percent to more than 99.6 percent, and latent and palm prints, a system with the ability to search through all criminal, civil, and Unsolved

Latent File repositories against ten-print, palm print, and supplemental fingerprints.

As more criminals attempted to alter or remove their fingerprints, further methods of identification were needed. NGI also includes the Repository for Individuals of Special Concern, a rapid search service available to law enforcement nationwide through the use of a mobile fingerprint device, which offers information on safety precautions, wants, and warrants. There is also a facial recognition search that accesses a database with the mug shots of more than 30 million criminals and suspects.

For as long as fingerprints have been used in forensic evidence collecting, criminals have made attempts to alter their

Fingerprinting has come a long way since the days of paper records and magnifying glasses.

FINGERING CROOKS

Criminals still use fingerprint mutilation to evade capture and identification to this day—and still to varying degrees of success:

• In 1999, Jose Izquierdo, arrested on drug charges under the alias Alexander Guzman, made Z-shaped incisions into his fingers, lifted and swapped the two flaps, and stitched them together.

• In 2007, a man arrested for car theft successfully bit off his fingerprints while in custody.

• Massachusetts police records from 2009 show 20 people were arrested with altered prints.

• In 2010, Dr. Jose Elias Zaiter-Pou was convicted on conspiracy charges for altering the prints of undocumented immigrants for $4,500.

• In 2015, a Florida man unsuccessfully attempted to chew off his prints in the back of a police car.

unique prints—with varying degrees of success. Some have turned to underground surgeons, like Wilhelm Loeser, who in 1934 agreed to alter gangster John Dillinger's fingerprints and also perform plastic surgery on him, for $5,000. Loeser cut away the outer layer of Dillinger's skin and treated his fingertips with hydrochloric acid before scraping away the remaining ridges. This method was only partially successful; when the skin grew back, the center of Dillinger's fingerprints were obscured, but the outer ridges were intact. The same year, gangster Creepy Karpis had mob doctor Joseph Moran remove his prints. Moran was successful enough that Karpis had trouble obtaining a Canadian passport because of the faintness of his ridges.

A 1935 article in the *Journal of Criminal Law and Criminology* recommended removing at least one millimeter of skin to ensure that ridges don't regenerate (a helpful tip from criminologists!).

In addition to those who mutilate their fingerprints, not everyone can leave them in the first place. According to Shari Forbes, a professor of forensic science at the University of Technology Sydney, people with very dry skin won't leave fingerprints.

The surfaces of a room also play a part in whether there will be fingerprints. An ideal scenario includes a criminal with oily skin and a crime scene enclosed by glass. But even if a killer doesn't leave prints, they leaves plenty of other traces, such as hair and skin cells.

SUNSHINE LAWS

D o you ever wonder why so many of the strangest crimes occur in Florida? The 2019 "Florida Man Challenge," which instructed participants to search for "Florida Man" followed by their birthdate, produced a plethora of gems, including "Florida Man Arrested After Hitting Dad with Pizza Because He Was Mad He Helped Birth Him" and "Florida Man Denies Syringes Found in Rectum Are His" Is there something in the water in Florida?

Turns out it's written in the laws—Florida has the strongest public record laws in the country. All arrest reports and mug shots, as well as state, county, and municipal records, are available to the public, including the media, who can turn these reports into very specific stories. The bizarre nature of these crimes may not be unique to Florida at all. Except perhaps "Florida Man Throws Alligator into Wendy's Drive-Thru Window" (see page 113).

ROCH THÉRIAULT: THE ANT HILL KIDS CULT

och Thériault was born Catholic and converted to Seventh-day Adventist in his youth. But in 1977, at age 30, Thériault decided to start a religious movement of his own. Employing only the force of his charisma, he began recruiting people from the Seventh-day Adventist community in Sainte-Marie, Quebec, Canada, enticing a group of about 25 adults to leave their jobs and homes and help him form a commune where they could listen to his motivational speeches and live free of sin in unity and equality.

His first order of business in establishing the free-living environment he promised his followers was to forbid them from contact with their families or any members of the Seventh-day Adventist Church. After cutting off his followers from the outside world, Thériault announced that God had told him the world would end on February 17, 1979. He then moved the commune to Saint-Jogues, in the remote Gaspé Peninsula, where he promised his flock they would be saved. Once there, Thériault sat back, drank all day, and watched as his followers built their commune, like ants building an anthill. He named his group the Ant Hill Kids.

When February 17 came and went and the world remained, some of the Ant Hill Kids began to question Thériault's authority. He chastised them, claiming it was a simple miscalculation—time on Earth and in God's realm were not parallel. He then renamed many of his followers with biblical names, choosing Moïse (Moses) for himself; married nine of the women; and fathered more than 20 children with them, tying them and their mothers to him and his cult.

But it wasn't all unité, égalité, and liberté under Thériault's reign. As his drinking worsened, he became more and more controlling, forbidding members from speaking to one another when he wasn't present, prohibiting them from having sex without his permission, and making all the women to whom he wasn't already "married" his concubines.

But all this was nothing compared to the abuse and murder to come.

The Ant Hill Kids sold baked goods in town and Thériault kept all the proceeds, controlling the cash flow of the group and subsequently how much food they were given. If members did not sell enough, he would beat them with a hammer. When one woman confided to her husband that she wanted to leave the cult after Thériault punched her for taking an extra pancake at breakfast, Thériault forced her husband to cut off his wife's toe. He would often make cult members harm one another, and sometimes themselves, in addition to the cruelty he personally inflicted on them. He retained enough of his charismatic personality to convince his underfed and terrified flock that the physical and sexual abuse he doled out—to adults and children alike—was meant to purify them of their sins so they would be strong enough to survive the inevitable doomsday.

Thériault also claimed he was a healer and, because he was an avid reader and collector of medical textbooks, performed surgeries on sick members, injecting ethanol into members' stomachs and performing circumcisions. It was one of these surgeries that would lead to his first stint in prison.

In March 1981, cult member Guy Veer brutally beat a two-year-old child for crying. The next day, Thériault operated on the boy, who then died. Thériault pinned the boy's death entirely on Veer and, as punishment, castrated Veer. In September 1982, Thériault pleaded guilty to criminal negligence for castrating Veer and was sentenced to two years in prison. Veer and seven other cult members were charged with criminal negligence in the death of the boy.

Thériault was released in June 1984 and moved his commune—at this point mostly consisting of his own wives and children—to Burnt River, Ontario, Canada. A few months later, local social workers began monitoring the commune, concerned about the welfare of the children. Despite the death of an infant in January 1985 (attributed to crib death, although some say the mother may have left the baby outside to freeze to save the infant from Thériault's abuse), local authorities did not raid the commune until December of that year. Fourteen children, ages 5 months to 16 years, were rescued, and many reported harrowing experiences of abuse.

Between 1986 and 1988, Thériault's followers gave birth to nine more of his children—all were taken by social services within days of their births.

Thériault's violent tendencies and grandiose delusions of medical knowledge escalated. In September 1988, Thériault "operated" on Solange Boilard, an Ant Hill Kid who complained of a stomachache, ripping out a piece of her intestines and mutilating her body before having Gabrielle Lavallée crudely stitch her up with a needle and thread. Boilard died the next day. Over the next four weeks, her body was disinterred twice and further mutilated by Thériault, in an attempt to resurrect her, before being cremated.

Lavallée herself was subject to especially harsh treatment at the commune—beatings, burns, tooth extractions. In the summer of 1989, Thériault cut off her arm after she attempted to escape the commune, then cauterized it with a hot iron a couple weeks later. Many members fled after this incident, and Lavallée was eventually able to escape and report to police the mutilation to which she'd been subjected. Meanwhile, police received a tip about Boilard's murder and searched the compound. They uncovered Boilard's remains and, aware that he was cornered, Thériault ran.

After a six-week search Thériault was taken into custody, charged with three counts of aggravated assault and one count of unlawfully causing bodily harm against Lavallée. He was sentenced to 12 years in prison for the crimes.

In 1993, Thériault pleaded guilty to the second-degree murder of Boilard and was sentenced to life in prison with no chance of parole until 2000. In 2002, he was denied parole because he was considered too high risk to reoffend. He never again applied for parole.

In 2011, Thériault's cell mate, Matthew Gerrard MacDonald, stabbed Thériault in the neck, killing him, then walked to the guard's station, handed over the shiv he used, and said, "That piece of shit is down on the range. Here's the knife, I've sliced him up." MacDonald, already serving a life term for a previous murder charge, was convicted of second-degree murder and given another life term.

THE VEGGIE HOLDUP

O n December 18, 2013, 28-year-old Gary Rough armed him-self and walked into a bookmaker in Glasgow, Scotland, with the idea of robbing the place. His weapon of choice: a cucumber covered in a black sock. Shortly after the woman at the counter refused his demand for cash, he was tackled to the ground by an off-duty police officer and taken into custody. Rough tried to play it off as a prank, claiming it was done on a dare. "It was a fucking cucumber," he said. "Am I going to jail for this?"

He admitted to assault with the intent to rob and received a 40-month sentence.

CELEBRITIES IN THE SLAMMER

Match the celebrity with the crime they did time for.

1. Wesley Snipes
2. Mark Wahlberg
3. Martha Stewart
4. Lil' Kim
5. Danny Trejo

a. Perjury
b. Insider trading
c. Willfully failing to file tax returns
d. Selling heroin to an undercover cop
e. Assault

Answers: 1C: *The Blade actor served 28 months of a 3-year sentence after years of tax resisting, claiming income tax is unconstitutional.* **2E:** *When he was 16 years old, Wahlberg was charged with attempted murder and pleaded guilty to assault after attacking two Vietnamese American men.* **3B:** *The domestic queen spent five months in federal prison in 2004 after selling a company's stock based on information that had not yet been made public.* **4A:** *The rapper served nine months for lying to a grand jury about a 2001 shooting.* **5D:** *Before he became an actor, Trejo served more than a decade in prison for selling heroin to an undercover cop. He decided to turn his life around after he injured a prison guard during a riot.*

THE MYSTERIOUS DEATH OF KEITH WARREN

eith Warren was just a month from starting college when he was found hanged on July 31, 1986, in a wooded area near his home in Silver Spring, Maryland. Police were alerted by a 911 call from a house party being held at the edge of the woods. The popular young man's death was ruled a suicide, but when his mother, Mary Couey, learned more about the circumstances surrounding his death, she began to question the police and coroner's ruling. There had been no signs that Keith was troubled leading up to his alleged suicide. Two ropes were used in the hanging and they were laid out in an elaborate configuration, anchored to the bases of two trees, not typical in a sudden suicide. The closer Couey looked, the more bizarre her son's death seemed.

It turned out the Keith Warren's case was odd from the start. Police took his body straight to a funeral home of their choosing after a friend of Warren's identified him at the scene of his hanging. No autopsy was performed. Warren's body was embalmed before Couey was even notified of her son's death, which was not until six hours after he was found. When Warren's grandmother wanted to pay her respects at the tree where he was found hanged, she, along with Couey and a friend of Warren's, discovered that the tree had been cut down. When Couey inquired with the police, she was told that it was being kept as evidence—in a closed case that was ruled a suicide.

According to Warren's friend Rodney Kendell, three unidentified men in a car were looking for Warren in the weeks leading up to his death. An acquaintance of Warren's, Mark Finley, was also urgently looking for him. Kendell, along with Warren's sister, Sherri, both found this strange because Warren and Finley were not close. In fact, Sherri recalled that the last time the two men were together they'd gotten into a fight.

Then, on April 9, 1992, which would have been Warren's 25th birthday, came perhaps the most remarkable twist in his story: a plain manila envelope that Couey found on her doorstep. Inside were five police photos of Warren's crime scene. After recovering from the initial shock of seeing the photos of her son, Couey and her daughter gave them a closer look.

The most disturbing detail was that Warren was not wearing his own clothing. After his death, Couey had received his jacket and brown boots from the police, but in the photos he was wearing a shirt, corduroys, and white sneakers—none of which he owned. He also had leaves on his back, indicating that he had been lying on the ground before he was hanged. Couey contacted the police but got no explanation from them. No one knew where the photos came from.

Affixed to one of the images was a message that read in part, "Don't worry, Mark Finley will be next." Shortly after Couey received the photos, she got a message from Finley. He claimed he had something to "unload," but before Couey could speak to him he was killed in what was ruled a bicycle accident. The damage to his face indicated more trauma than normal for a bike crash.

Warren's body was exhumed soon after Couey received the photos. Toxicology reports found high levels of deadly chemicals, suggesting foul play. Medical examiners were split—some believed the chemicals were from the embalming process, others noted that the original examiner did not note using these chemicals and that other chemicals not used in embalming were also found in Warren's system. Further, the substances found were typically inhaled.

Mary Couey died in 2009, but Sherri Warren continues to seek justice for Keith, pressing police to reopen her brother's case. "It's my responsibility," she says. "I am doing this to validate the last 23 years of my mother's life and . . . for my brother. He was loved. He wasn't a case number, double-0 whatever. He was a physical person whose life and spirit were cut short, and I want to know why."

ALEXANDER PICHUSHKIN: THE CHESSBOARD KILLER

oscow, 2001: People, mostly men, were disappearing from the lower-income neighborhood around Bitsevski Park. Though older women from the area pondered the whereabouts of the missing men, the police didn't investigate. Were they otherwise occupied, taking bribes, or did they simply not care about people who were missing? It's unclear. Many of the victims came from the same building complex where a young man named Alexander Pichushkin lived with his mother, Natalya.

As Natalya would later tell *GQ* magazine, "If he had killed people he didn't know, in another neighborhood, it wouldn't have been as bad, but he killed people he knew."

Pichushkin had a routine. He would invite his victims for a walk around Bitsevski Park and take them to a well. He would then pull out a hammer or wrench and strike them in the head. Sometimes he would pierce their skulls with a vodka bottle. Then he would push them down the well.

But the well wasn't an isolated water source—it was connected to a wastewater treatment facility. Some of the bodies resurfaced at the facility, though they weren't connected to the ongoing disappearances at first.

Pichushkin before a Moscow court hearing in 2007.

At least 13 of Pichushkin's victims vanished entirely. Authorities believe their remains are still decomposing in Moscow's sewage system.

> **"The closer a person is to you and the better you know them, the more pleasurable it is to kill them."**
> —*Alexander Pichushkin at his trial*

On February 23, 2002, Pichushkin pushed Maria Viricheva into the well. But Viricheva, who was pregnant at the time, summoned the strength to climb out and reach a hospital. When she told police of the attack, an officer asked for her papers. When she told them she didn't have papers, the police allegedly said that if she didn't report the attack, they wouldn't look into her legal status. So she didn't report the attack.

The next missed opportunity came with Mikhail Lobov. After Pichushkin threw the teenager to his likely death, Lobov's jacket caught on a piece of metal inside the well. He, too, managed to crawl out and inform police. But he, too, was dismissed. About a week after the attack, Lobov saw his attacker at the metro station and began screaming. Again, he told an officer. Again, police did nothing.

Continuing to prey on those close to him, Pichushkin invited his coworker Marina Moskalyova for a walk in 2006. Moskalyova accepted and left a note for her son, saying where she was going—and with whom.

A few hours later, a woman's body was found in the park. Moskalyova's son saw the news, feared the worst, and called his father. Finally, acting on the note, the police looked into nearby CCTV footage. Sure enough, there was video of Pichushkin and Moskalyova together near the time of her death.

Pichushkin was arrested on June 16, 2006. Initially, his mother assumed it had to be for burglary. She had no idea her son was capable of such atrocities.

Alexander Pichushkin confessed to murdering 63 people. His nickname, the Chessboard Killer, came from his habit of notching his victims off on each square of a chessboard. (A lead investigator in the case was confident Pichushkin would've continued killing past the board's 64 spaces.)

At his trial in 2007, where Pichushkin was housed in a glass cage for his own protection, prosecutors had only enough evidence to charge him with 48 murders. He was found guilty and, since Russia has a moratorium on all executions, was sentenced to life in prison, where he remains today.

JENNIFER MOREY AND THE FALSE SENSE OF SECURITY

ennifer Morey chose the Bayou Park Apartments in Houston, Texas, for their security, which included a guard on the premises 24 hours a day. But her sense of safety was shattered when she awoke at 4:00 a.m. on April 15, 1995, to find a man holding a knife to her throat. As she struggled to fight him off, he slashed several inches down her neck. He then threw her in the bathroom, threatening to kill her if she came out. After what felt like hours, Morey, bleeding heavily, pushed the door open and made a break for her cell phone. Richard Everett, working his first 911 shift that night, answered her call. After alerting police and paramedics, he stayed on the phone with her in an attempt to keep her conscious.

When there was a sudden knock on Morey's door followed by a man's voice claiming to be a guard, Everett, knowing police had not contacted building security, warned Morey not to open the door. His instincts were spot on—police found Bryan Wayne Gibson outside Morey's apartment, covered in blood.

Gibson, who *was* a security guard at Bayou Park Apartments, claimed he was attacked while on patrol by a man who then jumped off Morey's balcony. Police grew suspicious when they didn't find any footprints below Morey's balcony, suspicions that were confirmed when a Pinkerton Security cap and a pair of male underwear found inside Morey's home were linked to Gibson. He had apparently returned to Morey's apartment to retrieve his belongings, and possibly to silence her for good.

Gibson was sentenced to 20 years in prison. Morey has said of her recovery from the trauma of that night, "I have a theory that the Jennifer Morey that existed on April 15, 1995, died and that a new one had to come out of that." She eventually went on to marry and opened her own law firm. Richard Everett attended her wedding.

THE LALAURIE MANSION

Like many of history's high-society female serial killers, Madame LaLaurie had a taste for torture. The torture was a mere rumor though, until a fire broke out at her home on April 10, 1834. When the LaLauries refused to hand over the key to evacuate the slave quarters, rescuers broke in and confronted a horrifying sight. Enslaved people had been mutilated, flayed, and imprisoned in iron collars for months. The bodies of two enslaved people were unearthed on the property, but the true number of victims remains unknown.

Even in the pre–Civil War South, LaLaurie's cruelty toward those she enslaved was too much for the public. After an outraged mob sacked the home, the family fled to France and never returned.

The LaLaurie Mansion is considered one of the most haunted sites in New Orleans.

THE POISONOUS BLANCHE TAYLOR MOORE

he men in Blanche Taylor Moore's life tended to die. It began in her thirties with her father, Parker Davis Kiser, an alcoholic womanizer with a gambling addiction who forced Blanche into sex work to pay off his debt when she was a young girl in North Carolina. He died in 1966 of what was ruled a heart attack. At the time, Blanche had two children and was working as head cashier at a supermarket, married to a man named James Taylor, and having an affair with coworker Raymond Reid. In 1971, Taylor also died from a heart attack.

Soon after Taylor's death, Blanche began dating Reid openly. The couple was together for more than 10 years, but by 1985 the relationship had soured. That year, Blanche met Reverend Dwight Moore and the two began dating secretly while Blanche continued her relationship with Reid. In April 1986, Reid became ill with shingles and was hospitalized for months. Blanche visited him daily, often bringing him food such as her homemade banana cream pudding, which she spooned into his mouth. By October, Reid was dead.

Just as she did after her first husband died, Blanche started to date a new man openly, in this case Reverend Moore. The two got engaged soon thereafter. Their wedding was post-poned twice—once in 1987 because Blanche was diagnosed with breast cancer, and again in 1988, after Moore came down with

Moore with attorney David Tamer after she was sentenced to death in a North Carolina courtroom in 1990.

a mysterious intestinal illness that required two surgeries. The pair eventually married in 1989. Shortly after their honeymoon, Moore became severely ill after eating a sandwich Blanche had made him and was hospitalized after days of vomiting and nausea. His condition worsened in the hospital, his organs failing.

Blanche told Moore's doctors that he'd been working with an herbicide in their yard shortly after they returned from their honeymoon. When doctors learned about the use of herbicide they ordered a toxicology report, which revealed that Moore had 20 times the lethal dose of arsenic in his system. Blanche finally made a mistake.

Miraculously, Moore survived the poisoning and told investigators that Blanche's former boyfriend Reid had died of Guillain-Barré syndrome, the symptoms of which are similar to arsenic poisoning. This, in addition to Blanche's attempts to make herself the main beneficiary of Moore's pension, prompted investigators to exhume the bodies of Blanche's father, Kiser; her husband Taylor; and her ex-boyfriend Reid. All three bodies contained elevated levels of arsenic.

Blanche never confessed to the murders and claimed Reid and Moore were both depressed and had probably taken the arsenic themselves, an unlikely story. She was charged with the first-degree murders of Taylor and Reid and assault with a deadly weapon for the poisoning of Moore. Blanche was found guilty of Reid's murder on November 14, 1990, and sentenced to death. She was never put on trial for the additional charges. Blanche remains on death row, the oldest of all death row inmates in North Carolina and one of only two women. She maintains her innocence.

THE MURDER OF TUPAC SHAKUR

On November 30, 1994, iconic rapper Tupac Shakur was shot during an attempted robbery in the Manhattan building where he was recording his third album. Shakur survived, blaming the attack on fellow rappers Sean "Puff Daddy" Combs and rival rapper Christopher Wallace—aka the Notorious B.I.G. This accusation, along with Shakur's subsequent move to Los Angeles to join Death Row Records, would result in the East Coast versus West Coast feud that defined hip-hop in the 1990s.

Two years later, on September 7, 1996, Shakur and his entourage were seen engaging in a violent scuffle in the lobby of the MGM Grand Hotel in Las Vegas. Hours later, Shakur was riding in a car driven by Death Row Records head Suge Knight when a white Cadillac pulled up beside them at a red light. An unidentified shooter opened fire, shooting Shakur four times and grazing Knight's skull. Shakur succumbed to his wounds and died six days later, on September 13.

Six months later, Christopher Wallace was murdered in Los Angeles under similar circumstances. No arrests have been made in connection to either murder.

OPERATION FLAGSHIP

On December 15, 1985, 101 Redskins (now called "Washington Football Team") fans arrived at the Washington Convention Center for a brunch hosted by Flagship International Sports TV. They expected to walk away with tickets to the Redskins-Bengals game later that day but instead they left in handcuffs, courtesy of the US Marshals Service. The brainchild of Howard Safir, Operation Flagship was an ambitious sting that required the cooperation of 166 law enforcement personnel from seven different agencies.

Using the football game as bait, they sent invitations from the fake sports channel to the last known addresses of more than 3,000 fugitives with outstanding warrants in the DC area. It took six weeks of practice to get it right. When the fugitives arrived at the center, they were checked in and brought inside. Affectionate cheerleaders conducted pat-downs. The bulky mascot costumes concealed firearms. In small groups, attendees were led away from the party and arrested. That night, instead of celebrating the Redskins's victory they commiserated in jail.

THE WATCHER HOUSE

 In 2014, the Broaddus family bought their dream house in Westfield, New Jersey. But after moving in their belongings, they never ended up living there. The problem: Shortly after purchasing the $1.3 million home, they began receiving mysterious threatening letters from "The Watcher." The Watcher knew details about the house and the family—their car, the contractor they hired—explaining in one of the four letters that "My grandfather watched the house in the 1920s and my father watched in the 1960s. It is now my time." Another letter creepily threatened the three Broaddus children:

> *657 Boulevard is anxious for you to move in. It has been years and years since the young blood ruled the hallways of the house. Have you found all of the secrets it holds yet? Will the young blood play in the basement? Or are they too afraid to go down there alone. I would [be] very afraid if I were them. It is far away from the rest of the house. If you were upstairs you would never hear them scream.*

> *Will they sleep in the attic? Or will you all sleep on the second floor? Who has the bedrooms facing the street? I'll know as soon as you move in. It will help me to know who is in which bedroom. Then I can plan better.*

Upon learning that the previous owners, the Woods family, had received a letter from the Watcher shortly before they moved out, the Broadduses filed a lawsuit against them, claiming fraudulent concealment, intentional and negligent infliction of emotional distress, and several other issues related to the sale of the property. The lawsuit was dismissed, as was the Woods's counterclaim of defamation—they said the letter they had received was nonthreatening, and they had lived in the house for 23 years without incident. Whether other previous owners received similar letters is unknown.

The Broadduses were finally able to sell the house in 2019, at a loss of nearly half a million dollars—a blow certainly softened by their cut of a seven-figure Netflix deal for the rights to their story.

THE MURDER OF LANA CLARKSON

ctress Lana Clarkson was moonlighting as a hostess in early 2003 when she met music producer Phil Spector. Spector had produced some of the biggest names in music, including the Ronettes and the Beatles. He came off as charming and funny, and Clarkson accepted his invitation to go out for drinks after her shift. They eventually made their way back to his home, the Pyrenees Castle, in Alhambra, California. Soon after, Spector ran from the house, gun in hand, and told his driver, "I think I killed somebody." Clarkson sat slumped in a chair inside, dead from a single gunshot wound to the mouth. Spector quickly reversed his initial statement and claimed Clarkson had shot herself. In a July 2003 *Esquire* interview, Spector said Clarkson had "kissed the gun" and the episode was an accidental suicide.

Spector, who produced songs like The Crystals' "He Hit Me (And It Felt Like a Kiss)," was better known for his musical genius than his violent pattern of behavior toward women. But Spector's abuse was well-documented in *Be My Baby*, a memoir by Ronnie Spector, the Ronettes' frontwoman and Spector's ex-wife, in which she describes years of abuse and imprisonment. Ronnie also said that in her divorce settlement with Spector, she surrendered all future earnings on her Spector-produced records, as well as custody of their children, after Spector threatened to hire a hit man to kill her. Over the course

of two trials, a total of six women testified that Spector threatened them with a gun. He was convicted of second-degree murder in 2009 and sentenced to 19 years to life. He died in prison from complications of COVID-19 on January 16, 2021.

CRIMINAL CROONERS

M atch the singer to their crime.

1. Frank Sinatra
2. Billie Holiday
3. Barry White
4. Johnny Cash

a. Starting a forest fire
b. Stealing $30,000 worth of Cadillac tires
c. Adultery and seduction
d. Narcotics possession

Holiday, in a promotional image.

Answers: 1C: *Twenty-three-year-old Sinatra was arrested in New Jersey in 1938 for seducing a young woman with promises of marriage; charges were later dropped when it was discovered the woman was already married.* **2D:** *Holiday had been targeted by the Federal Bureau of Narcotics since 1939 because of a known heroin addiction. She was arrested three times for possession, including while she was lying in the hospital on her deathbed.* **3B:** *White was only 17 when he was jailed; he credits hearing Elvis Presley's "It's Now or Never" on a prison radio for turning his life around.* **4A:** *The 1965 fire in California's Los Padres National Forest destroyed 508 acres, burned the foliage off three mountains, and drove away 49 of the forest's 53 endangered condors; Cash eventually paid an $82,000 fine.*

THE GREAT CANADIAN MAPLE SYRUP HEIST

Just across the US border is a powerful cartel that controls 77 percent of the world's supply of a valuable substance— maple syrup. The Federation of Quebec Maple Syrup Producers also controls the marketing and sales of the product, which is valued at about $1,300 a barrel. Reserves are housed throughout Quebec, with warehouses storing up to 7,000 tons of syrup.

Over several months in 2011 and 2012, nearly 3,000 tons of syrup, worth $18.7 million CAD, were stolen from one of the warehouses. Barrels were moved to a remote sap house, drained, refilled with water, then returned. It wasn't until the annual inventory of reserves that the plot was discovered. Five people were convicted in what is now known as the Great Canadian Maple Syrup Heist.

FOOD FIGHT: CULINARY CROOKS

Fighting crime can be hard when the evidence is edible.

• **Cheese**—According to a 2011 UK study, cheese is the most commonly stolen food. Notable heists include $875,000 worth of Parmigiano-Reggiano wheels stolen during a single robbery in Italy, along with numerous vanished cheese trucks.

• **Beans**—In 2013, 6,400 cans of baked beans with sausages (worth about $10,000) were stolen from a Heinz delivery truck as the driver slept.

• **Avocados**—Tancítaro, Mexico, exports as much as a million dollars' worth of avocados in a day, a sum that caught the attention of Mexican drug cartels, who quickly moved in to extort money from farmers. After years of violence and fear, a trained and armed force of officers now patrols the town's farms, to keep the gangs at bay.

• **White Truffles**—Truffle hunters often rely on a keen canine sense to detect rare white truffles. These specially trained dogs are valuable, and also vulnerable to sabotage. They have been stolen from their owners, caught in traps, and even poisoned by competing foragers.

ROBERT CHAMBERS: THE PREPPY MURDERER

A cyclist found the body of 18-year-old Jennifer Levin on the morning of August 26, 1986. She had been strangled to death and left under a tree behind the Metropolitan Museum of Art in New York City's Central Park. Levin was last seen leaving a bar with Robert Chambers just two hours before she was found. When police arrested Chambers, a former student at York Preparatory School she'd been casually dating, his face and chest were covered with scratches.

At trial, Chambers claimed that he accidentally killed Levin while they were having rough sex in the park. The prosecution, meanwhile, said Chambers's "preppy" good looks and seemingly upper-class upbringing hid a drug-addicted thief who took Levin's life. When the jury deadlocked over his guilt, the prosecutor made a deal with Chambers. He pleaded guilty to first-degree manslaughter in exchange for just 15 years in prison.

Chambers was released in 2003 but was rearrested

Chambers appearing for trial in the murder of Jennifer Levin.

in 2007 for selling cocaine and sentenced to 19 years in prison. His next chance for parole is in 2024. Upon his latter conviction, Ellen Levin, mother of Jennifer Levin and victims'-rights advocate, commented that Chambers "got more time in prison for selling drugs than murdering my daughter, which is pretty amazing."

FIRSTS: ISABELLA GOODWIN, NYPD DETECTIVE

When Isabella Goodwin's husband, officer John Goodwin of the New York Police Department, died in 1896, he left her a widow with four children. To provide for them, Isabella decided to follow in John's footsteps and join the force herself. The 30-year-old Isabella passed the New York Police Department's exam and joined the force that same year, only 15 years after the NYPD began hiring women as "police matrons" to care for female and child prisoners. Goodwin served in that capacity for the next 15 years, though she was occasionally given the opportunity to go undercover.

Her big break came in 1912, when she took an undercover assignment as a scrubwoman in a boardinghouse to gather evidence on gangster Eddie "the Boob" Kinsman, who visited a love interest, Swede Annie, at the establishment. Police suspected Kinsman was behind a $25,000 midday bank heist in which two clerks were injured—and thanks to Goodwin's undercover surveillance of Kinsman, she confirmed that it was him. The bust earned her a promotion, making her the NYPD's first woman detective, with the rank of lieutenant first grade. She retired from the force in 1926 after 30 years of service. Of her years as a police officer she said, "My experience among the criminal classes has been that they are a very stupid lot. They do shrewd things sometimes and then nullify their efforts with the sheerest nonsense."

SEX IN THE CITY: PUBLIC PARKS

A 2019 *New York Times* article reported that New York City's public parks have become a lot less sexy: Only six public-sex summonses were issued in 2018, compared with 432 in 2007. Luckily, lewd-act complaints were also down: just 283 in 2018 compared with 483 in 2013.

New York City's
Central Park.

THE REAL HANNIBAL LECTOR

uthor Thomas Harris created one of the most chilling, disarmingly civilized fictional serial killers in Hannibal Lecter, who first appeared in Harris's 1981 novel, *Red Dragon*. Lecter's persona was based on an imprisoned doctor Harris met in Mexico while researching a story about another serial killer. In the late 1950s, Dr. Alfredo Ballí Treviño killed his lover, Jesús Castillo Rangel, dismembered his body, then packed it in a box and buried it. Ballí was the last man in Mexico to receive a death sentence, which was eventually commuted to 30 years in prison.

While serving his time, Ballí worked in the prison hospital, tending to fellow inmates as well as poor people from a nearby village. Harris, who didn't realize Ballí was a prisoner at first, invited him to have a drink. Harris would later described Ballí as "very still" and noted that he had "a certain elegance about him." Lecter's intellectual cunning mirrors Ballí in speech especially. During their interview, Ballí inquired of Harris, "You are a journalist, Mr. Harris. How would you put that in your journal? How do you treat the fear of torment in journalese? Might you say something snappy about torment, like 'It puts the hell in hello!'?"

THE MAD GASSER OF MATTOON

September 1, 1944, was a hot night in the small town of Mattoon, Illinois, with windows left open as residents listened to news of World War II on their radios. An elderly woman reported to police a perfumelike smell in her bedroom, which she thought was being pumped in from outside. It caused her to become ill and briefly paralyzed her legs. Her daughter, in another room, experienced no symptoms. In a headline the next day the local paper declared: "Anesthetic Prowler on Loose."

Over the next two weeks, 25 people claimed to have smelled the gas, causing them to experience nausea, vomiting, and paralysis. Some even said they saw a figure fleeing from their bedroom windows in the middle of the night. But despite patrols by armed vigilantes and local and state police, the phantom anesthetist was never found. A psychologist determined the symptoms were a result of mass panic and, after a stern warning from the police chief, reports of the gasser stopped.

THE MURDER OF KIM WALL

Peter Madsen was known throughout Denmark as an eccentric, a self-taught inventor whose launch of a home-made submarine, the *UC3 Nautilus*, from Copenhagen brought him international attention. So when Madsen agreed to a last-minute interview in August 2017, freelance journalist Kim Wall skipped her own good-bye party (she and her boyfriend were moving to Beijing) to meet him on his submarine.

Wall did not return home the next morning. Police found the *Nautilus* sinking in Køge Bay and rescued Madsen, but Wall

Madsen, at an engineering conference, 2010.

was not with him. When questioned, Madsen first claimed that he'd dropped Wall off the previous evening. But when her blood was found in the scuttled submarine, he said the 155-pound hatch had fallen on her head and he buried her at sea. When Wall's dismembered torso washed ashore 10 days later, Madsen changed his story again, claiming she died of carbon monoxide poisoning. Then her head and limbs, weighted down with metal, were found on the seafloor.

Madsen was charged with, and convicted of, Wall's murder and sentenced to life in prison. On October 20, 2020, Madsen escaped prison armed with what was described as a pistol-like object and what he claimed to be a bomb belt. Police apprehended him less than a mile from the prison and he was returned after the bomb squad determined the belt was a decoy.

DEATH ON SCREEN: FACT AND FICTIONALIZED

S ometimes the truth is even stranger than fiction. Compare these true crime documentaries with their dramatized counterparts.

• *The Act* and *Mommy Dead and Dearest*—The unbelievable story of Gypsy Rose Blanchard's involvement in the murder of her mother, Dee Dee (see page 9).

• *The People v. O. J. Simpson* and *O. J.: Made in America*— The 10-episode drama, which served as the first season of the *American Crime Story* anthology, focuses on the trial, while the 5-part docuseries elaborates on the cultural environment surrounding it.

• *Foxcatcher* and *Team Foxcatcher*—The 2014 movie about the murder of wrestler David Schultz by John du Pont was critically acclaimed; the Netflix documentary followed in 2016.

• *When They See Us* and *The Central Park Five*—The shocking injustice of the highly publicized case of five teenage boys convicted of rape in 1989, only to be exonerated by a confession and DNA evidence in 2001.

MELISSA DOHME: HAPPILY EVER AFTER...

 elissa Dohme was just 20 years old when her ex-boyfriend, Robert Lee Burton Jr., violently attacked her in the early hours of January 24, 2012. Despite a no-contact order from a previous assault, Burton had been inundating her with calls and messages for days, begging for closure and one final hug. Dohme, hoping to get rid of him for good, reluctantly agreed to meet one last time, outside of her home in Clearwater, Florida. As they embraced, Dohme heard the click of a switch-blade. Burton then stabbed her 32 times—in her face, head, neck, and arms, pausing only to retrieve a larger knife from his truck before continuing the attack. Burton then drove off as witnesses called 911. Dohme had to crawl out of the way to avoid being hit by Burton's truck.

First responder Cameron Hill got to the scene just in time, and resuscitated Dohme after she flatlined several times. She had a stroke due to the blood loss, her skull was cracked, and all of her teeth were knocked out. The trauma surgeon who later treated her said she was seconds away from dying. But Dohme survived.

Burton was apprehended only hours after the attack, when he overdosed on sleeping pills and crashed his truck. In 2013, he pleaded guilty to attempted first-degree murder and was

Melissa Dohme with her husband, Cameron Hill, a paramedic who helped save her after she'd been stabbed 32 times by her ex-boyfriend.

sentenced to life in prison without the possibility of parole. In a twisted display of the cycle of abuse and abusers, Burton's father was arrested in 2018 on charges of sexual battery with a deadly weapon, after his DNA matched evidence found at a January 21, 1993, rape scene.

Dohme underwent cognitive and speech therapy, facial-reconstruction surgery, and physical therapy to learn to walk again. She has since graduated from college and become a domestic violence prevention advocate and speaker. Dohme also went on to find love—two months after she was attacked she met Cameron Hill for lunch. Dohme and Hill fell in love and married on March 4, 2017. She wore a garter embroidered with the phrase *He's the reason my heart beats.*

TRULY CRAZY LOVE

Stories of victims falling in love with their rescuers can be heartwarming. But when a victim falls in love with their attacker, it's a little harder to swallow. That's exactly what happened with Burt and Linda Pugach. In 1959, Burt began dating Linda Riss, until Linda found out about Burt's wife and daughter and broke things off. Burt threatened her repeatedly, but the New York Police Department brushed off Linda's reports. Upon hearing of her engagement to another man, Burt hired three men to assault her. He maintains he "just" wanted them to beat her up, but they threw lye in her face, disfiguring and partially blinding her.

Burt was sentenced to 14 years in prison, during which time he continued to write to Linda. They resumed their relationship when Burt was released, and the two married in 1974. They remained married until Linda's death in 2013, even throughout Burt's 1997 trial for threatening a woman with whom he was

having an affair. Linda served as a character witness for Burt in that trial. A 2007 documentary, *Crazy Love*, documents their unbelievable story.

Burt and Linda Pugach at the 2007 premiere of *Crazy Love*, the documentary about their life.

TILL DEATH DO US PART

atch the killer to the spouse they married while incarcerated.

1. Ted Bundy
2. Charles Manson
3. Kenneth Bianchi
4. Angelo Buono Jr.
5. Richard Ramirez

a. Christine Kizuka
b. Doreen Lioy
c. Elaine "Star" Burton
d. Carole Ann Boone
e. Shirlee Joyce Book

Answers: 1D: Bundy (see page 21) married Boone in 1980 while she was on the stand during his trial. The two, who dated before Bundy's first arrest, had a child in 1982 and divorced in 1986. **2C:** Eighty-year-old Manson (see page 1) and 26-year-old Burton were engaged in 2014, but they never technically married. They were granted a marriage license, but Manson called it off after learning that Burton was planning to display his corpse after he died. **3E:** Hillside Strangler Bianchi married Book, who previously attempted to woo Ted Bundy, in 1989. **4A:** Angelo Buono Jr., Bianchi's partner in crime, wed Kizuka in 1986 after meeting her during a visit to her former husband in prison. **5B:** The Night Stalker (see page 71) and Lioy married in 1996 after meeting 11 years earlier. The two split in 2010.

THE DROWNING OF NATALIE WOOD

Film star Natalie Wood is known for iconic roles in high-profile movies, including *Miracle on 34th Street*, *Rebel Without a Cause*, and *West Side Story*. She's also known for her mysterious death. On November 29, 1981, her body was found floating a mile away from *Splendour*, a yacht that belonged to her husband, Robert Wagner. It is not known how she entered the water—she was terrified of drowning, because her mother had repeatedly told her that a fortune-teller foresaw someone in the family dying that way. Her blood

Wagner and Wood in 1976 on *Splendour*, the boat off which she would drown in 1981.

alcohol level was .14 percent, and there were traces of a motion sickness aid and a painkiller in her system, which would have increased the effects of the alcohol.

The other passengers of *Splendour*—Wagner, captain Dennis Davern, and Wood's *Brainstorm* costar Christopher Walken—were tight-lipped about the events of the night before, but two witnesses on a nearby boat claimed they had heard a woman screaming for her life. In November 2011, Davern came forward and admitted that he had heard Wood and Wagner fighting that night. Wood's cause of death was changed from accidental drowning to "drowning and other undetermined factors" in 2012, and Wagner was named a person of interest in February 2018 by the L.A. County Sheriff's Department.

THE FLIGHT ATTENDANT FREAKOUT

On August 9, 2010, after an argument with a passenger upon landing at JFK Airport in Queens, New York, flight attendant Steven Slater announced over the plane's PA system that he was quitting, grabbed two beers from the fridge, then deployed the evacuation slide and slid into infamy. Some lauded him as a working-class hero who snapped, but the airline and authorities stressed the danger of his actions—particularly because deploying an evacuation slide suddenly without regard for those on the ground could cause serious injury or death.

Slater was arrested later that day and charged with criminal mischief, reckless endangerment, and criminal trespass. Investigators noted that he seemed drunk and emotionally distressed. To avoid prison, he took a plea bargain and agreed to probation, drug testing, counseling, and payment of $10,000 in restitution to JetBlue.

MARTIN BRYANT: THE PORT ARTHUR MASSACRE

By most accounts, Martin Bryant led a strange life. As a young boy in Tasmania, Australia, he was described as "annoying"; as an adolescent he scored 66 on an IQ test and a psychiatrist noted he "could be schizophrenic and parents face a bleak future with him." By 19, he had become the companion of 54-year-old heiress Helen Mary Elizabeth Harvey. When Harvey died under dubious circumstances in a car accident, Bryant inherited her fortune and took up the habit of flying to destinations all over the world with the sole purpose of chatting incessantly with the captive passengers seated next to him.

Despite increasingly bizarre and erratic behavior, no one could have predicted the events of April 28, 1996, when Bryant went on a shooting rampage in Port Arthur, Tasmania. He ultimately killed 35 people ranging in age from 3 to 75 and wounded 18 others.

Bryant began his rampage by killing David and Noelene Martin, owners of the Seascape Cottage, an inn in Port Arthur that his father once attempted to purchase. By the morning of April 29, after tearing through the town of Port Arthur and killing 33 more people, Bryant was holed up at the same inn with several hostages, shooting at police who tried to approach. He was eventually captured 19 hours later, after being smoked out—by a fire he set himself. Bryant received 35 life sentences, one for each life he took.

The Port Arthur Massacre led to immediate, sweeping gun reform in Australia. Less than a month after the shooting, Australian legislators drafted the National Firearms Agreement. The agreement created strict licensing and registration procedures, including a 28-day wait period for purchasing a firearm. It also tightly restricted all automatic and semiautomatic weapons, allowing only licensed individuals who required them for a valid purpose other than "personal protection" to own them. All gun owners were required to keep all firearms stored securely. On October 21, 1996, the government began a gun buyback program for all firearms that had become illegal, resulting in the surrender of 700,000 weapons.

A 2006 study found that there had been no shootings of more than five people in the 10 years since the agreement. This trend continued until May 11, 2018, when seven people, including the shooter, were shot in Western Australia during an incident of familicide.

The Seascape Cottage hotel, where Bryant temporarily holed up before it caught fire and he surrendered to police.

MORE THAN A PUNCH LINE: THE LORENA BOBBITT STORY

he crime is infamous—on the night of June 23, 1993, as her husband, John Wayne Bobbitt, slept, Ecuador native Lorena Bobbitt got an eight-inch carving knife from the kitchen, entered their bedroom, and cut off John's penis. She then fled their home in Manassas, Virginia, with John's penis in her hand. After finding it hard to drive with just one hand, Lorena tossed the appendage out her car window. She made her way to the nail salon where she worked and called 911, reporting her crime and telling police where they could find the penis.

And find it they did. Police boxed it up on ice in a 7-Eleven Big Bite hot dog box and rushed it to a nearby hospital, where it was expertly reattached to John—who had been rushed to the emergency room—during a nine-and-a-half-hour surgery overseen by a urologist and a plastic surgeon.

The media went wild over what they perceived as a sensational crime, and the investigation and subsequent trials were both highly publicized and the butt of more than a few jokes. John maintained that he had told Lorena that night he was divorcing her, that they had had consensual sex, and afterward, in a jealous rage, she attacked him while he slept. The image of Lorena as a jealous, vengeful, and unsatisfied wife was further supported by a widely reported initial interview with police in which Lorena claimed, "He always have orgasm and he doesn't wait for me to have orgasm. He's selfish. I don't think it's fair, so I pulled back the sheets then and I did it."

The full story Lorena eventually told was more harrowing. She said that John began sexually and physically abusing her shortly after their 1989 marriage, and that he repeatedly raped her, including on the night of the crime. While he was in surgery, Lorena was just down the hall getting a rape kit examination.

John was charged with marital sexual assault—at the time, the more serious charge of marital rape was reserved for couples living apart and victims who were seriously physically injured. Marital rape had only recently been declared a crime in all 50 states in 1993, and it was nearly impossible to prove in Virginia. The two-day trial in November 1993 focused only on the five days before the mutilation, a period during which Lorena admitted she and John had also had consensual sex.

The jurors, who deliberated for nearly four hours, were initially split but they eventually found John not guilty. Lorena would be tried in the same court, prosecuted by the same attorney, and overseen by the same judge just three months later.

The defense in Lorena's January 1994 trial was able to establish a clearer pattern of John's escalating physical, sexual, and emotional abuse toward his wife. Forty-six witnesses testified to the volatility of their marriage, many confirming that they had frequently heard the couple fighting and seen Lorena with bruises. Some of John's friends revealed that he had bragged on several occasions that he enjoyed having sex with women without their consent. Lorena's testimony was painful to watch as she shakily recounted the violence she suffered in the marriage.

Much of John's testimony contradicted facts established throughout the trial, which further weakened the prosecution's case against Lorena. The defense argued a mix of self-defense and temporary insanity, saying Lorena had depression and PTSD and lived in constant fear of John, who claimed that he would find her and rape her even if they divorced. After seven hours of deliberation, the jury found Lorena not guilty by reason of insanity. She underwent a 45-day psychiatric evaluation, after which she was released.

The Bobbitts' divorce was finalized in 1995. John went on to form a band, the Severed Parts, and star in two adult films, *John Wayne Bobbitt: Uncut* and *Frankenpenis*. In the years since the trial, he has been arrested a number of times and has served time on battery charges against two different women. He lives in Las Vegas, Nevada.

Lorena, who now goes by her maiden name, Gallo, continues to live and work in Manassas with her longtime partner and teenage daughter. Her trial is said to have shifted the national conversation on spousal abuse, and she continues to advocate for victims of domestic violence. She vows, "I'll put myself through the jokes and everything as long as I can shine a light on domestic violence and sexual assault and marital rape." The case received new attention in 2019 when a four-part documentary, *Lorena*, was released.

Bobbitt on trial in 1994. She was acquitted on the grounds of temporary insanity.

IN THEIR DEFENSE

Match the defendants to their defense attorneys.

1. Leopold and Loeb
2. O. J. Simpson
3. Lyle and Erik Menendez
4. Sam Sheppard

a. Johnnie Cochran
b. F. Lee Bailey
c. Leslie Abramson
d. Clarence Darrow

Answers: 1D: *Darrow is best known for his defense of the young murderers—including a twelve-hour closing statement—as well as the 1925 Scopes "Monkey" Trial, in which he defended science teacher John T. Scopes, who was on trial for teaching human evolution in a Tennessee public school.* **2A and B:** *Cochran and Bailey were among a team of six defense attorneys who represented Simpson during his 1995 trial for the murders of Nicole Brown Simpson and Ron Goldman.* **3C:** *Abramson was the subject of controversy during the highly publicized Menendez trial, when she was accused of instructing Erik's psychiatrist to delete recordings and rewrite notes from their sessions; she later went on to briefly represent Phil Spector during his trial for the murder of Lana Clarkson (see page 232).* **4B:** *The sensational Sam Sheppard case was a career-maker for Bailey; he was responsible for Sheppard's exoneration in 1966.*

LEOPOLD AND LOEB: THE ÜBERMENSCH MURDERERS

 athan Leopold and Richard Loeb were both exceptionally intelligent young men in the early 1920s. Leopold was studying law at the University of Chicago by age 19, having already finished his undergraduate degree there. He studied 15 languages, 5 of which he spoke fluently, and had received national attention for his work in ornithology, the study of birds. Loeb had skipped several grades in school and become the youngest graduate of the University of Michigan, at age 17.

The young men grew up two blocks from each other in Chicago's affluent Kenwood neighborhood in the early twentieth century, but they became especially close after Loeb began taking graduate classes at the University of Chicago. They bonded over a shared fascination with crime and an obsession of Leopold's: German philosopher Friedrich Nietzsche's concept of the Übermensch, or superman. An Übermensch is an individual with extraordinary talents and superior intellect who is therefore exempt from the laws that apply to ordinary people. Leopold believed he was an Übermensch, and he soon convinced Loeb that he was one, too. Combined with their interest in crime, this proved a toxic recipe for criminal behavior.

Leopold and Loeb began exploring their perceived superiority with petty theft, vandalism, and arson, but they quickly grew bored. Even worse for the attention-hungry pair, none of their crimes were being reported in the newspapers.

On the evening of November 10, 1923, they drove six hours from Chicago to Ann Arbor, Michigan, to burglarize Loeb's former fraternity, Zeta Beta Tau. On their way back, disappointed by their loot of $80, some watches, a few penknives, and a typewriter, Loeb told Leopold of his wish to commit the perfect crime that was sure to get the city's attention: the kidnapping and murder of a wealthy child. The two spent that winter perfecting a plan.

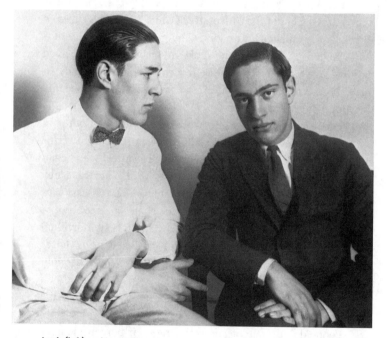

Loeb (left) and Leopold were the sons of millionaires.

LEOPOLD AND LOEB ON SCREEN

The story of Leopold and Loeb has inspired many writers and filmmakers—as much for its intellectual airs as for its brutal murder.

• *Rope* (1929)—The three-act British play by Patrick Hamilton sets the murder in London, England.

• *Rope* (1948)—James Stewart stars in the famous Alfred Hitchcock movie adapted from Hamilton's play.

• *Compulsion* (1959)—Leopold unsuccessfully tried to block production of this movie starring Orson Welles, which was adapted from the 1956 novel of the same name by University of Chicago classmate Meyer Levin.

• *Swoon* (1992)—This film focuses more on the killers' purported homosexuality than the crime itself.

• *Murder by Numbers* (2002)—A high-budget Hollywood retelling is loosely based on this case.

On May 21, 1924, Leopold and Loeb prowled the streets of Kenwood in a rental car until they spotted 14-year-old Bobby Franks, Loeb's second cousin. Franks was only two blocks from home, but Loeb, sitting in the back seat, lured him into the car by asking him about a tennis racket. Once Franks was in the front seat, Loeb hit him in the head four times with a chisel as Leopold drove. Franks continued to struggle, so Loeb gagged him. Franks quickly suffocated.

The two drove several miles south of Chicago to Indiana and dumped the body in a remote spot near railroad tracks. They mailed a ransom note—made on the typewriter they stole from Zeta Beta Tau—to the Franks family for delivery the next morning. By the time Leopold and Loeb returned to Chicago, the neighborhood was already buzzing about Franks's disappearance, and their perfect crime was already starting to show flaws.

Franks's body was found the next day, voiding the ransom plot. Also found near his body was a pair of eyeglasses with unusual hinges. In fact, only three pairs like them had been sold in the Chicago area—one to Nathan Leopold.

Leopold and Loeb were brought in for questioning on May 29. When asked about the eyeglasses, Leopold suggested he may have lost them on a bird-watching trip near the crime scene. The two claimed they'd spent the night with two women (whose last names they couldn't remember) whom they'd picked up in Leopold's car. The alibi was soon debunked, however, when the family chauffeur informed investigators that he'd been repairing the car that night.

By May 31 both men confessed, and both blamed the other for planning and executing the murder.

The trial of Leopold and Loeb was a media sensation dubbed the "trial of the century" (the third such trial at that point in the twentieth century, after those of Harry Thaw and Sacco and Vanzetti). Loeb's family hired renowned criminal defense lawyer Clarence Darrow to represent both men. Darrow entered a plea of guilty, hoping to persuade the judge to sentence his clients to life in prison instead of death. He succeeded after a memorable 12-hour closing argument about the cruel punishments of the American justice system and the youth and naïveté of the accused. Leopold and Loeb were sentenced to life in prison for the murder of Bobby Franks, plus 99 years for kidnapping.

The pair managed to maintain their friendship while incarcerated together in Joliet Prison and later in Stateville

Penitentiary, eventually adding a high school and junior college curriculum to the prison school system. Both men were targeted because of their wealth, with Loeb even paying an allowance to fellow prisoner James E. Day in an effort to stay safe. This effort failed, however, and on January 28, 1936, Day killed Loeb in the shower room.

Leopold went on to become a model prisoner, working in the library, teaching fellow inmates, and volunteering in the hospital. He was paroled in March 1958 and moved to Puerto Rico, where he married and worked as a technician in a hospital. He died of a heart attack on August 29, 1971, at the age of 66.

A TRUE HALLOWEEN MONSTER

I f you've ever had your Halloween candy inspected by your parents before you could dive in, you may know the urban legend of the Candy Man—the monster who hands out poisoned candy to trick-or-treaters. Only this isn't just a legend. On Halloween night 1974, Ronald Clark O'Bryan gave Pixy Stix to his son and daughter, two children he was chaperoning, and one child from his local church. O'Bryan's eight-year-old son ate his before bed and died within an hour. The candy had been replaced with enough cyanide to kill two adults. Police were able to warn the parents of the other children in time. O'Bryan's daughter also survived.

O'Bryan claimed an arm reached out of a house the children had thought was empty and handed them the Stix, but his story soon unraveled. The owner of the house was at work, which 200 people confirmed. O'Bryan had more than $60,000 in life insurance policies on his children, which proved to be damning. He was convicted of murder and given the death penalty. He was executed on March 31, 1984.

THE SYDNEY RIVER MCDONALD'S MURDERS

ighteen-year-olds Derek Wood and Darren Muise, along with their 23-year-old friend Freeman MacNeil, spent the winter of 1992 watching cheap movies and concocting plans for armed robberies in Sydney River, Nova Scotia. In March, Wood got a job at the local McDonald's and, after getting a glimpse of a large safe in the basement and a second smaller one upstairs, the men set their sights on the fast-food restaurant. Wood would leave a little-used basement door ajar so Muise and MacNeil could sneak in with guns, force the night manager to open the safes for them, then make off with what Wood claimed would be upwards of $200,000. The weapons were meant for intimidation only. The three did not plan on using violence—they just wanted to make off with some easy money.

On May 6, the night of the robbery, Wood opened the door as planned and waited for Muise and MacNeil to enter. When they didn't arrive, Wood tried calling the pay phone near where they were supposed to be parked, but there was no answer. He then propped the door open with his backpack and found his co-conspirators at the nearby Tim Hortons restaurant, reminding them that it was time to put their plan into action.

The men entered the basement door, stepping over Wood's backpack. Muise was wearing a mask, MacNeil was carrying a shovel handle, and Wood had a stolen .22-caliber pistol. When Arlene MacNeil (no relation to Freeman), 20, saw Wood while waiting for her friend Donna Warren, 22, she laughed and said, "Is this supposed to be funny?" In response, Wood shot Arlene in the head.

Wood then left Warren with the other men and went upstairs, where Neil Burroughs, 29, was washing dishes. Wood shot him, then returned downstairs to retrieve Warren, who could access the safes. As Warren opened the smaller upstairs safe, Muise and MacNeil brutally beat, stabbed, and then fatally shot Burroughs. Wood, having given up on the big safe downstairs, cleaned out the upstairs safe and shot and killed Warren. In the end, the men took $2,017, leaving bills scattered on the floor.

As the three made their escape out of the employee entrance, they ran into maintenance man Jimmy Fagan, 27, who arrived to work by taxi an hour early. MacNeil shot him, and they stepped over his body as they fled. The cabdriver who dropped off Fagan called the police.

Wood, Muise, and MacNeil fled in their getaway car after MacNeil dropped the shovel handle in a drain. As they sped away, Wood remembered that he had left his backpack, with his uniform and name tag inside, jammed in the basement door. The three concocted a cover story—that Wood had been smoking at the door and ran when he heard shots. Wood got out of the car and ran to a convenience store, where he called the police to say he had been working at McDonald's and heard shots. Police were suspicious of the story but weren't quite sure how Wood fit into the crime, so they questioned and released him.

The three men ultimately implicated one another. Muise eventually took a polygraph test and failed, despite his belief that his martial arts training would help him pass.

With MacNeil already in custody, an emergency response team was dispatched to arrest Wood and Muise. Within 10 days of the massacre, all three men were arrested. Wood was found guilty of the attempted murder of Arlene MacNeil, the first-degree murders of Donna Warren and Neil Burroughs, robbery, and unlawful confinement. He received 25 years to life and was denied his first request for parole, in 2015. MacNeil was convicted of the first-degree murder of Neil Burroughs, the second-degree murder of Jimmy Fagan, and other crimes. He remains in prison but has been granted escorted temporary absences. Muise pleaded guilty to second-degree murder and robbery and struck a plea bargain with prosecutors. He was granted parole in 2015, but he is banned from ever going to Sydney River again.

Arlene MacNeil is the sole survivor, though she remains permanently physically and mentally disabled from the attack.

The McDonald's in Sydney River, Nova Scotia, where the murders took place.

THE HERMIT OF NORTH POND

In 1986, 20-year-old Christopher Thomas Knight disappeared into the wilderness of the North Pond area of Maine. Except for two brief encounters—a simple "hi" to a passing hiker, and when a fisherman and his son stumbled on his camp and were sworn to secrecy—he would not be seen or heard from again for years. Knight survived all those bitter Maine winters by waking up during the coldest time of night (as low as –25°F) and pacing until he was warm again. He avoided building fires, instead cooking with propane tanks stolen from nearby campsites. He stockpiled supplies, also stolen from local camps and residences, and stayed inside his camp between November and March so he could not be tracked by footprints left in the snow.

Knight was arrested on April 4, 2013—27 years after he vanished—while burgling a camp in Rome, Maine. Locals were relieved to finally learn where their mysteriously disappearing items had gone. Some cabins had been broken into up to 50 times, with stolen items varying from batteries to flashlights to steaks from the fridge. Knight received seven months in jail and was ordered to pay $2,000 in restitution to the victims of his burglaries.

ALBERT DESALVO: THE BOSTON STRANGLER AND THE GREEN MAN

O n January 4, 1964, 19-year-old Mary Sullivan was found dead in her apartment. A card reading *Happy New Year* was found lying against her foot. She had been raped and then strangled to death with a pair of stockings, which were left tied around her neck in a neat bow. Sullivan would be the last of 13 women who were raped and murdered by the Boston Strangler. The murderer evaded capture during his four-year reign of terror, his identity remaining a mystery for almost a year after Sullivan was found dead. Then, 29-year-old Albert DeSalvo, an inmate at a Boston-area mental hospital, confessed to his cell mate that he was the guilty party.

The Boston Strangler was the third iteration of Albert DeSalvo's escalating serial criminal career. He started as the Measuring Man, a "modeling scout" who went door-to-door and groped unsuspecting women as he took their measurements. He spent a year in prison for those crimes. Next were the brutal Green Man rapes—in which DeSalvo broke into hundreds of apartments in New England dressed in a green handyman's outfit, tied women up, and raped them. In 1962, he began killing his victims, and the Boston Strangler was born.

In October 1964, DeSalvo, as the Green Man, raped one last woman but left her alive and well enough to describe him to police. DeSalvo was arrested, and shortly thereafter confessed to his cell mate about his murders. He was never tried for any of them—there wasn't enough evidence linking him to the crimes. Instead, he received a life sentence for the Green Man rapes. That sentence was cut short in 1973, when he was killed in prison by another inmate.

DeSalvo after he was captured, following his escape from Bridgewater State Hospital in 1967.

TRUE CRIME MEMOIRS

In these powerful autobiographies, survivors share their stories in their own words.

• *Bloodsworth* by Tim Junkin. The first death-row prisoner exonerated by DNA evidence, Junkin reveals his side of the trial and conviction for the murder of a nine-year-old girl.

• *Down City* by Leah Carroll. Carroll lost both her parents before she turned 18: her father to alcoholism, and her mother to a mob hit.

• *A Stolen Life* by Jaycee Dugard. Dugard's story of being kidnapped and held captive by Phillip and Nancy Garrido for 18 years (see page 12).

• *Whipping Boy* by Allen Kurzweil. Kurzweil finds the man who relentlessly bullied him as a kid and discovers he is in prison for an elaborate fraud scheme.

THE #1 *NEW YORK TIMES* BESTSELLER
"Brave, dignified and painstakingly honest . . ." —*New York Times*

a stolen life

a memoir

jaycee dugard

author of *freedom*

WITH A NEW AFTERWORD FROM THE AUTHOR

The cover of Dugard's
A Stolen Life

• *The Fact of a Body* by Alexandria Marzano-Lesnevich. An intern at a law firm defending child murderer Ricky Langley, Marzano-Lesnevich is reminded of abuse she herself suffered as a child.

• *Lucky* by Alice Sebold. The novelist tells the true story of how her life was shaped by her own brutal rape.

• *Terror by Night* by Terry Caffey. A father's shocking tale of the murder of his family by his daughter's boyfriend.

ELIZABETH SHOAF AND THE FOREST BUNKER

Elizabeth Shoaf was on her way home from school on September 16, 2006, when a man posing as a police officer stopped her. He said she was under arrest, cuffed her, placed a small bomb around her neck, and led her into the woods. The 14-year-old soon realized that the man, later identified as 36-year-old fugitive Vinson Filyaw, was not a police officer, as he led her in circles to disorient her. She slipped off her shoes to leave evidence for the police. When Filyaw finally stopped leading Shoaf around, he reached toward the ground and pulled up a door, indistinguishable from the forest floor. Shoaf was forced down into a 15-by-15-foot bunker, where Filyaw would rape and abuse her for the next 10 days.

But Shoaf was a fighter, and a clever one. She befriended Filyaw, pretending to like him and share interests with him, despite the abuse she endured. She gained Filyaw's trust, and eventually he allowed her out for brief forays into the forest. There, she pulled out strands of her hair and draped them on branches as evidence she was still alive. In so doing, she began the process of rescuing herself.

In what would turn out to be a lifesaving gamble, eight days into her imprisonment Shoaf worked up the courage to ask to borrow Filyaw's phone to play a game. While he slept, she texted her mother that she was being held underground and provided geographic markers. The search parties, which had slowed in the days before Shoaf sent the text, were renewed. The police notified the media, and, while watching TV that night, Filyaw learned about the text and realized the police were closing in on him. He was furious at Shoaf but had also become so dependent on her he asked for her help. Shoaf convinced him to flee the bunker to avoid getting caught.

After Filyaw fled, Shoaf waited until she felt like he was far enough away to come out of the bunker. By the time she emerged the police had triangulated her location via local cell towers, and she heard them calling her name. Filyaw was arrested the same day. He pleaded guilty to multiple crimes, including one count of first-degree criminal sexual assault for each of the 10 days Shoaf was imprisoned. On September 19, 2007, he was sentenced to 421 years in jail and died there in May 2021.

ANNA DELVEY: THE ERSATZ HEIRESS

Anna Delvey lived a lavish lifestyle. From her Celine sunglasses to her Gucci sandals, she deftly fit the role of a New York socialite. A German heiress set to inherit millions, Delvey lived in hotels and dined at the trendiest restaurants around Manhattan, where she picked up exorbitant checks for herself and her friends. She spent her free time working at her art foundation and traveling to exotic destinations.

But in 2017, Delvey's glamorous façade cracked when she was arrested on six charges of grand larceny. It turned out Delvey was actually a Russian-born con artist named Anna Sorokin who had bilked various New York businesses and several friends out of a total of $275,000, cashing bad checks, taking out loans, and convincing others she would reimburse them. She ran up tabs of $503.76 at the W New York hotel, $11,518.59 at the Beekman hotel, $30,000 at the 11 Howard hotel, and $62,000 at La Mamounia hotel in Morocco, which was fronted by a friend who expected to be paid back. In 2019, she was sentenced to four years in prison.

Fake heiress Anna Sorokin in 2019 after being sentenced for larceny in a Manhattan court.

COURTROOM COUTURE: HOW TO DRESS TO IMPRESS

During her trial, con artist Anna Sorokin (see page 275) became as well known for her courtroom attire as for her crimes. Her lawyer confirmed that she worked with stylist Anastasia Walker to decide on her designer duds. Sorokin is hardly the first defendant to work with a stylist or turn to a favorite designer in her time of need—it's a common practice among celebrities facing judge and jury. Lil' Kim, Courtney Love, and Winona Ryder showed up to court for their various infractions in tasteful Marc Jacobs looks. Michael Jackson toned down his usual style in Willie Scott suits when he was on trial. And Cardi B wore a white Christian Siriano tunic with matching pants when she declined a plea deal in an assault case against her.

Here are a few fashion rules from Shawn Holley, a Los Angeles attorney (her clients include Lindsay Lohan, Kris Jenner, and Justin Bieber), and Jason Bloom, the president of a firm that advises clients on jury selection and courtroom behavior.

- **Color coordinate**—Consider wearing white, a color associated with virtue and innocence.

- **Soften it up with a sweater**—Sweaters are often worn by defendants on trial for violent crimes, like the Menendez brothers and Casey Anthony.

- **Be professional**—A good suit always does the trick; it's especially helpful in cases that hint at possible substance abuse issues, like DUIs and drug offenses.

- **Don't seem too rich**—Too much bling can give an impression of lying, cheating, and stealing, especially in financially based crimes.

ANDREAS LUBITZ: MURDER BY PILOT

here weren't any distress calls or responses to air traffic control before Germanwings Flight 9525, en route to Düsseldorf from Barcelona on March 24, 2015, crashed into a mountain in the French Alps, killing everyone on board—144 passengers and 6 crew members. An investigation into the crash revealed the chilling reason why: Copilot Andreas Lubitz had deliberately flown the plane into the mountain, at 435 miles per hour. It was a devastating case of suicide by copilot.

A voice recording was recovered that captured what happened inside the cockpit in the final minutes. At some point during the flight the pilot left the cockpit and Lubitz immediately locked the door behind him. The pilot is later heard banging on the door, demanding that Lubitz let him back in. When Lubitz did nothing, the pilot attempted to break the door down but was unsuccessful. Special reinforcements added to all cockpit doors after the September 11 attacks rendered the door impenetrable. Along with the pilot's futile efforts, the recording captured unanswered transmissions from air traffic control and Lubitz's quiet, steady breathing—then, just moments before the crash, the screams of passengers.

A search of Lubitz's home yielded more disturbing evidence. In his trash was a doctor's note declaring Lubitz unfit for work; on his tablet were searches for "ways to commit suicide" and "cockpit doors and their security provisions."

German-born Lubitz had been treated for suicidal tendencies before his pilot's training and was denied a US pilot's license because of the treatments. Germany has strict privacy laws preventing employers from accessing their employees' medical records. Lubitz also believed he was losing his eyesight and had consulted more than 40 doctors over the 5 years leading up to his suicide. He feared that impending blindness would cause him to lose his pilot's license.

The French Bureau of Enquiry and Analysis for Civil Aviation Safety (BEA) concluded that Lubitz had psychotic depression and his fear of blindness prompted him to research ways to kill himself. The BEA also questioned German medical privacy laws, stating this may have been a case in which the risk to the public outweighed the individual's right to privacy.

Echoing BEA's statement, Carsten Spohr, CEO of Germanwings's parent company, Lufthansa, proposed random psychological testing of employees and called for the loosening of Germany's physician-patient confidentiality laws in extreme cases like that of Lubitz. German politicians began to call for this as well. The British Psychological Society offered psychological testing and monitoring to pilots, and the European Federation of Psychologists' Associations expressed their support for psychological testing, though they stressed that such testing would not necessarily provide blanket protection against similar aviation tragedies.

A photo of Lubitz shown by his father, Gunter, at a news conference in 2017.

The airline regulatory agency in Germany, as well as those in Australia,

New Zealand, and Canada, enacted a "rule of two," which is already used in the United States and China. This rule ensures that two people are in the cockpit at all times, in case of an emergency. Individual airlines around the world also adopted this policy.

The 150 passengers of Germanwings 9525 were citizens of at least 18 countries, mostly Germany and Spain. Among the victims were 16 high school students and 2 teachers returning from a Spanish exchange program to their town of Haltern am See, north of Düsseldorf. The mayor of Haltern am See described the crash as "the darkest day in the history of our town."

A memorial held a month after the crash was attended by 1,400 people—including friends and relatives of the victims, politicians, rescue workers, and airline employees. Lubitz's parents were invited but did not attend. Two months after the crash, the bodies of the 2 teachers and 15 of the 16 students were returned to Haltern am See for burial. The remains of 44 German victims were returned to Düsseldorf the same day.

Negligence on the part of Lufthansa could not be proven; insurance specialists determined that Lubitz withheld information about his illness from his employer and the airline was not liable. The airline promised to pay up to €85,000 (around $103,000 USD) to each victim's family and up to €25,000 (around $30,000 USD) pain and suffering compensation to every close relative of a victim.

DEAD-END JOBS

 atch the serial killer to his day job.

1. Dean Corll	**a.** Chocolate mixer
2. Jeffrey Dahmer	**b.** Contractor
3. John Wayne Gacy	**c.** Journalist
4. Dennis Rader	**d.** Security alarm installer
5. Jack Unterweger	**e.** Vice president of a candy factory

Answers: 1E: As vice president of his family's candy factory, Corll gave treats to children, which earned him the nickname "The Candy Man" (see page 146). **2A:** Dahmer (see page 45) worked as a chocolate mixer at Ambrosia Chocolate Factory in Milwaukee. **3B:** Gacy (see page 120), best known for his hobby of dressing as a clown for children's parties, found a lot of his victims through his contracting company. **4D:** Rader, the BTK Killer, worked there to disarm security systems at his victims' houses. **5C:** Instead of writing about the sex workers in Los Angeles he claimed to be researching, journalist Unterweger murdered them.

FOURTEEN FEET IN THE SALISH SEA

Since 2007, 14 human feet, still in socks and shoes, belonging to 10 individuals, have been found on the beaches of the Salish Sea, between Seattle and Vancouver. They drift ashore one at a time, months apart, until they are spotted and reported to the police. Only seven have been identified. A right foot clad in a black boot, for instance, was found in November 2011, 26 years after the man it belonged to was reported missing. Online sleuths at first suspected a serial killer, but it's more likely that the feet belong to victims of drowning and suicide.

The area surrounding the Salish Sea is home to more than 7 million residents, and some of those people end up dead in the sea. As a body decomposes in water, it comes apart at the joints, and the feet, buoyed by the rubber sole of a shoe, will float to the surface. So feet are the body parts most likely to be found.

FAMOUS FOOTWEAR

• When 39 members of the Heaven's Gate cult died by suicide in San Diego in 1997, they did so in matching outfits, including black-and-white Nike Decade tennis shoes.

• A key piece of evidence in the murders of Nicole Simpson and Ronald Goldman was a bloody print from a size 12 Bruno Magli boot. Costing $160, only 200 pairs were sold in the United States. A Bloomingdale's employee testified that he showed O. J. Simpson the shoes but couldn't prove he bought them. After his acquittal, a photograph of Simpson wearing the boots at a Buffalo Bills game surfaced.

• As Richard Ramirez (see page 71), the Night Stalker, raped and murdered his way through Los Angeles in 1985, he left behind impressions of his Avia aerobics shoes, including one on a victim's face. The recurrence of these prints helped investigators connect the crimes and conclude that a serial killer was on the loose.

COLLEEN STAN:
THE GIRL IN THE BOX

olleen Stan had already refused three rides while hitch-hiking to a party on May 19, 1977, when Cameron Hooker stopped to pick her up. Hooker was with his wife, Janice, and their baby, so Stan felt she would be safe with them. But Hooker and Janice were on the hunt to imprison someone as part of their sexual fantasies, so they kidnapped Stan and held her hostage for seven years.

Hooker and Janice tortured and dehumanized Stan, lock-ing her in a coffin-sized box under their bed for up to 23 hours a day, referring to her only as "K," and forcing her to address Hooker as "Master." Hooker also brainwashed Stan, convincing her that he was a member of a powerful organization known as "the Company" that would kill her whole family if she attempted to escape. Stan complied with Hooker's demands to gain tempo-rary freedoms like jogging and working in the yard, but her fear of "the Company" kept her bound to Hooker for the time being.

In 1981, Hooker allowed Stan to visit her family, introduc-ing himself as her boyfriend. After the visit, Hooker worried that he'd given Stan too much freedom, and he resumed locking her in the box under the bed for 23 hours a day. Years passed, and toward the end of 1983 Hooker started giving her more freedom again, which included her working as a housekeeper at a local motel.

In 1984, Hooker informed Janice that he intended to make Stan his second wife. This revelation prompted Janice to tell

Stan that Hooker was not a member of "the Company," though she maintained that the organization existed. That day Stan left her job at the motel and phoned Hooker from a bus station to tell him she was leaving. At Janice's request, Stan did not contact the police.

Three months later, Janice turned Hooker in, while also confessing to the kidnapping, rape, torture, and imprisonment of Stan. She further claimed that she had been tortured and brainwashed by Hooker since their first date and received full immunity in exchange for testifying against him. Hooker received 104 years in prison for kidnapping and sexually assaulting Stan.

Of the varying degrees of freedom given to her during her time in captivity, Stan says, "People don't understand all the threats made against me, my family. There's a lot more to it than just walking away. When you're sexually abused, these things solidify the fact that if you don't do what I say, I can take your life. I thought, 'What if he catches me when I try to escape?' It wasn't like I never thought about these things. I did but I never felt safe to act on them until his wife came to me and said, 'We have to get out of here.'"

THE SUSPICIOUS DEATH OF MARSHA P. JOHNSON

Marsha "Pay It No Mind" Johnson was a well-known gay rights activist widely believed to be the first person to throw a brick during the Stonewall uprising (see page 117) on June 28, 1969—though Johnson later said she didn't show up to the uprising until 2:00 a.m., when the nightclub was already in flames. Johnson was also a founding member of the Gay Liberation Front, as well as STAR (Street Transvestites Action Revolutionaries), a radical political collective that provided housing and support to gay and transgender homeless youth and sex workers in the early 1970s in Greenwich Village.

Shortly after the NYC Pride parade in 1992, Johnson's body was found floating in the Hudson River. Her death was initially ruled a suicide—Johnson's struggles with mental health began in 1970, and her friend Randy Wicker, with whom she lived, said Johnson was in a fragile state at the time of her death. However, friends and members of the community claimed Johnson was not suicidal and that police ignored a massive wound present on the back of Johnson's head when her body was found.

Wicker agreed. He said that despite the state of her mental health, Johnson would not have taken her own life, suggesting instead that she may have walked into the river during a hallucination or jumped in to escape harassers. Witnesses came forward to report they had seen a group, who was known to rob people in the neighborhood, harassing her. Another witness saw a neighborhood resident arguing with Johnson two days before her body was found. The resident called Johnson a homophobic slur, and the witness later heard the same person in a bar bragging about "killing a drag queen named Marsha." The witness went to police with this information but was brushed off.

In 2012, Johnson's cause of death was officially changed from "suicide" to "undetermined," due to the efforts of New York State Senator Tom Duane, who believed the initial investigation was closed too quickly and also cited the fact that Johnson did not leave a suicide note. In 2016, Victoria Cruz of the NYC Anti-Violence Project tried to get the case reopened. She gained access to previously unreleased documents and statements and sought new interviews with those familiar with Johnson's probable murder. These efforts were documented in the 2017 film *The Death and Life of Marsha P. Johnson*. As of 2021, Johnson's case is open but remains unsolved.

Gay rights activist Marsha P. Johnson at a Pride March in New York City, 1975.

THE WANDERING COP

wandering cop is an officer who frequently transfers between police departments despite a record of misconduct or often unsuitable or subpar job performance.

The wandering cop phenomenon is the result of several factors, including:

• lack of communication among the 18,000 police agencies on the federal, state, and local levels in the United States.

• It is easier to hire an officer who has already been trained and certified than it is to recruit rookies.

• There is pressure on police departments to cover up misconduct to avoid lawsuits, investigations, bad press, etc.

A well-known example of a wandering cop is Cleveland officer Tim Loehmann, who shot 12-year-old Tamir Rice as he played with a toy gun in a public park. Loehmann had previously been "allowed . . . to resign" from a job after displaying a "dangerous loss of composure" during firearms training. After killing Rice, Loehmann was fired from the Cleveland Police Department but managed to get yet another job at a police department in Ohio a year later. There are parallels between the wandering cop phenomenon and the Catholic Church's practice of "priest shuffling."

CHARLES STARKWEATHER: MICK AND MAYBE MALLORY

Teenage spree killer Charles Starkweather was a likely murderer—despite a relatively happy home life. He was bullied at school over his stutter and bowleggedness. Channeling his rage into physical activity, he soon became a bully himself and eventually graduated to murder. Among his first victims were the family of his 14-year-old girlfriend Caril

Starkweather (right), 19, and Fugate, 14, were considered accomplices in crime, but Fugate's innocence is debated.

Fugate in January 1958. After killing her stepfather, mother, and young half sister, Starkweather took Fugate along with him on his crime spree, which ended when he was injured in a high-speed chase with police.

Once captured, Starkweather and Fugate spun vastly different stories, with Starkweather claiming Fugate aided him in several of the murders, and Fugate declaring herself his hostage, taken by Starkweather after he murdered her family.

Starkweather received the death penalty and was executed in 1959. Fugate received a life sentence for first-degree murder, becoming the youngest person in the US at the time to be charged with the crime. She was released on parole after serving 17 years.

Charles Starkweather became the inspiration for Woody Harrelson's character, Mickey Knox, in the film *Natural Born Killers*. Whether Fugate was an accomplice, as an all-male jury of her peers believed, or a hostage is still debated.

LINDA TAYLOR:
THE "WELFARE QUEEN"

In August 1974, Linda Taylor reported $14,000 worth of valuables stolen from her home. But Detective Jack Sherwin recognized her from a similar scene two years earlier—she had a different name and look then, but the circumstances were similar enough to jog his memory. Taylor was again trying to commit insurance fraud. Sherwin charged her with falsifying a report, but the run-in piqued his interest. In the months that followed, he identified dozens of false identities, multiple husbands, and evidence that she'd stolen at least $150,000 from public assistance. All the while Taylor lived in opulence, wearing fur coats and jewels, and driving one of her luxury cars to the public aid office.

Future president Ronald Reagan and press in Chicago called her the "Welfare Queen." In a campaign speech, Reagan warned about the "woman who holds the record. She used 80 names, 30 addresses, 15 telephone numbers to collect food stamps, Social Security, veterans' benefits for four nonexistent deceased veteran husbands, as well as welfare. Her tax-free cash income alone has been running $150,000 a year." The term "welfare queen" quickly devolved into a racist stereotype against Black single mothers, when in reality it referred to just one person: the con artist Linda Taylor.

Taylor was born Martha Miller, or maybe Martha Louise White, in either Alabama or Tennessee in the late 1920s.

According to the 1930 census, she was white, but ex-husbands said she could easily pass as Black, Hispanic, or even Asian if she desired, and the press labeled her Black when she was tried for welfare fraud in 1976. She spent time in Ohio, Texas, and California before moving to Chicago in the early 1960s.

While living in Chicago, Taylor befriended underground lottery kingpin Lawrence Wakefield. He treated her like a daughter, giving her money and bodyguards. When Wakefield died in 1964, Taylor tried to lay claim to his $763,000 inheritance, presenting herself as Constance Wakefield. She had a birth certificate and a will that identified her as his daughter, but the judge found the documents suspect. Her fingerprints revealed previous

Linda Taylor is considered the original "Welfare Queen," which became a racist stereotype for those who defraud public assistance.

arrests under other aliases for prostitution, assault, and delinquency of a minor, so the judge dismissed her claim. The money went to Wakefield's common-law wife instead.

Taylor had four children when she moved to Chicago in the 1960s, though she often left them alone for long periods of time. Because of her neglect, Taylor's oldest son moved out when he was a teenager. She gave her second son to another family, leaving her with a son and daughter who often ran away.

Even without her biological children, there were a lot of kids going in and out of Taylor's house. Some, she kidnapped, like Raymond Pagan. She babysat him for his 16-year-old mother, refusing to return him for two years. Others, like a baby named Tiger, would suddenly appear and disappear just as quickly. The press theorized she was taking (or buying) the kids to support her welfare claims, then selling them afterward. Police charged Taylor twice with kidnapping, but didn't pursue human trafficking claims.

In 1977, Taylor was convicted of using four aliases to steal $8,000 from the government, though the actual amount of money is likely higher. She was sentenced to two to six years in prison.

Taylor is also suspected of the mysterious kidnapping of baby Paul Joseph Fronczak in April 1964. The day after Fronczak was born to Dora and Chester Fronczak in Chicago's Michael Reese Hospital, a woman dressed in a white nurse's uniform took the baby from Dora. Instead of bringing him to a doctor, though, the "nurse" took the baby down a back staircase and disappeared into a cab on the street. Hospital staff notified police, but neither baby Paul nor the kidnapper were found despite an exhaustive search of the city.

Fourteen months later, in July 1965, a baby boy was abandoned at a shopping center in Newark, New Jersey. His ears were similar to those of the Fronczak baby and blood tests did not exclude a match, so Dora and Chester raised him as their missing son. A DNA test in 2012 proved the abandoned baby boy was actually Jack Rosenthal, who vanished along with his still-missing twin sister, Jill, in 1965. Despite this revelation, the adopted Paul still considers himself a Fronczak, and along with the rest of the family awaits the day the original Paul—and Jack's twin sister, Jill—are found.

Taylor is also a person of interest in the death of Patricia Parks by barbiturate overdose in 1974.

After she was released from prison in 1980, Taylor moved to Illinois with her husband, Sherman Ray. In 1983, Willtrue Loyd accidentally shot and killed Ray during a fight. With the money from Ray's life insurance policy, Taylor moved to Florida with Loyd.

In Florida, Taylor lived with Loyd and his new wife, Mildred Markham. When Markham died in 1986, Taylor presented herself as Markham's daughter and collected on two life insurance policies.

Taylor died of a heart attack in Chicago in 2002.

BY THE NUMBERS: PRISON LABOR

The 13th Amendment of the US Constitution abolished slavery "except as punishment for crime whereof the party shall have been duly convicted." This constitutional loophole allows for prison labor, which is often criticized as institutionalized slavery. Here are some typical wages for prison labor:

$2.90 to $5.12 per day for inmate firefighters

$1 per hour for inmate firefighters in an active emergency

$.14 to $.63 per hour: the national average for nonindustry prison jobs

$.33 to $1.41 per hour: the national average for labor done for state-owned businesses

$.93/$4.73 per day: the national average minimum/maximum prison wages in 2001

$.86/$3.45 per day: the national average minimum/maximum prison wages in 2017

2 weeks: How long it takes inmates on an average prison salary to save up to buy a box of tampons

LATIN CRIME TERMS

 Match the criminal terminology with its English definition.

1. *in flagrante delicto*
2. *locus delicti*
3. *mens rea*
4. *actus reus*
5. *cui bono*

a. Scene of the crime
b. As a benefit to whom?
c. In blazing offense
d. Guilty mind
e. Guilty act

Answers: 1C: *Often used as a euphemism for being caught having sex, in the courtroom this term means to be caught in the act of a crime.* **2A:** *The location where the crime took place.* **3D:** *Mens rea is one requirement for an event to be classified as a crime—proving intent and competence to commit the crime.* **4E:** *Actus reus is the other requirement for an event to be classified as a crime—proving criminal liability.* **5B:** *A perpetrator can be found by investigating those who benefit financially from the crime.*

CORAZON AMURAO ATIENZA

Not only did Corazon Amurao Atienza witness the unthinkable, she had to remain silent and still the entire time. On July 14, 1966, Richard Speck forcibly broke into a Chicago home shared by nine nursing students and murdered eight of them. Atienza hid under her bed, eluding Speck's murder spree. From her vantage point she saw him clearly enough to provide police with a sketch that helped catch the killer.

In the ensuing trial, Atienza was a crucial witness for the state, leading the prosecutor to refer to her as "95 pounds of steel and lace." Speck spent the rest of his life in prison. Atienza finished her nursing degree, got married, worked as a critical care nurse, and now spends time with her grandchildren.

THE GREYHOUND BUS MURDER

im McLean was sleeping peacefully on a Canadian Greyhound headed from Edmonton to Winnipeg in Canada on the evening of July 30, 2008, when the unthinkable happened. Another passenger, Vincent Li, moved from the front of the bus to sit next to McLean, then began viciously stabbing him in the neck and chest with a large knife. When the bus driver pulled to the side of the road to let the other passengers out, Li decapitated McLean and displayed his head to the passengers as they watched, horrified, from the side of the road. Li then began cannibalizing McLean.

The nightmare lasted nearly five hours. The bus driver and two other passengers initially tried to subdue Li, but the extreme violence of his attack forced them to retreat. They ultimately ended up barring him in the bus, using only a crowbar and a hammer as they waited for police to respond to the remote area.

Li was still trapped in the bus when police arrived. He tried to escape by driving the bus away, but the driver had activated the emergency immobilizer. Special negotiators and a heavily armed tactical unit were summoned to the scene. The standoff between Li and the police lasted until 1:30 a.m., during which time Li continued to pace the bus and consume parts of McLean's body. Li was captured shortly after attempting to escape through a broken window. Parts of McLean's body were found in Li's pockets, while others were retrieved from the bus.

Li was arraigned at a nearby courthouse, where his only response were pleas for someone to kill him. At his trial the following spring, a judge determined that Li was not criminally responsible for the killing. A psychiatrist testified that Li had heard God's voice instructing him to kill McLean, who was a force of evil intent on executing him. Li was eventually discharged from psychiatric care on February 10, 2017, after years of reduced supervision.

THE HOLLOW NICKEL CASE

J ingling coins in his palm, Jimmy Bozart continued his rounds collecting payments for delivery of the *Brooklyn Eagle*. But something was off. One of the coins didn't sound right. He found the misfit, but accidentally dropped it on the floor. To his surprise the coin split open. Inside was a piece of microfilm marked with 10 columns of 21 five-digit numbers. Through the daughter of a police officer, the coin found its way to the FBI. But it took four more years—until 1957—for the mystery of the Hollow Nickel to be solved, when Reino Hayhanen arrived at the US embassy in Paris and told agents he wanted to defect from Soviet Russia. He was able to identify what Bozart had found as a piece of misplaced correspondence between two Soviet spies operating in New York City. With Hayhanen's help, the FBI was able to arrest Rudolf Ivanovich Abel, working under an alias out of a Brooklyn photo studio, for espionage. Abel remained in prison until 1962, when he was exchanged for an American pilot.

DRUG-FUELED DOCUMENTARIES

Check out these drug-related documentaries:

• *Heroin(e)*—A mini Netflix documentary explores the opioid crisis in West Virginia and three women who are fighting against it and saving lives.

• *Cocaine Cowboys*—This flashy documentary depicts the Miami Drug War of the 1970s and '80s.

• *Murder Mountain*—A look at the mysterious and sometimes deadly marijuana-growing business in Humboldt County, California.

• *Icarus*—While researching the inefficiency of anti-doping drug tests in sports, filmmaker Bryan Fogel uncovers an international doping scandal.

THE CHICAGO TYLENOL MURDERS

I n 1982, seven victims died from simply taking their medicine. Several pharmacies in the Chicago area had been unknowingly selling Tylenol laced with potassium cyanide. Someone had been placing the poisoned bottles on store shelves. Although no one was ever charged with the poisonings, a New York resident named James William Lewis was convicted of extortion for sending a letter to Johnson & Johnson claiming responsibility for the murders and demanding a $1 million ransom to stop them. As a result of the deaths, the pharmaceutical industry changed the way it packages medications and the government introduced anti-tampering laws.

STELLA NICKELL:
THE EXCEDRIN
MURDERS

 s Susan Snow got ready for work on Wednesday, June 11, 1986, she took two extra-strength Excedrin capsules. Fifteen minutes later, she collapsed. Snow passed away later that day at a hospital in Auburn, Washington, with her husband and two daughters at her side. Tests revealed that the pills were laced with cyanide. When police announced the findings, Stella Nickell came forward to suggest that her husband, Bruce, may also be a victim, as he took Excedrin shortly before he died. An autopsy confirmed her suspicions. Fearing that their product had been tampered with, as in the 1982 Chicago Tylenol Murders that killed seven people, the manufacturer issued a recall.

Police found five contaminated bottles of Excedrin. Examination of the tainted capsules under a microscope revealed green crystals. Whoever mixed the cyanide did so in a bowl used to crush algae destroyer tablets for a fish tank. Two of the bottles were found in Nickell's home. She also had an aquarium . . . and three life insurance policies on her husband.

Stella Nickell was 16 when she gave birth to her daughter, Cynthia. Growing up, Cynthia moved with her mother from Oregon to California to Washington. Along the way, Nickell was convicted of forgery, fraud, and beating her daughter. Eventually, Cynthia moved away, got married, and had a daughter of her own.

But divorce brought her back home to live with her mother and her mother's husband, Bruce, in a small trailer in Auburn.

She quickly learned that Nickell was not happy there. Cynthia caught her reading about poisons, once suspecting her mother of giving Bruce something that made him lethargic. Nickell also talked openly about how easily she could kill him with a drug overdose. Most revealing though, was Nickell's fantasy of something like the Chicago Tylenol Murders happening to Bruce.

When Bruce died, the coroner said it was from pulmonary emphysema, so Cynthia had no reason to suspect her mother was culpable. But that changed after Snow's death and Bruce's toxicology report. So in January 1987, Cynthia went to the police.

With Cynthia's information, things clicked into place for the cops. The insurance policies Nickell had on her husband would net her $176,000, but only if Bruce's death was ruled accidental. When his death was misattributed to emphysema, Nickell's payout was cut by more than half. In order to change his cause of death without attracting suspicion, someone else had to die. So Nickell contaminated three more bottles of Excedrin and planted them in local stores. Snow just happened to be one of the unlucky ones.

In May 1988, Nickell was sentenced to 90 years in prison for the product-tampering deaths of Bruce Nickell and Susan Snow. No physical evidence connected her to the crimes, so the prosecution's case relied heavily on the testimony of Cynthia. Bristol-Myers, the manufacturer of the drug, gave Cynthia a $250,000 reward for her contributions to the case. Nickell, meanwhile, maintains her innocence.

A DEADLY KISS

W hen Melissa Ann Blair greeted Anthony Powell in prison, the couple exchanged a lengthy kiss. The PDA wasn't just affectionate—it was practical. Blair had seven balloons of methamphetamine stored in her mouth and was passing them to her boyfriend. Powell, who was serving a life sentence for killing his mother-in-law, later died when two balloons ruptured in his stomach.

Blair was sentenced to two years in prison for the incident.

TERRY JO DUPERRAULT AND THE SINKING OF *BLUEBELLE*

On November 12, 1961, 11-year-old Terry Jo Duperrault was sleeping on the *Bluebelle*, a ship chartered by her father from captain Julian Harvey, when she woke to screams. Duperrault went to investigate and found the stabbed bodies of her mother, father, brother, sister, and Harvey's wife. A bloody knife was lying nearby. Harvey yelled for her to stay below deck, and Duperrault retreated as he began to scuttle the ship. She escaped on a small cork float just before the ship went down and survived adrift on the float for four days without food or water, until she was rescued by a shipping freighter.

Julian Harvey was picked up three days before Duperrault was found. With him was the body of her younger sister, Renee. He claimed a squall had sunk the *Bluebelle*, and that he had found Renee's body in the water and attempted to revive her. After he heard of Duperrault's rescue, he checked into a motel and died by suicide with a razor blade. Investigators believe that Duperrault's father may have witnessed Harvey killing his wife, prompting the *Bluebelle* massacre.

Terry Jo Duperrault shortly before her rescue at sea in 1961.

DAYTIME DRAMA: THE MURDER OF SCOTT AMEDURE

I t was the low point of trashy 1990s daytime TV: On March 6, 1995, Scott Amedure appeared on an episode of *The Jenny Jones Show*, where he admitted to having a secret crush on his straight friend Jonathan Schmitz. Three days later, Amedure was shot dead at his home by Schmitz, who tearfully phoned the police immediately after to confess, claiming he'd been publicly humiliated.

Schmitz's crime seemed particularly deliberate—he drove to the bank to take out money, then to the gun store to buy a shotgun, then to Amedure's house, where he verbally confronted Amedure. After this first confrontation, Schmitz retrieved the new shotgun from his car, returned to Amedure's home, and shot him with it. Despite the clear premeditation, Schmitz was only found guilty of second-degree murder, and sentenced to 20 to 25 years in prison. He was released on August 22, 2017.

Amedure's family decided to sue *The Jenny Jones Show* and the production company, Warner Bros., for wrongful death, retaining the services of Geoffrey Fieger, an attorney on high-profile cases such as the defense of Dr. Jack Kevorkian. Fieger thoroughly and aggressively questioned the producers of the show and Jenny Jones herself. After Fieger's eight-hour closing statement, the jury found that all parties involved in the production of the show acted irresponsibly and negligently.

Jonathan Schmitz in court for killing Scott Amedure after learning on *The Jenny Jones Show* that Amedure had a crush on him.

Warner Bros. was found liable for Amedure's death and ordered to pay his family $29,332,686.

The decision was later overturned in appeals. The Amedure family had far fewer resources than the WarnerMedia corporation and could not afford to fight back. In the end, they received no settlement money. Jenny Jones never admitted any responsibility or apologized. The trials were widely publicized on Court TV, a cable channel owned by WarnerMedia, meaning the company once found criminally liable in Amedure's death profited off the tragic event, while Amedure's family got nothing.

BANNING THE PANIC DEFENSE

 ince the early 1960s, criminal defense attorneys have frequently employed the discriminatory "gay panic" or "transgender panic" legal strategy when defending clients accused of assaulting or murdering LGBTQIA+ victims. The strategy hinges on the theory that learning an individual is gay, bisexual, or transgender renders the defendant temporarily insane and spurs their violent action. This stemmed from the notion that same-sex attraction and gender dysphoria were mental illnesses, an idea disproved in the 1970s. The panic defense has received widespread media coverage in the United States on several occasions, including the 1998 murder of Matthew Shepard and the 2013 beating of Islan Nettles, a transgender woman who later died from her injuries.

The same year Nettles died, the American Bar Association called on state governments to outlaw the use of panic defenses. California was the first to issue a ban in 2014, followed by Illinois in 2017, Rhode Island in 2018, Nevada, New York, Connecticut, Hawaii, and Maine in 2019, and New Jersey, Washington, and Colorado in 2020.

Akin to the panic defense in the United States is Australia's "provocation defense," which also includes the "homosexual advance defense," nonviolent sexual advances that relate to sexual orientation and gender identity. Tasmania led the ban in 2003. Previously known as "Bigot's Island" for its resistance to LGBTQIA+ rights up until the late 1990s, the state is now known worldwide for its extensive LGBTQIA+ law reforms. Bans followed in Victoria in 2005, Western Australia in 2008, and Queensland in 2017. New South Wales, Australian Capital Territory, and the Northern Territory took a different approach in 2012 and banned defenses that used nonviolent sexual advances of any kind. South Australia, ironically, the first state to legalize consensual gay sex, was the last to ban the panic defense, in 2020.

OPERATION BROKEN GLASS

In 2012, eel prices soared to $1,900 a pound, putting *unagi* (a type of eel) everywhere at risk. Restrictions were already in place on exports of eels from the European Union and the United States because of declining eel populations. Like most restricted items, a black market developed for the small, transparent delicacy known as glass eels. Poachers lined the East Coast of the United States as turf wars and fistfights erupted between fishermen.

In 2013, eel poacher Alan Perkins broke into a seafood business in Maine and tried to steal a five-gallon bucket of eels worth $10,000. He was caught a month later; charged with burglary, theft, and violating release; and sentenced to seven years in jail. In 2019, US Fish and Wildlife arrested more than 20 people in a sting operation known as "Operation Broken Glass." Among those arrested were Tommy Zhou, a seafood dealer in Brooklyn who mixed illegal eels with legally caught ones and threatened to kill anyone with a "big mouth" who thought of blabbing (reportedly, he claimed he would pay hit men $200,000 to kill people who snitched on him), and Bill Sheldon, a Maine fisherman charged with seven counts of illegally smuggling eels. Sheldon was ordered to surrender all vessels associated with his smuggling operation, including a pickup truck with the license plate "EEL SZN."

SPORTS EDITION

Match the (proven) crime to the athlete.

1. Hindering the prosecution in the investigation of an attack on a competitor

2. Kidnapping and theft of memorabilia

3. Shooting his limo driver

4. Criminal possession of a handgun

a. O. J. Simpson

b. Jayson Williams

c. Tonya Harding

d. Plaxico Burress

Answers: 1C: *After the infamous attack on fellow ice skater Nancy Kerrigan was orchestrated by Harding's ex-husband, Jeff Gillooly, Harding accepted a plea bargain and pleaded guilty to hindering prosecution.* **2A:** *Football legend Simpson was convicted in 2008 in connection with a 2007 Las Vegas robbery of sports memorabilia, which he claimed was stolen from him.* **3B:** *Williams, a basketball player, pleaded guilty to assault for the accidental shooting death of Costas "Gus" Christofi.* **4D:** *Burress, a football player, turned himself in to face charges after accidentally shooting himself in the leg at a nightclub before learning that the hospital where he was treated had not reported the shooting to the police.*

OSCAR PISTORIUS AND THE MURDER OF REEVA STEENKAMP

After losing both of his legs when he was 11 months old, Oscar Pistorius grew up to compete in both the Olympic and the Paralympic games as "the fastest man on no legs." But Pistorius became infamous on February 14, 2013, when he shot and killed his girlfriend, model and aspiring lawyer Reeva Steenkamp, at his home in Pretoria, South Africa. Pistorius claimed that he mistook Steenkamp for a late-night intruder—break-ins are a common occurrence in South Africa—but neighbors heard them fighting for hours before Steenkamp locked herself in the bathroom with her cell phone. When Pistorius fired at Steenkamp through the bathroom door, he said he thought she was still in bed.

Steenkamp was shot multiple times by Pistorius in 2013, and died from her wounds.

Pistorius was convicted of culpable homicide and sentenced to a maximum term of five years in prison and, for a separate incident with a firearm at a restaurant, was convicted of reckless endangerment and given a concurrent three-year sentence. The culpable homicide charge was eventually overturned and he was found guilty of murder in 2017 and sentenced to 13 years and 5 months, less the time he already served.

MING OF HARLEM

I n October 2003, Antoine Yates visited a New York City emergency room with what he claimed were bite wounds from a pit bull, though attendants noted the width of the bite marks suggested an attack by a much larger animal. Soon after, police received a tip and headed to Yates's five-bedroom apartment in Harlem public housing. They heard loud growling noises coming from the apartment and enlisted a police sniper to rappel down the side of the building with a tranquilizer gun. When he reached the window, a 425-pound tiger lunged at him, nearly breaking the glass.

Ming the tiger had been living in Yates's apartment for three years, since Yates purchased him when he was just an eight-week-old cub. By 2003, neighbors were aware of Ming only as a sort of urban legend, and it was a standing joke in the building that Yates could eat the 20 pounds of raw chicken he bought at the local supermarket every day.

Ming had bit Yates in the arm and leg after Yates attempted to block Ming from attacking his new house cat, Shadow. Also found in the apartment was a five-and-a-half-foot alligator named Al. They had all been living in harmony, along with a couple of human roommates, until Yates brought Shadow into the mix. Yates was charged with reckless endangerment and possession of a wild animal. His mother was charged with endangering the welfare of a child when it was discovered that she had been babysitting in the apartment alongside the dangerous menagerie. As part of a deal to reduce the charges against his mother,

Yates pleaded guilty to reckless endangerment and served five months in prison and five years' probation.

Upon his release, Yates attempted to sue New York City for the loss of his pets (including Ming, Al, Shadow, and an unnamed rabbit). The suit was dismissed, though the judge noted Yates's "chutzpah." Yates has been living and working at a big cat sanctuary in Las Vegas since 2010. Ming was safely tranquilized the day he was rescued and he lived out his life at Noah's Lost Ark Animal Sanctuary in Ohio. He died from natural causes in February 2019 and was laid to rest in a pet cemetery in Hartsdale, New York.

ESCAPING THE TOY-BOX KILLER

n March 1999, just north of Truth or Consequences, New Mexico, Cynthia Vigil Jaramillo escaped the home of David Parker Ray and Cindy Hendy wearing nothing but a dog collar and a chain. She had been held for three days by Ray, the Toy-Box Killer, named for the torture chamber in the semitruck trailer behind his home. On the day she escaped, Ray had removed her handcuffs and shackles and left her in the living room with a padlock chained around her neck.

Hendy was watching soap operas nearby when the phone rang. When she got up to answer it, Jaramillo noticed a set of keys on the coffee table. She grabbed them and began trying them in the lock at her throat. Hendy caught her, dropped the phone, and began attacking Jaramillo with a lamp and an ice pick. Jaramillo fought to stay conscious—then found the right key. She freed herself, grabbed the phone and ice pick, and called 911. She then dropped the phone and stabbed Hendy, grazing her forehead. Jaramillo ran out the front door and to a neighboring trailer to seek help. The 911 dispatcher heard the fight and sent authorities to Ray and Hendy's home.

Jaramillo and Hendy were taken to the same hospital. There, Hendy tried to explain that she and Ray had picked up Jaramillo from Albuquerque to help her detox, which is why Jaramillo was chained up in their house. But it was too late—the police had already found Ray's "toy box," with its whips, chains, pulleys, straps, clamps, leg-spreader bars, syringes, surgical blades, saws, and more. Later, they found the "welcome" video Ray played for Jaramillo and his other victims, which began with "Hello, bitch." They also discovered his journals, which detailed the torments he inflicted on his victims, as well as some tapes with video recordings of murders he had committed. Jaramillo would be his final victim, and she made it out alive.

None of Ray's murder victims were found, though the investigation that began after Jaramillo escaped led to the identification of a local John Doe as Billy Ray Bowers, who may have been killed by Ray. Ultimately, Ray was charged with the kidnapping, torture, and rape of Jaramillo and two other women who managed to escape the toy box, Angelica Montano and Kelly Garrett. Both reported the torture to police after they escaped, but neither was believed.

Ray was tried separately for his crimes against the three women and found guilty on 12 counts for his crimes against Jaramillo. He pleaded guilty to crimes against Kelly Garrett. Angelica Montano died before Ray went to trial for what he did to her, and there was no conviction due to lack of evidence without

Ray, at a 1999 hearing where he was charged with 25 criminal counts, from kidnapping to aggravated battery.

Montano's testimony. In 2001, Ray received 224 years in prison. He died the next year.

In 2000, Cindy Hendy received a 36-year sentence, but was released in 2019. Two of Ray's other accomplices served time as well. His daughter, Jesse Ray, served 30 months for kidnapping. Dennis Roy Yancy was convicted of the 1997 murder of Marie Parker, which Ray recorded on video. Yancy was paroled in 2011 but returned to prison 3 months later to serve his full 20-year sentence.

Jaramillo went on to have two sons and found the non-profit Street Safe New Mexico, an organization that focuses on harm reduction for women affected by sex trafficking, homelessness, and addiction.

TATTOO ANALYSIS

Tattoos are some of the most unique identifying marks on a person's body and have played a role in forensic investigations for centuries. Despite this, there isn't much published research about forensic tattoo analysis.

Forensic scientist Michelle D. Miranda is changing that, with academic articles and a book, *Forensic Analysis of Tattoos and Tattoo Ink*—the first of its kind. Miranda covers everything from the ink found on mummified bodies of antiquity and the role of tattoos in contemporary investigations and prosecutions to the tools, techniques, and various styles of tattoos, which can reveal information about a person's identity and cultural practices.

She also breaks down the science behind tattoo forensics, including the chemical analysis of tattoo ink, the photodecomposition processes of pigment particles, and the historical role body art has played in criminology since the nineteenth century.

Miranda's work is poised to become the academic cornerstone of this identification tool that has already been used for so long by criminologists, forensic experts, investigators, and lawyers.

THE TATTOO CONFESSION

I n October 2008, 25-year-old Anthony Garcia, a Rivera 13 gang member, was arrested and charged with the January 2004 murder of John Juarez. Garcia avoided capture for four years, though he had been arrested on other charges. Each time he was picked up, police would take photos of his tattoos because he was an active gang member. After Garcia was arrested in 2008 for drunk driving, Detective Sergeant Kevin Lloyd connected the detailed tattoo on Garcia's chest with Juarez's murder. The tattoo depicted the crime scene, Mr. Ed's Liquor store in Pico Rivera, California, with Juarez as Mr. Peanut—the peanut being a common symbol of a rival gang in the area. An anthropomorphic helicopter is seen spraying bullets into Mr. Peanut. Garcia's nickname in Rivera 13 is "Chopper."

Los Angeles police officers and gang experts believe this is the first time such a literal depiction of a crime was found tattooed on a criminal, and they called it a "nonverbal confession." Garcia received a 65-year sentence for the murder.

THE OSAGE INDIAN MURDERS

In 1870, the Osage Nation purchased 1.57 million acres of land in present-day Oklahoma from the Cherokee Nation, which the US government designated as the Osage Reservation. Because the Osage purchased the land outright and held a deed to it, they retained more sovereignty than many other tribes, whose land was typically held in trust by the government. So when oil was first discovered on the reservation in 1897, the Osage residents, who also owned the mineral rights to the land, were poised to become extremely wealthy. As the US government prepared Oklahoma for statehood a decade later, 657 acres of the reservation were allotted to each Osage on the tribal rolls. Each tribal member and their heirs—Osage or not—received royalties and headrights (legal rights) to the oil their land produced.

The activities of the wealthy Osage were reported in papers across the country, and they were hailed as "the richest nation, clan, or social group of any race on earth, including the whites, man for man."

In 1921, Congress passed a law requiring most Osage residents to have a court-appointed guardian who managed their wealth until they proved their "competency." This guardian system attracted many opportunists to Osage County, and many of the guardians were white lawyers and businessmen who swindled and defrauded the Osage.

Many believe this law was the product of opportunism, lobbied for by whites who wanted a piece of the Osage wealth. In 1924, just a few years after the guardianship law was enacted, two dozen guardians were charged with corruption. All those accused skirted punishment by settling out of court. A reported $27 million was held by the guardian system, which was set up to protect the Osage.

The corruption didn't stop there. Along with the swindlers came those with even more nefarious intentions. Between 1921 and 1925, an estimated 60 Osage were murdered, and the US government did very little to deliver justice for the killings.

An investigation into the suspicious deaths of the Osage in the late twentieth century revealed massive corruption among the white law enforcement and government officials in the county, including failure to conduct postmortem exams and falsifying death certificates. The incentive to murder the Osage was high—guardians could establish themselves as next of kin and inherit the deeds to an Osage's land, effectively gaining a steady income of millions of dollars, with little recourse to remedy the injustice by way of the law.

By 1925, the Bureau of Indian Affairs and the US Department of the Interior had still not solved any of the murders, so the Osage sought help from the nascent Bureau of Investigation (later known as the FBI), which discovered a low-end market for murderers-for-hire to kill wealthy Osage. Also discovered was a ring of petty thieves let by William King Hale, who the Osage had suspected was responsible for many of the deaths. Of all those who cheated the Osage out of life and livelihood, Hale was the most infamous.

William Hale moved to Osage County shortly before the turn of the twentieth century and quickly rose to prominence through bribery, extortion, and intimidation. In 1921, he conspired with his nephew Ernest Burkhart and several others to kill multiple Osage in a single family in order to gain their land and headrights.

Hale persuaded Burkhart to marry Mollie Kyle, a full-blooded Osage. He and his accomplices then began murdering Kyle's family one by one. The first was Kyle's sister Anna Brown, who was found dead in a ravine. Her death was initially attributed to alcohol poisoning, but an associate of Hale's later confessed to killing her at Hale's request. On the same day Brown was found, her cousin Charles Williamson was also discovered shot in the

Members of the Osage Nation.

head. Brown and Kyle's mother, Lizzie Q. Kyle, was killed two months later. A year and a half after Lizzie's death, the murders continued with another cousin, Henry Roan, who was found shot to death in his car. A month after Roan's murder, Kyle's sister Rita Smith and Rita's husband, Bill, were killed when a bomb containing five gallons of nitroglycerine demolished their house.

After the spate of killings, Mollie Kyle, along with her husband, inherited all of the land and headrights from her deceased family, leaving Kyle vulnerable to Hale's murderous intentions. Kyle soon fell ill, and it was discovered that she was being poisoned. Suspecting Burkhart, she moved away from him. The two later divorced after she recovered. She and their children were left to inherit the wealth of her decimated family.

After a lengthy FBI investigation, Hale, Burkhart, and several contract killers were arrested and put on trial. Burkhart quickly turned on Hale, accusing him of spearheading the murder conspiracy. He also named two accomplices who were both killed before they could testify. Burkhart pleaded guilty and received life in prison, but was later paroled. Hale was tried and convicted only for the murder of Kyle's cousin Henry Roan.

In an effort to prevent further criminality and protect the Osage, Congress passed a law in 1925 that prohibited non-Osage from inheriting land and headrights from those with half or more Osage ancestry, effectively ending the "Reign of Terror," as one paper dubbed it, against the tribe members. In 2000, the Osage filed a lawsuit against the Department of the Interior, alleging mismanagement of the tribe's trust assets, leading to historic monetary loss. The US government settled the lawsuit for $380 million in 2011, the largest trust settlement with any tribe in history.

THE BLOODY BENDERS

abette County, Kansas, 1871: Weary travelers along the Great Osage Trail could stop at the Bender family inn, a modest one-room cabin with just a curtain dividing the dining and guest quarters from the family's living space.

It was like something out of *Little House on the Prairie*: Ma and Pa Bender and their children, Kate and John, were German or Dutch immigrants, eking out a life in the American West. Only unlike *Little House*, all of Ma's *seven* previous husbands had died of "head wounds," and Kate, a spiritualist, held séances and was likely John's wife instead of his sister.

One more thing: Travelers who passed through Labette County had a habit of disappearing. . . .

If you checked in at the Benders' inn, your stay would likely go as follows: You'd drop your bag and survey the space. *You must be starving*, Ma would say. *Sit here*. Kate would pull out a chair with its back to the curtain. As you enjoyed your meal, the fabric behind you would slowly part, a hammer peeking through the slit. Then, before you could finish your potatoes, your bludgeoned head would be bleeding out on your plate. To make sure you were dead, Ma or Kate would then slit your throat.

Two visitors recounted that Ma grew irate when they refused to sit in front of the curtain. It likely saved their lives.

To be fair, anything could happen to someone traveling through the American West in the late nineteenth century—encounters with robbers or animals, accidents. So, at first, the disappearances were written off as the unfortunate consequences of Manifest Destiny.

George Loncher and his daughter were among the unlucky visitors to the Benders' inn. After embarking on their journey from Independence, Kansas, to Iowa in 1872, they vanished. But when the Benders killed the man sent to look into their disappearance, Dr. William York, they definitely murdered the wrong person.

Colonel Ed York, William York's brother, went looking for answers, even questioning the Benders themselves. It was clear that Loncher, his daughter, and York had disappeared somewhere in Labette County. Locals grew suspicious, even holding a town meeting where they all agreed to open up their homes for searches.

As the investigation closed in on the Benders, Kate had one last card to play: spiritualism. As the *Chicago Tribune* later reported, Kate volunteered that "she would consult the spirits if time would be given her to do so, and would, through her agency, be able to disclose the whereabouts of the missing persons." Kate then used this time to abscond with her family.

Neighbors noted that the Benders were always plowing their garden. They weren't planting seeds, it turned out—they were burying bodies. William York plus nine more corpses were found in the garden.

Why did they do it? Although money seems like an obvious motive, most of the travelers had few possessions at the time of their murder. Some cite the sheer thrill of the kill as the Benders' motive.

A railroad employee testified that he saw the family heading to Humboldt, Kansas. Some accounts placed Kate and John in Texas or New Mexico, whereas Ma and Pa were allegedly in St. Louis. But despite the many sightings of people who looked like the Benders in the years that followed, there is no conclusive evidence of the family's fate.

Perhaps more mysterious than their whereabouts were the actual identities of the Benders. They were not, it seems, the Benders. Pa was born John Flickinger, and Ma was born Almira Mark. Kate, a daughter from one of Ma's previous marriages, was born Eliza Griffith, and John Bender Jr. was born John Gebhardt.

With their track record of hiding their past, it's little surprise that the "Benders" slipped into obscurity, likely changing their names, starting new identities, and, perhaps, killing again.

KILLERS, COME ON DOWN!

Match the convicted murderer with the game show they appeared on.

1. Rodney Alcala	**a.** *Jeopardy!*
2. Stephen Port	**b.** *The Dating Game*
3. John Cooper	**c.** *Celebrity MasterChef*
4. Edward Wayne Edwards	**d.** *Bullseye*
5. Paul Curry	**e.** *To Tell the Truth*

Answers: 1B: Aptly named the *Dating Game Killer*, Alcala won an episode of the show in 1978. The woman who chose him was not harmed, but he is believed to have killed up to 130 others. **2C:** Port assisted singer JB Gill in a 2014 episode of the show. A year later he was arrested for poisoning four men. **3D:** Cooper killed two people a month after his 1989 appearance on the show. He was also linked to the 1985 murder of two others. **4E:** Edwards was a supposedly reformed criminal when he appeared on the show in 1972, but his killing career continued well into the '90s, when he was sentenced to death for killing his stepson. **5A:** Paul Curry was a two-time Jeopardy! champion when he met his wife, Linda, in 1989. He was later convicted of her 1994 death from nicotine poisoning.

PHILIP MARKOFF:
THE CRAIGSLIST KILLER

Philip Markoff was in over his head. The 23-year-old medical student had a gambling problem that led him to rack up massive debt. So he hatched a plan. Markoff responded to an escort's ad on Craigslist and the pair arranged to meet. On April 10, 2009, Markoff bound, gagged, and robbed Trisha Leffler at gunpoint at a Boston hotel.

Just four days later, Markoff struck again. Only this time, his victim fought back. In a panic, Markoff fatally shot Julissa Brisman and fled the scene. With the police closing in, Markoff moved to a new location. But his next meeting also went awry when an exotic dancer's husband showed up.

Police soon connected the crimes and located hotel security footage that showed Markoff. He was indicted on first-degree murder and robbery charges but died by suicide in prison on August 15, 2010, while awaiting trial.

Markoff (left) robbed his first victim but killed his second and third victims.

THE LANA TURNER AFFAIR

Lana Turner was one of the most popular actresses in the Golden Age of Hollywood, appearing in dozens of films and receiving an Academy Award nomination for Best Actress in the movie *Peyton Place*. She married and divorced seven times and had a daughter, Cheryl Crane, from her second marriage.

In 1958, Turner was dating Johnny Stompanato, a former bodyguard to mobster Mickey Cohen. He was possessive and violent, once threatening to disfigure her face with a razor. After months of abuse, Turner finally decided to end things. A violent argument ensued in the bedroom of her Beverly Hills home, where Stompanato threatened to kill Turner and her 14-year-old daughter. Fearing for her mother's life, Crane grabbed a butcher knife from the kitchen and rushed to her aid. When Turner opened the door, Crane saw Stompanato behind her mother with his arm raised and stabbed him in the stomach. Turner called for a doctor, but Stompanato bled to death before he arrived. Police arrested Crane at the scene.

The Hollywood press sensationalized every detail of the Lana Turner affair, culminating in the coroner's inquest into Stompanato's death. While Crane was imprisoned at a juvenile detention center, Turner appeared before a 12-man jury to recount, through tears, everything that happened that night. Turner testified that "I was walking toward the bedroom door and he was right behind me, and I opened it and my daughter

Lana Turner testifying at the coroner's inquest into the death of Johnny Stompanato.

came in. I swear it was so fast, I ... I truthfully thought she had hit him in the stomach. The best I can remember, they came together and they parted. I still never saw a blade." The jury unanimously decided the death was the result of justifiable homicide.

Despite getting cleared of murder charges, Crane was made a ward of the state and spent time in a boarding school and sanatorium. She struggled with drugs and alcohol before moving to Hawaii, marrying a model, and becoming a real estate agent. Though her relationship with Turner was strained after Stompanato's death, her 1988 memoir brought her close with her mother again. Turner continued acting until 1985. She died in 1995 of throat cancer.

FORENSIC FORAYS

• *Death's Acre* by Dr. Bill Bass and Jon Jefferson. An inside look at the world's first body farm, at the University of Tennessee, as told by its founder.

• *Mindhunter* by John E. Douglas and Mark Olshaker. A retired FBI agent looks back on his time at the agency, and the different serial killers and criminals he profiled there.

• *Dead Men Do Tell Tales* by William R. Maples and Michael Browning. A forensic anthropologist discusses the science he uses to help solve cases when the only thing left to study is bone.

• *The Killer of Little Shepherds: A True Crime Story and the Birth of Forensic Science* by Douglas Starr. The story of French serial killer Joseph Vacher and the two men, Emile Fourquet and Alexandre Lacassagne, who stopped him with revolutionary science.

NATASCHA KAMPUSCH

atascha Kampusch was only 10 years old when she was abducted by Wolfgang Přiklopil, who dragged her into his van while she was on her way to school in Austria in 1998. For the next eight years, Kampusch spent most of her time in the 54-square-foot-cellar where Přiklopil kept and abused her. Little by little, Přiklopil gave her more freedom, believing Kampusch too brainwashed by him to ever escape.

Kampusch at the premiere of the movie about her captivity, *3096 Days*.

She watered his garden and cleaned his house, and they went on several outings together. She once tried to escape by jumping out of a car but was unsuccessful. Then, in August 2006, Přiklopil received a call while Kampusch was vacuuming the interior of his BMW. When he stepped away to take the call, Kampusch made a run for it. She knocked on a neighbor's door and declared, "I am Natascha Kampusch."

Unwilling to face his crimes, Přiklopil died by suicide by jumping in front of a train shortly after Kampusch escaped. Though Kampusch had the cellar filled with cement, she now owns the house where she was held. In her book, *3,096 Days in Captivity*, Kampusch said, "We live in a world in which women are battered and are unable to flee from the men who beat them, although their door is theoretically standing wide open. One out of every four women becomes a victim of severe violence. One out of every two will be confronted by sexual harassment over her lifetime. These crimes are everywhere and can take place behind any front door in the country, every day, and barely elicit much more than a shrug of the shoulders and superficial dismay."

WOMEN BELIEVE WOMEN

Less than 40 percent of women around the world who survive violence seek help. Less than 10 percent of those seek help from police. In Brazil, a country with one of the highest rates of violence against women in the world, some police departments are trying to change this sorry statistic. They created women's police stations (WPS), entire precincts staffed with only women personnel and officers. Studies have shown that the women living in municipalities with WPS have better relationships with police and feel safer. Women in these areas are more likely to be comfortable reporting abuse and seeking help, and WPS are subsequently associated with a 17 percent reduction in homicide among women ages 15 to 49 in the municipalities where they're located.

THE THEFT OF THE
MONA LISA

On August 21, 1911, Leonardo da Vinci's most famous painting, *Mona Lisa*, was stolen from the Louvre in Paris. Vincenzo Peruggia, a former employee of the museum, hid in a broom closet until closing, removed the painting from its frame, wrapped it in his coat, and walked out. The theft was discovered the next day, when an artist sketching in the gallery asked when *Mona Lisa* would be returned. The theft made front-page news around the world, and visitors lined up at the museum just to view the empty space where the painting had hung.

Authorities questioned many people, including Pablo Picasso, who was viewed as a possible modernist enemy to classical art. Peruggia was caught two years later when he tried to sell the painting to an art dealer in Florence. Peruggia said he stole *La Gioconda*, as the masterpiece is known in Italy, because it belonged in Italy. He hoped that he'd be hailed as a hero for returning the painting to its native land. Instead, he was arrested. He spent a short time in jail for the theft but was released to serve in World War I.

When the *Mona Lisa* was returned, the media sensation, combined with that mysterious smile, cemented its now-legendary status. The masterwork currently resides in the Louvre behind bulletproof glass, as the most famous painting in the world.

PRICIEST SINGLE-ITEM HEISTS

Mona Lisa
Estimated worth: $2 billion.

The Empire State Building
The $1.89 billion building was stolen in 2008, when the *New York Daily News* filed fake paperwork with the city to prove a point about lax processes around city clerks verifying such paperwork. The *Daily News*, posing as "Nelots Properties LLC" (Nelots is *stolen* spelled backward), forged a notary stamp. The notary was signed in the name of bank robber Willie Sutton, and *King Kong* star Fay Wray is listed as the notary witness. The building has since been returned to its owners.

The Concert
Part of the 1990 Isabella Stewart Gardner Museum heist, this Vermeer is valued at $200 million. It is still missing.

The Scream
Edvard Munch painted four versions of this famous work. The most well-known, worth $120 million, was stolen in 1994 and again in 2004. It was recovered both times.

The Saliera
The $57 million statue by sixteenth-century sculptor Benvenuto Cellini went missing from a Vienna museum in 2003 but has since been returned.

GORDON CUMMINS:
THE BLACKOUT RIPPER

Royal Air Force leading aircraftman Gordon Cummins had no prior criminal or violent history when he began killing and mutilating women in World War II London. But in the wartime blackout conditions he saw a sinister opportunity, which manifested in a five-day killing spree in February 1942. During this time Cummins killed four women and attacked two others. One of them, Greta Hayward, escaped when a delivery boy interrupted the attack. Cummins left his RAF-issued gas mask case, marked with his service number, when he fled. Police found even more conclusive evidence when they arrested him on February 16, including trophies from his victims and fingerprints that matched those on the murder weapons.

Cummins was put to death on June 25, 1942. His gruesome habit of mutilating his victims earned him comparisons to Jack the Ripper, along with the moniker the Blackout Ripper.

All of Cummins's murders happened during London's WWII blackout orders.

EDWARD JOSEPH LEONSKI: THE BROWNOUT STRANGLER

Edward Joseph Leonski had an obsession with female voices, particularly those that sang. He would later claim that he strangled women to "get at their voices." Psychologists eventually determined that the New Jersey native's killing spree was "symbolic matricide," inspired by his resentment of his mother.

After the United States entered World War II, the army stationed Leonski in Melbourne, Australia. Unfortunately, getting a world away from his family did not fix things. In May 1942, he strangled Ivy Violet McLeod, Pauline Thompson, and Gladys Hosking. Since all the murders took place during Melbourne's wartime brownout period (like a blackout, but with low lighting), Leonski became known as the Brownout Strangler. He was tried and hanged on November 9, 1942.

WHO KILLED JONBENÉT?

 hristmas will forever be intertwined with one of history's most disturbing unsolved murders: the killing of JonBenét Ramsey. The six-year-old beauty pageant queen was strangled and bludgeoned in the basement of her family's Boulder, Colorado, home on the night of December 25, 1996, or early on December 26.

Throughout the investigation, police suspected several members of the Ramsey family. There have been several theories, including the following: The ransom note left in the Ramseys' kitchen was written by her mother, Patsy; the crime scene was staged to cover something up; or her father committed the murder. In 2003, the discovery of DNA linking the murder to an unidentified male led the district attorney's office to issue a letter of apology to the Ramseys.

Speculation about suspects outside the Ramsey family abound, ranging from the unlikely to the enduring. (A small "foreign faction" occupies the former category.) That ransom note Patsy said she found referenced "a group of individuals that represent a small foreign faction," and demanded $118,000 for the safe return of JonBenét—the exact amount John Ramsey received as his Christmas bonus:

Listen carefully! We are a group of individuals that represent a small foreign faction. . . . At this time we have your daughter in our posession. She is safe and unharmed and if you want her to see 1997, you must follow our instructions to the letter. . . .

You will withdraw $118,000.00 from your account. $100,000 will be in $100 bills and the remaining $18,000 in $20 bills. . . . Any deviation of my instructions will result in the immediate execution of your daughter. You will also be denied her remains for proper burial. . . .

Ramsey's death remains unsolved.

Nearly 10 years after JonBenét's murder, 41-year-old schoolteacher John Mark Karr confessed to the crime. Karr was extradited from Bangkok, Thailand, where he was living, in an attempt to escape child pornography charges. Those charges were eventually dropped, and police were unable to hold him for JonBenét's murder. Despite a gruesomely detailed confession of the girl's murder and the "relationship" that preceded it, investigators could find no link between JonBenét and Karr, and Karr only provided details that were previously made public, leading the confession to be widely believed as false. Karr resurfaced in 2010 under the alias Alexis Reich, who was wanted by police in the Pacific Northwest in connection with a stalking case.

Bill McReynolds, who played Santa Claus at Patsy Ramsey's Christmas party the week before JonBenét's death, was rumored as a possible suspect. But there was no evidence linking McReynolds with the murder, though he allegedly took a "special interest" in JonBenét and may have arranged a Christmas Day visit. Another rumor speculated that McReynolds guarded a vial of glitter JonBenét gave him, even bringing it with him when he underwent heart surgery and requesting that it be mixed with his ashes if he died. These claims were unsubstantiated—McReynolds was most likely a friendly acquaintance who made the mistake of volunteering to play Santa for a group of neighborhood kids days before tragedy struck.

The case remains unsolved.

HOLIDAY HORRORS

Six-year-old JonBenét Ramsey was famously killed in her Boulder, Colorado, home on, or the day after, Christmas in 1996. Can you match these other crimes with the holidays on which they occurred?

1. Egan Family murder
2. Isabella Stewart Gardner Museum heist
3. Lana Turner affair
4. Lawson Family massacre
5. Murder of Reeva Steenkamp

a. New Year's Eve
b. Valentine's Day
c. St. Patrick's Day
d. Good Friday
e. Christmas Day

Answers: 1A: *Peter, Gerald, and Barbara Ann Egan were killed by an unknown person in Watertown, New York, on New Year's Eve, 1964.* **2C:** *Two thieves stole 13 works of art from the Isabella Stewart Gardner Museum in Boston, Massachusetts, on the night of St. Patrick's Day, 1990.* **3D:** *Cheryl Crane, Lana Turner's daughter, killed Johnny Stompanato in Beverly Hills, California, on Good Friday in 1958 (see page 331).* **4E:** *Charles Davis Lawson killed his wife and seven of his children, and then himself, in Germantown, North Carolina, on Christmas Day, 1929.* **5B:** *Reeva Steenkamp was killed by Oscar Pistorius (see page 314) in Pretoria, South Africa, on Valentine's Day, 2013.*

THE MAN AT THE ATM

Matthew Chase left his Los Angeles home on the evening of June 8, 1988, to deposit his paycheck at a local bank and pick up cat food. The next morning, when the 22-year-old still hadn't returned from the errands, his roommates grew concerned. One called Chase's bank pretending to be him, to see if his ATM card had been used. When the bank said the card had been used several times at different locations, Chase's roommates called the police, who uncovered surveillance footage of a man standing uncomfortably close to Chase at the ATM.

Chase's body was found three months later in a ravine near Pasadena. He was shot in the head. The case went cold for 30 years until the LAPD and Chase's family announced in 2018 that they believed David "Bear" Meza, who died the day after Chase's disappearance, was responsible for the murder.

HOW SCIENTIFIC IS FORENSIC SCIENCE?

n 2009, the National Academy of Sciences released the results of a two-year review of forensic techniques. They found that most methods weren't actually based on science and that they lacked standardized methodology and terminology and often relied on the subjective opinion of the person reviewing the evidence. Major issues were cited in the fields of fingerprinting, hair and fiber analysis, bite-mark analysis, ballistics, arson investigation, and blood-spatter analysis.

Hair analysis, the science of comparing hair samples under a microscope to determine if they match, was originally popularized by Sir Arthur Conan Doyle's Sherlock Holmes series. By the 1950s, it was accepted as legitimate forensic science. However, doubts about its accuracy began to surface in the '70s. In 1984, the FBI reported that it couldn't positively match one person through hair analysis. With the rise of DNA profiling in the '90s, the FBI began to review cases in which hair analysis had been used. A study of cases between 1996 and 2000 found that 11 percent of hair analysis cases were contradicted by DNA evidence.

After an outcry from defense attorneys who were angry at the use of faulty science to convict their clients, the FBI conducted further studies, including a review of 21,000 more cases in July 2013. By 2015, they found 32 death penalty cases where

BAD HAIR DAY

These prisoners were convicted largely based on hair analysis—and later exonerated.

- **Santae Tribble**—Released after serving 28 years for the 1978 murder of John McCormick. Tribble had an alibi with four witnesses, but investigators said a stocking mask nearby contained 13 hairs that all matched Tribble. A 2012 DNA profile disproved this and found that one of the hairs belonged to a dog.

- **Kirk Odom**—Convicted of the 1981 rape and robbery of a woman in Washington, DC, in part because Special Agent Myron T. Scholberg testified that hairs found on the woman's nightgown were indistinguishable from Odom's. Odom served 20 years before DNA analysis proved the hairs could not be his.

- **Donald E. Gates**—Served 28 years for rape and murder before he was exonerated by DNA testing in 2009. Gates's hair analysis was done by prominent hair analyst Michael Malone, whose 6,000 cases had been investigated and found to be flawed in 1997.

FBI experts had overstated the reliability of hair analysis—and 14 of those defendants had been executed or died in prison. A separate study by the Department of Justice reviewed 268 trials and found that experts exaggerated the accuracy of hair analysis in 257 cases (95 percent of the total).

Blood pattern analysis (BPA) is the scientific study and analysis of bloodstains at a crime scene. BPA uses biology, physics (fluid dynamics), and mathematical calculations. It interprets the size, color, and shape of bloodstains to determine timing, angle of impact, blood origin, force of impact, and other information

A BPA TIMELINE

1880—In the first known mention of BPA in court, Mississippi's Supreme Court rules to exclude the testimony of blood-spatter experts on the grounds that their analysis would add nothing to the jury's common-sense inferences.

1895—Polish doctor Eduard Piotrowski publishes the first study on bloodstains, "On the Formation, Form, Direction, and Spreading of Blood Stains After Blunt Trauma to the Head."

1957—California's Supreme Court is the first American court to accept BPA testimony at trial.

1971—Herbert Leon MacDonell publishes *Flight Characteristics and Stain Patterns of Human Blood*, which is based on research funded by a grant from the US Department of Justice.

1973—MacDonell teaches the first 40-hour course on BPA.

1983—The International Association of Bloodstain Pattern Analysts is founded.

2009—The National Academy of Sciences publishes a study criticizing BPA and the credentials of analysts, and calls the findings of these analysts "more subjective than scientific."

2013—A paper published in *Forensic Science International* finds that many of the central hypotheses of BPA remain untested and questions the assumptions of analysts.

about a crime. Specialized BPA software, like HemoSpat, can also aid in processing crime scene photos to calculate the origin of impact patterns, which can further assist in determining posture and position of suspects and victims, sequence of events, corroborating or refuting a testimony, and crime scene reconstruction. Results can be viewed as top-down, side, and front views in 2D or exported to 3D formats.

The use of BPA as forensic evidence in criminal cases was rejected by the court systems in several states for many decades until it eventually gained wide use in the mid-twentieth century. It remains in use today, despite increased scrutiny since the 2000s.

That isn't to say that these techniques are *completely* bunk. A hair follicle found at a crime scene will look like the follicle of the person who left it there. In 2019, paleogeneticist Ed Green discovered a way to extract DNA sequencing from hair without a root attached.

However, reviews of old cases have helped free people wrongly convicted by faulty techniques, but there are potentially many more. According to the Innocence Project, the misapplication of forensic science contributed to 45 percent of wrongful convictions in the United States proven through DNA evidence, including 161 of the 375 exonerees represented by the Innocence Project. False or misleading forensic evidence was a contributing factor in 24 percent of all wrongful convictions nationally.

BY THE NUMBERS: DNA EXONERATIONS IN THE US

 ccording to the Innocence Project:

1989: The year the first DNA exoneration took place.

375: The number of DNA exonerees to date (as of 2020).

14: The average number of years served by exonerees.

5,284: The total number of years served by exonerees.

26.6: The average age at the time of wrongful conviction.

43: The average age at exoneration.

44 of 375 exonerees pleaded guilty to crimes they did not commit.

45 percent of cases involved misapplication of forensic science.

165: The number of actual assailants identified after someone was exonerated. Those individuals were later convicted of 154 additional violent crimes, including 83 sexual assaults, and 36 murders while innocent people sat behind bars.

THE CSI EFFECT

Do forensic science crime shows influence American jurors? That's what many prosecutors and law enforcement personnel believe. *CSI: Crime Scene Investigation*, along with similar shows such as *NCIS* and *Cold Case Files*, depict forensic science wizardry, much of which has been described by actual forensic scientists as pure fiction. Frequent viewers then place a high premium on forensic evidence in actual court cases, and prosecutors seeking criminal convictions aren't always able to meet the jurors' expectations.

Although some studies show that the *CSI* effect has been exaggerated, circumstantial evidence appears to hold less weight than it once did, and jurors want DNA traces or other forensic evidence.

COMMUNITY SUPERVISION

Community supervision, or community corrections, refers to two systems: probation and parole. Probation, the primary form of correctional control, allows a person to remain in their community under the supervision of a probation officer in lieu of incarceration. Parole is conditional supervised release from prison.

In the United States, there are twice as many people on probation and parole than there are incarcerated people. This means the total population under correctional control is actually triple the number usually given in statistics, which only accounts for those incarcerated. Disproportionately affected by community supervision are Black Americans, who make up 30 percent of those on probation and parole but just 13 percent of the US population; poor people, who are burdened by probation fees; and women, who often have trouble complying with conditions that involve travel and program participation because of caregiving obligations. Increased community supervision does not necessarily correlate with a lower crime rate—New York City reduced its probation population by 60 percent between 1996 and 2014, and violent crime also dropped by 57 percent during that period.

BETTY LOU BEETS

Betty Lou Beets allegedly endured years of sexual and physical abuse throughout her five marriages. This, she explained, was the reason for her violent behavior toward her husbands. Beets shot her second husband twice in the back of the head in 1970. Eight years later, she tried to run over her third husband with her car. Both men survived. Her fifth husband, Jimmy Don Beets, was not so lucky.

On August 6, 1983, Betty Lou called 911, attempting to mislead the police into thinking Jimmy had drowned. This proved futile, as a tip pointed them toward the new widow. With a search warrant in hand, they scoured the property and found not only Jimmy Don's buried remains, dead from two gunshots, but the remains of Doyle Wayne Barker, Betty's fourth husband.

Beets had a long history of abuse by, and violence toward, her five husbands.

CRIME AND PUNISHMENT:
THE DEMISE OF CAPTAIN COOK

Captain James Cook is believed to be the first European to visit the Hawaiian Islands. When he and his crew landed there in 1778 they were welcomed by the Hawaiians, who were fascinated by Cook's ships, HMS *Resolution* and *Discovery*, and the Europeans' use of iron. Cook traded the metal for provisions, and his crew traded iron nails for sex, before leaving the islands.

Hawaiians attached a religious significance to Cook's second visit to the islands in 1779, because the arrival of the captain and his crew coincided with a festival dedicated to the Hawaiian fertility god, Lono. Cook and his crew were treated as gods, and they took advantage of the Hawaiians' generosity. Then one of Cook's crew members died, exposing the Europeans as mere mortals. Cook and his crew sailed from the island on February 4, 1779, but bad weather forced them to return within a week. This time, Hawaiians hurled rocks at the ships, then stole a small boat from *Discovery*. Relations fell apart when a Hawaiian chief was shot by one of Cook's men. Cook and most of his men were killed by a mob, but a few made it back to *Resolution*. The Europeans retaliated a few days later, firing cannons and muskets at the shore and killing 30 Hawaiians before heading back to Britain.

ELIZABETH SMART

Elizabeth Smart's story gripped the nation, from her abduction in June 2002 until well after she was found in March 2003. Fourteen-year-old Smart was taken by Brian David Mitchell from her home in Salt Lake City, Utah. Mitchell and his wife, Wanda Barzee, held Smart at an encampment near the city, where they shackled her to a tree, alternately starving her and feeding her drugs, alcohol, and garbage. Mitchell raped Smart every day and made her change her name. Eventually, he began taking her out in public, making her cover her face with a veil. Smart missed several chances to escape, afraid of Mitchell and worried that her Mormon community would reject her because she had been raped.

Smart's sister eventually placed Mitchell's voice, which she heard on the night of the abduction, as a man who had worked odd jobs for the Smart family. Mitchell's family recognized a composite sketch on TV and contacted law enforcement, leading to Smart's rescue.

Barzee was sentenced to 15 years in 2009; she was released in September 2018. Mitchell was given two life sentences in 2011.

Elizabeth Smart has gone on to receive a degree in harp performance from Brigham Young University, serve a mission in Paris, and become a successful journalist and child safety activist. In 2011, she founded the Elizabeth Smart Foundation, which works with the Internet Crimes Against Children task force, educates children about violent and sexual crime, and fights human trafficking in partnership with Operation Underground Railroad. She and her husband have three children.

HEAVENLY CREATURES: THE PARKER-HULME MURDERS

On June 22, 1954, 16-year-old Pauline Parker and 15-year-old Juliet Hulme bludgeoned Pauline's mother, Honora, to death on a walking path in Christchurch, New Zealand. The girls had become obsessed with each other and created a rich fantasy life together, including their own religion. But Juliet's parents were planning to send her to South Africa, and the girls believed the only way they could stay together was to kill Honora so Pauline could run away with Juliet.

Their guilt was clear, but their sanity was called into question at trial. Was their fantasy life delusional? Was their fear of being separated paranoia? The jury didn't think so, and both girls were found guilty of murder. Juliet and Pauline were both under the age of 18, so neither was eligible for the death penalty. Instead, they were sentenced to five years in prison—a logistical challenge for the penal system, as there was only one youth correctional facility in New Zealand at the time. They served their time and were released, allegedly with a provision that they never contact each other again. Both Pauline and Juliet were given new identities. Juliet later became a successful writer of historical detective fiction under the name Anne Perry.

POLITICAL INSTINCTS

M atch the politician to his crime.

1. Ted Kennedy
2. David Petraeus
3. Dennis Hastert
4. Anthony Weiner

a. Improperly sharing classified information

b. Sending sexual text messages to a minor

c. Leaving the scene of a crash

d. Illegally structuring bank transactions to pay millions to quash sexual misconduct allegations

Answers: 1C: *Kennedy (see page 83) later expressed his regret for failing to immediately report the crash that caused the death of Mary Jo Kopechne, but he received only a two-month suspended license for the incident.* **2A:** *The charge against General Petraeus stemmed from his affair with US Army vet and writer Paula Broadwell.* **3D:** *Hastert served 13 months in prison for molesting four boys during his time as a high school wrestling coach.* **4B:** *Weiner was involved in his first sexting scandal with an adult woman in 2011; despite a political comeback after that scandal, he was convicted in 2017 for sexting and threatening a minor.*

THE ROCKEFELLER RINGER

When Clark Rockefeller abducted his daughter on July 27, 2008, it may have seemed at first like a case of a well-to-do popular preppy gone wrong. But after his apprehension, a much more sinister and complex web came to light. He was *not* the grand-nephew of John D. Rockefeller after all—in fact, he had no connection to the Rockefeller family. His name was Christian Gerhartsreiter, a German exchange student who had emigrated from Germany 30 years prior. Since then, he had lived many lives by many names, including Chris Gerhart, University of Wisconsin film student; Christopher Chichester, the 13th baronet; Christopher C. Crowe, TV producer; Clark Rockefeller, grand-nephew of John D. Rockefeller; and Chip Smith, the alias Gerhartsreiter was using when he was apprehended by police. While living in San Marino County, California, in the mid-1980s, he was implicated in the murder of his landlady's son, John Sohus, and John's wife, Linda.

After fleeing California, he eventually resurfaced in New York, where he married and lived under his Rockefeller identity for many years until his wife began to suspect he wasn't who he said he was. Things unraveled quickly when she divorced him and gained full custody of their daughter, Snooks. Gerhartsreiter fled with Snooks during a supervised visit, injuring a social worker in the process. He was charged with kidnapping, assault, and the first-degree murder of John Sohus and is currently serving a life sentence in prison.

TRUE CRIME CLASSICS

• *Bad Blood: Secrets and Lies in a Silicon Valley Startup* by John Carreyrou. Elizabeth Holmes's biotech startup, Theranos, promised to improve blood testing for all medical sciences, but her miracle machine turned out to be fake.

• *Killers of the Flower Moon* by David Grann. In the 1920s, Native Americans on the Osage Indian Reservation began dying mysteriously, and the newly created FBI stepped in to help solve the crimes (see page 322).

• *The Feather Thief* by Kirk Wallace Johnson. In June 2009, 299 rare bird skins were stolen from the Natural History Museum at Tring in the UK to satisfy the demand for feathers to re-create Victorian-era salmon flies (see page 28).

• *The Monster of Florence* by Douglas Preston and Mario Spezi. Preston, an American author, and Spezi, an Italian journalist, are themselves investigated by the Italian police as they research a serial killer known as the Monster of Florence.

THE MATTHEW SHEPARD AND JAMES BYRD JR. HATE CRIMES PREVENTION ACT

n the night of October 6, 1998, 21-year-old Russell Henderson and 22-year-old Aaron McKinney offered Matthew Shepard, a 21-year-old gay college student, a ride home. They instead drove Shepard to a remote area near Laramie, Wyoming, where they brutally beat and tortured him before setting him on fire and leaving him to die. He was found the next morning by a cyclist who initially thought he was a scarecrow. He was still alive when police arrived, but he succumbed to his injuries six days later.

After Henderson and McKinney left Shepard, they returned to town and picked a fight with two other men. When police responded to that scene, they found a gun covered in Shepard's blood along with his shoes and credit card in McKinney's truck. Both men were eventually charged with first-degree murder, kidnapping, and aggravated robbery. Henderson pleaded guilty to murder and kidnapping, received two consecutive life sentences, and also agreed to testify against McKinney. McKinney's lawyers attempted to mount a gay panic defense (see page 310), but it was rejected by the judge. He was found guilty of felony murder and sentenced to two consecutive life terms as well.

Shepard's murder, widely believed to have been a hate crime, came just months after the shockingly cruel murder of a Black man named James Byrd Jr., 49, in Jasper, Texas, by three white supremacists. On June 7, 1998, the three men, Shawn Berry, 23, Lawrence Brewer, 31, and John King, 23, offered Byrd a ride home. Instead, they took him to a remote area outside of town and beat and tortured him before tying him by his ankles to Berry's truck and dragging him for about three miles. An autopsy suggested Byrd was alive for half the time he was being dragged. Berry, Brewer, and King then dumped Byrd's body in front of a Black church and went to a barbecue.

All three men were convicted of Byrd's murder. Berry was given life in prison after it was determined that he participated very little in the crime. Brewer was sentenced to death and was executed on September 21, 2011. King was also sentenced to death and was executed on April 24, 2019.

On October 22, 2009, Congress passed the Matthew Shepard and James Byrd Jr. Hate Crimes Prevention Act, which President Barack Obama signed into law six days later. The law

Byrd (left) was killed by white supremacists who dragged his body behind their truck for three miles. Shepard (right), who was gay, was beaten and tortured by two men and later died from the assault.

was initially conceived as a response to the Shepard (see page 360) and Byrd (see page 361) murders and expands the Civil Rights Act of 1968 to include crimes motivated by gender, sexual orientation, gender identity, or disability as hate crimes, in addition to race, color, religion, or national origin. It also removes the prerequisite that the victim be engaging in a federally protected activity, gives federal authorities greater ability to engage in hate crimes investigations, and requires the FBI to track crime statistics based on gender and gender identity in addition to the other groups.

Commemorating along with the president and other proponents of the bill were Shepard's mother, Judy, and James Byrd Jr.'s sisters, Louvon Harris and Betty Byrd Boatner.

WRESTLING WITH MURDER

As a luchadora (wrestler), Juana Barraza was known as La Dama del Silencio (The Silent Lady), but she would become infamous in Mexico under a different moniker—Mataviejitas (The Old Lady Killer). Barraza was charged with the murder of 11 women over the age of 60, though it's believed she may have killed more than 40 between 1998 and her arrest in 2006. She claimed to have been motivated by a deep resentment of her mother, who gave her away when she was 12 to a man who abused her.

Barraza may have gotten away with her crimes for so long because police and the general public believed that Mataviejitas was a man dressed in women's clothing. When she was finally tried and convicted, she received 759 years in prison.

THE SLENDER MAN ATTACK

 n 2009, the internet forum "Something Awful" challenged users to doctor real photos to appear paranormal. Eric Knudsen created two such photos that showed an unnaturally tall, thin, dark-suited male figure looming ominously behind groups of children. The photos were accompanied by "testimony" describing the children's abductions. The so-called Slender Man soon went viral, inspiring more images, stories, and videos online.

The horror legend of Slender Man caught on quickly and turned deadly in the hands of 12-year-olds Anissa Weier and Morgan Geyser. Weier and Geyser believed that Slender Man was real and they both idolized and feared him, seeing him as a threat to their families. They became convinced that they needed to prove their loyalty to him, becoming his "proxies" so they could live in his mansion, confirm his existence to the world, and protect their families.

To do this, they decided they had to kill someone, targeting a classmate and friend, Payton Leutner, who was also 12. They attacked her on May 31, 2014, during a game of hide-and-seek in a local forest, stabbing Leutner 19 times. After the attack, they told Leutner to lie down, in order to "slow the flow of blood," while they went to get help. Instead, they left her to die.

Leutner crawled to a nearby road where she was found by a cyclist. She suffered wounds to her diaphragm, liver, and stomach.

Another wound missed a major artery in her heart by less than a millimeter. She went home a week after the attack and returned to school in September 2014. Her advice on friendship: "Get out before something bad happens to you. Even if you're guilted into it, if you've been friends with them for years. . . . If you feel something is bad, you need to get out while you still can. . . . But I'm not blaming myself at all. Because who could ever see something like this coming?"

Weier and Geyser were caught the day of the attack, wandering down I-94, looking for Slender Man. The knife they used to stab Leutner was in a bag they carried. Weier felt guilty for the attack, but Geyser showed no remorse. She was convinced it was necessary to appease Slender Man. The two had planned the attack for months. Weier pleaded guilty to being a party to attempted second-degree homicide but was diagnosed with schizophrenia and found not guilty by mental disease or defect. She was given an indeterminate sentence of 25 years to life, including at least three years in a psychiatric hospital followed by supervision until age 37. Geyser accepted a plea deal that involved a psychiatric evaluation and received 40 years to life, a sentence similar to Weier's.

Slender Man, a viral meme taken to an even darker place.

BODY SNATCHING

I n the late eighteenth and early nineteenth centuries, medical schools in England were increasing in number, but there was a lack of corpses to help teach their students. The legal way to procure a body for study was to wait for a murderer to be executed. If you didn't want to wait until then, you had another option: body snatching.

Anatomists could either go to the graveyard and dig up recently buried bodies themselves or hire resurrectionists to do it for them. The job paid well, and while highly unethical, it wasn't *exactly* illegal. Resurrectionists worked in teams to dig a small hole at the top end of a grave, break open the coffin, and pull the body out using a rope. As long as you left the clothing and jewelry behind, you would get at most a misdemeanor charge for possession of a stolen corpse. Bodies would then be smuggled to medical schools in boxes or sacks, where they'd be exchanged for money.

Body snatching went on for a century unimpeded. In 1828, when a lodger died in William Hare's Edinburgh boardinghouse, he and his friend William Burke sold the body to Dr. Robert Knox for £7. It was easy money, so when a sick person came to stay with them a few weeks later, they decided to help him along by smothering him with a pillow. The pair killed at least 15 other people, their murder spree only ending when another lodger discovered one of their victims in a haystack before the body could be delivered to Knox, and notified police.

Burke was hanged and dissected; his skin was used to make a snuff box and bind a book. His last name became a verb meaning "to smother," as well as shorthand for body snatching. When similar crimes occurred in England, the culprits were named the London Burkers. Hare, however, was merely jailed, and Knox only suffered public derision. As a result of these crimes, British Parliament passed the Anatomy Act of 1832, which allowed medical schools to use unclaimed bodies for dissection.

THE BIZARRE BODY SNATCHING OF GRAM PARSONS

 few years before musician Gram Parsons died of multiple drug intoxication on September 19, 1973, he confided to Phil Kaufman that he wished to be cremated and have his ashes scattered in Joshua Tree National Park. Unaware of these plans, Parsons's family made arrangements to have him transferred home to New Orleans via Western Airlines. Determined to respect his friend's last wishes, Kaufman enlisted Parsons's assistant, Michael Martin, to help him snatch Parsons's body from the airport. What ensued was a morbid comedy of errors. After borrowing a hearse, the two men impersonated mortuary workers sent by the family of the deceased to convince the airline cargo manager to release Parsons's body to them. Kaufman signed the release papers as "Jeremy Nobody" and loaded the casket into the hearse. Then they took Parsons on a final wild ride through the California desert.

Before leaving the airport, Kaufman and Martin enlisted a patrolman to help them load the casket into the hearse after the two struggled to move it themselves. Martin, who had consumed a large amount of alcohol in an unsuccessful attempt to calm his nerves before the heist, then proceeded to crash into a wall of the hangar directly in front of the patrolman. The patrolman did not deem any of this behavior suspicious and let the men leave with Parsons's body. When they reached Joshua Tree, Kaufman

Parsons's family didn't know about his wishes to be cremated.

attempted to cremate Parsons by pouring five gallons of gasoline on the casket and setting it on fire. Then he and Martin sped away from the scene, forcing other cars off the road in their haste. They headed back to Los Angeles, stopping on the way to sleep off their drunkenness.

After awakening from their slumber, Kaufman and Martin got back on the highway and were involved in a pileup after they rear-ended a car. A police officer responding to the accident handcuffed both men after several beer cans fell out of the hearse—but the two slipped out of their cuffs and fled once again. The officer had failed to ask either man for his driver's license, so he couldn't identify them.

Meanwhile, back at Joshua Tree, Parsons's remains were spotted by campers, who alerted park authorities. Witnesses, including the airline worker who released the body, identified Kaufman and Martin from prior mug shots.

Kaufman was arrested on September 25 and Martin surrendered the next day. They were both charged with grand theft, but because there was no law in California at that time against stealing a dead body, they were ultimately found guilty of misdemeanor theft and fined only $300 for stealing the casket. The two also received 30-day suspended sentences and were ordered to pay $708 for funeral expenses. To raise money for the fees, Kaufman held a fundraiser. He dubbed the event "Kaufman's Koffin Kaper Koncert" and sold bottled beers with the inscription "Gram Pilsner: A stiff drink for what ales you."

The remains of Gram Parsons were returned to his family in New Orleans, and they were interred at Garden of Memories in Metairie after a short service. An unofficial monument to Parsons can be seen at the site of his "cremation" in Joshua Tree National Park.

"THE UNREPENTANT NECROPHILE"

O n December 17, 1979, apprentice embalmer Karen Greenlee was driving to the cemetery in Sacramento, California. The corpse of a 33-year-old man who died a week prior was in the back of the hearse, on his way to be laid to rest. But when Greenlee glimpsed the family of the departed, she turned the hearse around and fled. She was found the next day, unconscious from an overdose of codeine. Police also found a note in the deceased's casket—four and a half pages worth—in which Greenlee professed her love for the departed and confessed to relations with 20 to 40 other dead young men. "Why do I do it? Why? Why?" the letter asked. "Fear of love, relationships. No romance ever hurt like this. . . . It's the pits. I'm a morgue rat. This is my rathole, perhaps my grave."

Laws banning necrophilia did not exist in California at the time, so Greenlee was only charged with stealing the hearse and interfering with a funeral. She spent 11 days in jail, paid a $225 fine, and received probation that included mandatory therapy.

THE SOAP MAKER
OF CORREGGIO

After losing thirteen children—three to miscarriage and ten more to childhood illnesses—Leonarda Cianciulli vowed to protect her four surviving offspring at any cost. When she found out her eldest son, Giuseppe, was joining the Italian army at the onset of World War II, she had a mental breakdown and became convinced that the only way to ensure his safety was through human sacrifice. Between 1939 and 1940, Cianciulli used her reputation as a fortune-teller to lure three unsuspecting women into her shop in Correggio, Italy, gain their trust, and then murder them. Most disturbingly, to dispose of their bodies, she turned them into soaps, cakes, and cookies.

Cianciulli eventually confessed to the murders when Giuseppe became a suspect. At her 1946 trial she remained unrepentant, offering explicit descriptions and correcting the prosecutor about the details of her crimes while on the stand. Of her third victim, Virginia Cacioppo, Cianciulli remarked, "She ended up in the pot, like the other two . . . her flesh was fat and white, when it had melted I added a bottle of cologne, and after a long time on the boil I was able to make some most acceptable creamy soap. I gave bars to neighbors and acquaintances. The cakes, too, were better: that woman was really sweet."

Cianciulli was found guilty and sentenced to thirty years in prison and three additional years in a psychiatric hospital.

THE BENNINGTON TRIANGLE

I n 1992, Vermont author and folklorist Joseph A. Citro coined the term "Bennington Triangle" to describe the site of a series of mysterious disappearances in southwestern Vermont. The triangle centers on Glastenbury Mountain and includes the surrounding towns of Glastenbury, Bennington, Woodford, Shaftsbury, and Somerset. Glastenbury and Somerset were successful logging towns in the nineteenth century, but are now essentially ghost towns with populations of eight and two, respectively, according to the 2010 census.

Five people disappeared in the Bennington Triangle between 1945 and 1950. These are their stories.

On November 12, 1945, a group of five hunters led by 74-year-old Middie Rivers embarked on an expedition up Glastenbury Mountain. Rivers was an experienced hunter and fisherman familiar with the area. On the way down the mountain, Rivers got far ahead of the group and was never seen again. The area was thoroughly searched, but the only thing Rivers left behind was a single rifle cartridge from his gun, found in a nearby stream.

Paula Welden is perhaps the best-known victim of the Bennington Triangle. The daughter of a wealthy industrial engineer, Welden was an 18-year-old sophomore at local Bennington College and an avid hiker. On December 1, 1946, she set out around 2:30 p.m. to hike the Long Trail on Glastenbury Mountain. At

4:00 p.m., she encountered a fellow hiker and asked him how far the trail went. He replied that it ran all the way to Canada. That was the last confirmed sighting of Welden.

Some believe she wasn't prepared for the hike and, because she wasn't dressed for a late autumn night in Vermont, simply got lost and succumbed to the elements. Others believe there was foul play or that she may have run away. Regardless, Paula Welden disappeared and no trace of her was ever found.

James Tedford disappeared on December 1, 1949—exactly three years after Paula Welden. A veteran and resident of the Bennington Soldiers' Home, Tedford had been visiting relatives in St. Albans, about three hours north of where he lived. Witnesses reported seeing him on the bus after the last stop before Bennington. Upon arriving in Bennington, however, all that remained of Tedford was a bus schedule on his seat and his luggage still on board.

Paul Jephson, 8 years old, was the youngest of the Bennington victims. Jephson was left unattended in a truck on October 12, 1950, while his mother went to feed pigs at the farm where she worked. When she returned an hour later, Jephson was gone. Search parties looked for the child, who was wearing a red jacket that should have made him more visible, but no trace of him was found.

Sixteen days after Jephson's disappearance, 53-year-old Frieda Langer also vanished. Langer was camping with her family near the Somerset Reservoir when she and her cousin Herbert Elsner decided to go hiking. During the hike, Langer fell into a stream. Elsner waited for her while she doubled back for dry clothes. When Langer didn't return, Elsner went back to the campsite, to find that Langer never made it back. Two weeks, five search parties, aircraft, helicopters, and 300 searchers later, no trace of Langer had been discovered.

Her body was eventually found on May 12, 1951, near the Somerset Reservoir, in an area that had already been thoroughly searched. No cause of death could be determined. Frieda Langer is the only Bennington Triangle victim whose body has been found.

ADAM WALSH AND *AMERICA'S MOST WANTED*

On July 27, 1981, Revé Walsh left her 6-year-old son, Adam, at a video game kiosk in a Hollywood, Florida, Sears while she went shopping. When she finished, she returned to the kiosk to learn that Adam had been kicked out of the store by a 17-year-old security guard, along with a group of rowdy older boys. Revé would never see Adam again. Two weeks later, Adam's head was found in a drainage ditch 130 miles away. Serial killer Ottis Toole would later confess to the murder, along with many others. Toole's involvement was never proven.

In 2007, there was a widespread theory that serial killer Jeffrey Dahmer, who was living in Miami Beach at the time, had killed Adam. There were several witnesses who saw a man who looked like Dahmer at the shopping mall the day Adam was abducted. Part of Dahmer's modus operandi was decapitation, though Adam was much younger than his average victim. Dahmer had been questioned about Adam in 1992 in the midst of his many graphic confessions, and he said, "I've told you everything—how I killed them, how I cooked them, who I ate. Why wouldn't I tell you if I did someone else?"

When the case was closed in 2008, police announced they were satisfied that Ottis Toole was Adam's killer. The Walshes also believed that Toole killed Adam.

Adam's abduction and murder was one of the earliest high-profile cases of its kind, and it would spawn a public-safety movement led by his father, John Walsh.

John Walsh became well known after the murder of his son and his subsequent commitment to help missing and exploited children. In 1988, he began production on the TV show *America's Most Wanted*, which he also hosted. *America's Most Wanted* featured reenactments with actor portrayals of dangerous criminals, on-camera interviews with victims and witnesses, and voice-overs by Walsh. Each episode also featured photographs of fugitives and a toll-free hotline number, 1-800-CRIME-TV, for viewer tips.

Over the course of 25 seasons, *AMW* collected viewer information that led to the arrests of more than 1,200 criminals, including:

• **David James Roberts** (rape, murder, arson)—the first fugitive profiled and first captured. Caught on February 11, 1988, in Staten Island, New York. He had been hiding for four days after seeing himself on the show.

• **Rickey Allen Bright** (kidnapping, rape)—caught after a viewer called in a tip that he was playing drums in Nashville, Tennessee. Apprehended on January 6, 1996, at a hotel where his band was playing.

• **Tony Ray Amati** (burglary, murder)—captured on February 27, 1998, for murders committed in the summer of 1996.

• **Chaunson Lavel McKibbons** (murder)—captured on October 24, 2004, before his addition to the FBI's Ten Most Wanted list was made public.

The Adam Walsh Child Protection and Safety Act was signed into law by President George W. Bush on the 25th anniversary of Adam's abduction. The Walsh Act organizes sex offenders into three tiers based on the crime they committed and requires them to register based on their tier. The sex offender registry is available to the public. States and territories in the US are required to post offender data, including name, address, date of birth, place of employment, and photograph, online.

The long title for the act is: An act to protect children from sexual exploitation and violent crime, to prevent child abuse and child pornography, to promote internet safety, and to honor the memory of Adam Walsh and other child crime victims.

THE MORRIS WORM

O n November 2, 1988, just months before the World Wide Web launched, the first cyberworm was released from a computer at the Massachusetts Institute of Technology. Within 24 hours, 10 percent of the 60,000 computers that were connected to the internet at that time were affected—the internet was grinding to a halt at Harvard, Princeton, Stanford, Johns Hopkins, NASA, the Lawrence Livermore National Laboratory, and many other institutions.

Shortly after the attack, a programmer contacted friends saying he had launched the worm and was unable to control it. He asked one friend to send out a plea for help along with an apology. Ironically, most of those who could help had already been knocked offline by the worm. Through talking to another of the friends, the *New York Times* discovered the programmer was Robert Tappan Morris. Morris became the first person to be convicted under the 1986 Computer Fraud and Abuse Act. He received a fine, probation, and 400 hours of community service, but no jail time.

THE DOGNAPPING OF KID BOOTS ACE

Kid Boots Ace was a lucky dog. His owner, Louis Rudginsky, was riding high as the Boston terrier won three championships by the time he was 18 months old, including the February 1934 Westminster Kennel Club Dog Show. Less than two weeks later he took the prize again, this time at the Western Boston Terrier Show in Chicago. It was here that Rudginsky's luck ran out. While his owner was being interviewed by *Boston Terrier Magazine*, Kid Boots Ace vanished. Shortly afterward, Rudginsky received a call in his hotel room: "We have your dog. We want $5,000 to give it back."

Two days later, Rudginsky received a message that he would receive another call. This time the dognappers asked for $500, a more reasonable sum. But they hung up and never called back. Months passed and Rudginsky gave up hope until the phone rang on July 27, 1934. A couple had stolen the dog and, after breaking up, had left him in the care of a friend who recognized him as Kid Boots Ace. He was safe and in good health and was reunited with Rudginsky.

MCGRUFF THE CRIME DOG

Take a Bite out of Crime" was the motto of this trench coat–clad anthropomorphic cartoon bloodhound. Created by the ad agency Dancer Fitzgerald Sample, McGruff debuted in July 1980 as a response from the Ad Council and the National Crime Prevention Council to rising crime rates in the US through the 1960s and '70s. He continues to this day to educate the nation about ways to prevent crime.

McGruff had his own sort of brush with the law in 2014, when John R. Morales, an actor who had donned the McGruff suit to play the crime dog at live events, was sentenced to 16 years in prison for possession of 1,000 marijuana plants and 27 weapons—including a grenade launcher and 9,000 rounds of ammunition.

McGruff was memorialized on a US postage stamp in the 1980s.

THE VAMPIRE ATTACK

O n November 17, 1994, 23-year-old Lisa Stellwagen saw *Interview with the Vampire* with her boyfriend, Daniel Sterling, 25. When she woke up the next morning, she found Sterling staring at her. When asked what was wrong, Sterling replied, "I'm going to kill you and drink your blood."

Later that night, he attempted to do just that. He stabbed Stellwagen nine times and drank her blood "for several minutes." Stellwagen was able to get away and survived the attack.

Sterling was found guilty of attempted first-degree murder, aggravated mayhem, battery, assault, and domestic violence after a jury rejected the defense's claims that he was mentally ill and highly suggestible. He was sentenced to life in prison.

CRIME RATES HAVE FALLEN—BUT PEOPLE DON'T THINK THEY HAVE

T he Pew Research Center reported that according to annual reports from the FBI, violent crime, such as rapes, robberies, and assaults, decreased by 51 percent between 1993 and 2018. Property crime, such as burglary, theft, and auto theft, also decreased—by 54 percent. Nationally representative annual surveys by the Bureau of Justice Statistics found even steeper declines in crime rates over the same period—71 percent less violent crime and 69 percent less property crime.

However, the majority of Gallup surveys conducted during 1993 and 2018 show that public perception of crime rates clashes with the data—about 60 percent of Americans believe crime has increased, especially on a national level. Fewer think crime has increased on a local level. The disparity between data and public perception on crime is often attributed to the 24-hour news cycle and the dramatic increase in crime reporting.

PHOTO CREDITS

ACKNOWLEDGMENTS

Thanks first and foremost to my co-contributors, Sam O'Brien and Steven Bucsok, without whom this book would be missing many classic serial killer stories and forensic facts, among other great stories.

I would thank everyone at Workman Publishing by name if I could. As it is, I'll limit myself to those whose talents directly made this book possible: editor John Meils; designer Galen Smith; typesetters Annie O'Donnell and Barbara Peragine; production manager Erica Jimenez; production designer Jac Atkinson; publicity and marketing team Rebecca Carlisle, Diana Griffin, and Cindy Lee; and, last but first in my heart, copyeditor Jessica Rozler and production editor Angie Chen.

And to everyone else at Workman Publishing who makes true crime content possible, namely Marta Jaremko, Barbie Altorfer, Gracie Elliott, and Alexis August.

Eternal gratitude to all my beloved family and friends who support my writing and my true crime fixation (even, and maybe especially, those who don't understand it) and to everyone who's sent me an obscure true crime gem or two (to twenty) over the years.

And most of all to H, BD, and M, who make me feel safe whenever I get too scared during *Unsolved Mysteries*.

Kim Daly writes about pop culture, true crime, and mystery when not working as copy chief at Workman Publishing. She holds a master's degree in English with a focus on trauma studies, and previously worked as a rape crisis counselor. She lives across from Green-Wood Cemetery in Brooklyn, New York.